NOMAD CITIZENSHIP

Nomad Citizenship

FREE-MARKET COMMUNISM AND THE
SLOW-MOTION GENERAL STRIKE

Eugene W. Holland

University of Minnesota Press
Minneapolis
London

Portions of chapter 1 were previously published as "The Utopian Dimension of Thought in Deleuze and Guattari," in *Imagining the Future: Utopia and Dystopia,* ed. Andrew Milner, Matthew Ryan, and Robert Savage, 217–42 (North Carlton, Australia: Arena, 2006); "Studies in Applied Nomadology: Jazz Improvisation and Postcapitalist Markets," in *Deleuze and Music,* ed. Ian Buchanan and Marcel Swiboda, 20–35 (Edinburgh: Edinburgh University Press, 2004); "Affirmative Nomadology and the War Machine," in *Gilles Deleuze: The Intensive Reduction,* ed. Constantin Boundas, 218–25 (London: Continuum, 2009); and "Schizoanalysis, Nomadology, Fascism," in *Deleuze and Politics,* ed. Ian Buchanan and Nick Thoburn, 74–97 (Edinburgh: Edinburgh University Press, 2008). Portions of chapter 2 were previously published as "Affective Citizenship and the Death-State," in *Deleuze and the Contemporary World,* ed. Adrian Parr and Ian Buchanan, 161–74 (Edinburgh: Edinburgh University Press, 2006). Portions of chapter 4 were previously published as "Nonlinear Historical Materialism and Postmodern Marxism," *Culture, Theory, Critique* 47, no. 2 (2006): 181–96.

Published by the University of Minnesota Press
111 Third Avenue South, Suite 290
Minneapolis, MN 55401–2520
http://www.upress.umn.edu

Library of Congress Cataloging-in-Publication Data

Holland, Eugene W.
  Nomad citizenship : free-market communism and the slow-motion general strike / Eugene W. Holland.
    p. cm.
  Includes bibliographical references and index.
  ISBN 978-0-8166-6612-6 (hc : alk. paper) — ISBN 978-0-8166-6613-3 (pb : alk. paper)
  1. State, the—Philosophy. 2. Citizenship—Philosophy. 3. Communism—Philosophy. 4. Utopias—Philosophy. I. Title.
  JC11.H645 2011
  320.01—dc23
                    2011028083

Printed in the United States of America on acid-free paper

The University of Minnesota is an equal-opportunity educator and employer.

18 17 16 15 14 13 12 11   10 9 8 7 6 5 4 3 2 1

To Eliza, *nomade par excellence*

CONTENTS

This book is a creature of circumstance. It has been said that genuine thinking begins with a scream—not of fear, but of outrage. (And if you're not outraged, so another saying goes, you're simply not paying attention.) If thinking does begin with a scream of outrage—outrage at all that is intolerable in this world—then there is plenty to scream about. This book was born of outrage at the presidency of George W. Bush. Who would have believed that a U.S. government, supposed global beacon of freedom and democracy, would resort to preemptive war, rendition and torture, the suspension of habeas corpus, domestic wiretapping, and innumerable presidential signing statements to circumvent federal and international law and consolidate practically unchecked power in the executive branch? Of course, the abrupt turn to militarism and authoritarianism was justified in the name of restoring national honor after the shock and humiliation of the September 11 attacks on the World Trade Center and the Pentagon. But this in turn justified considering the Bush regime as a latter-day variant of palingenic populist ultranationalism—the category utilized in current scholarship to characterize the popular program of nation rebuilding in response to a humiliating defeat that was instituted in Nazi Germany after World War I. But that was only part of the cause for outrage: there was also blatant disregard for the looming environmental catastrophe; a general disdain for empirical evidence and scientific findings; a massive transfer of wealth to the already wealthy, coupled with record federal budget deficits; an unholy electoral and policy alliance with religious fundamentalism—the list could go on and on.

And yet, had this book been written a decade earlier, there would have been plenty of cause for outrage at the Clinton presidency, too—callous disregard for the damage to progressive causes stemming from sexual impropriety being the least of it: passage of global trade pacts favoring transnational capital over American workers; refusal to finally deinstitutionalize homophobia in the military; capitulation to the pharmaceutical and insurance industries in the abandonment of health care reform; the evisceration of welfare and its transformation into work-fare—this list, too, could go on and on.

So the book is not partisan in *that* sense: once the screams subside, *both* regimes are understood to be variants of neoliberalism, the latest stage of global capitalism. But the differences between the two varieties—the neo-Conservative and the neo-Liberal, as I label them—turn out to be significant, for they reveal a fundamental bipolarity of the modern State-form. Deleuze and Guattari and Foucault (among others) distinguish analytically between an apparently more archaic, "despotic" or "sovereign" form and an apparently more modern, "civilized" or "biopolitical" form of State power. The temptation, and the danger, would be to consider them stages in a historical progression replacing the archaic with the modern. For what if they more closely resemble business cycles of boom and bust (to which they may not be unrelated)? What if the contemporary State oscillates between the two forms, without ever leaving the less desirable (presumably the older) one definitively behind? This is the view propounded by Deleuze and Guattari in *A Thousand Plateaus* (especially when read as a corrective to *Anti-Oedipus*) and registered in my psychohistorical study of Baudelaire (see especially the preface to *Baudelaire and Schizoanalysis*). Comparison of the neo-Liberal Clinton regime with the neo-Conservative Bush regime confirms this view and lends it added urgency: if history can no longer be conceived in linear fashion as evolving from one stage to the next, nor thought of dialectically to accommodate backsliding or steps backward in the course of a process that nonetheless leads inexorably forward, then it must be conceived in nonlinear fashion as oscillating between two (or among several!) basins of attraction in an open process that has no single predictable direction or final outcome. The sovereign or neodespotic State-form represents one basin of attraction, into which Nazi Germany fell between the wars while the United States (narrowly) avoided it; the biopolitical or axiomatizing State-form represents another basin of attraction, which Germany now occupies, while the United States, at least under George W. Bush, moved closer to the neodespotic form. Bush's immediate successor, perhaps because of constraints imposed on him by the two wars and banking fiasco he inherited, has not moved the country appreciably closer to the axiomatizing State-form, but neither has he wielded executive power as neodespotically as Bush did. Yet even if Obama or one of his successors were to succeed in repositioning the

United States closer to or within the axiomatizing basin of attraction, on this view, there is no guarantee that it would remain there, nor indeed that it might not subsequently fall back into the neodespotic basin again and perhaps remain there indefinitely.

Hence the urgency of thinking through the outrage philosophically, rather than simply taking sides for one State-form against the other, as important as that may be politically or practically speaking. Thinking philosophically means thinking creatively—looking outside the State and the mode of production for perspectives and categories to analyze contemporary political and economic developments. The main philosophical categories created for this purpose in what follows are *nomad citizenship* and *free-market communism,* developed primarily from conceptual resources provided by the two volumes of Deleuze and Guattari's *Capitalism and Schizophrenia.* In *Anti-Oedipus,* for example, schizoanalysis construed schizophrenia as the outside of the Oedipus complex and normal neurosis. In *A Thousand Plateaus,* nomadology construes nomadism as the outside of the State-form. This is not a kind of libertarianism or State-phobia: the point is to *transform* citizenship, not eliminate it; to renew, enrich, and invigorate it by displacing the monopoly of State citizenship with plural nomad citizenship, not abandon it altogether. It would be foolish to refuse on principle to use any weapons the State offers (e.g., rights, labor contracts) to resist political oppression and economic exploitation, even if the main objective of nomad citizenship is to develop superior weapons (abilities, autonomy) outside the ambit of the State. In a somewhat different but related sense, nomadology construes so-called primitive accumulation as the outside of the capitalist mode of production and seeks to displace capital-controlled "free markets" with *truly* free ones. This is not a kind of neoliberalism: the point is to rescue market exchange, not perpetuate capitalism, and to enable noncapitalist markets to coordinate socialized production on a global scale, with an eye to the Common Good, by freeing them precisely from capitalist control.

Categorically distinguishing nomad citizenship and free-market communism from libertarianism and neoliberalism is important and necessary because both sets of conceptions of political and economic life have a single underlying utopian impulse in common: freedom. One of the great strengths of utopian thinking, as Fredric Jameson and Ernst Bloch have shown, is the ability to discern the positive ideals or desires secretly animating even the most degraded or misguided of political or economic programs. In the idiom of the affirmative nomadology developed here, freedom is a key Problem of social organization that admits of a wide variety of actual solutions, some of which are more desirable—inasmuch as they actually realize greater degrees of freedom—than others. The concepts of nomad citizenship and free-market communism are created in response to that Problem. But they don't pretend to solve it in and by themselves: they are philosophical thought experiments and call as such for practical experimentation in the real world to see if and how well they work— thereby putting thought once again in touch with its outside, not only as source of Problems but also as proving ground for various potential solutions. I develop the concept of the *slow-motion general strike* as a guide for pursuing such experimentation, for if the nonlinear view of history adumbrated previously is true, the long-term effects of experiments in social change will be practically impossible to predict, and so such experiments must be *immediately* advantageous in their own right *while also* improving the prospects for widespread social change and greater degrees of freedom in the *longer* term: these are the twin imperatives of the slow-motion general strike.

The Problem of degrees of freedom in social organization is by no means peculiar to the Bush and Clinton regimes, of course, even if they provided the immediate circumstances from which my thinking about it took off and represent (unlike the Obama regime, so far) recent clear-cut examples of the two main tendencies of the bipolar modern State-form. (Degrees of freedom, in fact, is a Problem humans share with many other forms of life—which is why herds and packs, colonies, flocks, and schools can enter into consideration.) Behind the dizzyingly rapid alternation between the two poles of the modern State-form that took place in the United States around the turn of the twenty-first century lie two other solutions to the Problem of freedom in social organization that developed over the course of the last few centuries: the social contract and the labor contract. Situated at the outside (nomadic, "primitive") edges of the State-form and the mode of production, nomadology is able to diagnose these so-called contracts as myths or screen narratives serving to obscure the founding and continuing violence that vitiates the very freedoms they, as solutions, are supposed to secure. Acute dissatisfaction and thorough analysis of the two variants of the neoliberal State expose the contract solutions underlying both of them as undesirable, with examination of the immediate circumstances serving as a springboard for farther-reaching diagnoses of two of the foundational myths of modern Western civilization. Diagnosing them as myths, in turn, provides impetus to transform societies based on them beyond recognition.

This book is a creature of circumstance in another sense. I had started work on the third volume of the trilogy that will eventually complement my schizoanalytic study of a single individual (Baudelaire) and my introduction to schizoanalysis itself with a schizoanalytic study of modern Western culture of the last few centuries, seen through the lens of a number of perversions that, for me, constitute the cultural logic of capitalism. But then I started receiving, and ended up accepting, so many invitations to address the topic of citizenship from the perspective of schizoanalysis and nomadology that it soon became apparent that I had the makings of a book-length study at hand. First and foremost, I am grateful to the Center for Cultural Studies at the University of California, Santa Cruz, and especially to its codirectors, Chris Connery and Gail Hershatter, for enabling me to spend a year as resident fellow there, assembling a set of wide-ranging conference papers and essays into the first draft of a book manuscript. I would like to take this opportunity also to thank the following groups for the occasions they provided to share my thinking about citizenship, utopia, and nomadology with them and for the insightful feedback they provided: the Australasian Society for Continental Philosophy; the Canadian Society for Continental Philosophy; the Trimble Lecture Fund at Colorado State University; the Copenhagen Business School; the Deakin University Centre for Citizenship and Globalisation (Melbourne); the Duke University Graduate Program in Literature; the Empire State College (New York) All Areas of Study Committee; the Erasmus University Institute for Philosophy and Economics (Rotterdam); the Harvard University Romance Languages and Literatures Department; the University of Melbourne School of Philosophy, Anthropology, and Social Inquiry; the Miami University French and Italian Department; the University of Minnesota International Relations Colloquium; the Monash University Center for Comparative Literature and Cultural Studies (Melbourne); the Royal Danish Academy of Fine Art (Copenhagen); the Trent University Philosophy Department; and the Utrecht University Centre for Humanities. I would also like to express gratitude to a number of interlocutors and fellow Deleuze scholars for their continuing friendship and support: Costas Boundas, Rosi Braidotti, Ian Buchanan, my graduate research ally Andrew Culp, Paul Patton, John Protevi, Brian Rotman, Dan Smith, and Charles Stivale. Later in the process, I found the readers and editors at the University of Minnesota Press a pleasure to work with and want to thank them for their challenging responses and kind assistance. Finally, my most sincere thanks go to Eliza Segura-Holland for her great patience and support for the completion of this project and thanks to whom all things seem possible—and most things actually get done.

Assays in Affirmative Nomadology

The point of doing philosophy is to create new concepts, and political philosophy creates concepts in response to social problems that confront the philosopher in a given historical milieu. The concepts define the problems in responding to them. Philosophical concepts extract from actual historical states of affairs what is philosophically "Interesting, Remarkable, or Important," as Deleuze and Guattari say: "what belongs to philosophy by right."[1] At the same time, and conversely, it is the historical milieu that provokes philosophical thought to begin with: something in the milieu has become unbearable, Intolerable, Problematic; it forces the philosopher to think anew, to break old habits of thought (that have almost inevitably become bad habits of thought). Hence the particular value in philosophy of constructing paradoxical concepts: they force us to think something through afresh. There is thus a secret family resemblance between philosophical concepts and surrealist metaphors: sparks of astonishment and perplexity are supposed to fly.

The two main concepts under construction here are *nomad citizenship* and *free-market communism*. By most definitions, *citizenship* applies to an exclusive group of people identified by their belonging to a clearly demarcated, well-defined, and well-defended state territory. Nomad citizenship is designed to break with that definition and its territorialization of the concept of citizenship: *nomadism*, by most definitions, broadly applies to groups that are precisely not identified with state territory; Deleuze and Guattari's concept of nomadism, as we will see, is broader still. But the point of combining nomadism with citizenship in this way is to smash the State's territorializing monopoly on belonging and redistribute it globally, in alternative or minor forms of sociality both within and beyond the boundaries of the State.[2] The paradox of free-market communism is even more dramatic: the terms are strongly charged, ideological polar opposites, designating a kind of Mexican standoff between capitalism, on one hand, and its archenemy and would-be grave digger, on the other. But the point of combining the terms *free market* and *communism* in this way is to deploy selected features of the concept of communism to transform capitalist markets to render them truly free and, at the same time, to deploy selected features of the free market to transform communism and free it from a fatal entanglement with the State. The concept is thus designed to cut both ways: it forces orthodox Marxism to acknowledge that hitherto existing communism has featured a centralized authoritarian State and that the free market offers an essential corrective to State-governed social relations; at the same time, the concept forces orthodox champions of capitalism to acknowledge that hitherto existing capitalism has inexorably produced exploitative oligopolies and monopolies that ruin free markets and that communism offers an essential corrective to the wage relation on which capitalist exploitation is based. The point of the paradoxical concept is to force us to think about free markets and about communism in new, more productive ways, just as nomad citizenship is designed to oblige us to think about territories and belonging in new and more productive ways.

A question inevitably arises, however: why keep the term *citizenship* at all, if the point is to radically detach it from the nation-State? For one thing, citizenship defined in relation to the nation-State is, in historical terms, a fairly recent and specific version of a much broader phenomenon, often involving cities or municipalities instead of states.[3] But for our current situation, in which the State, practically speaking, monopolizes citizenship, why not use a term like *social movement*—or *community*, or even *subculture*—to name nonstate social groups to which people in fact belong and feel a strong sense of belonging? There are basically two responses to this question, one of which is urgent, dramatically forced on us by a contemporary historical situation that has become absolutely Intolerable, and the other of which is less so. The simple fact is that the term *citizenship* has already begun detaching itself from the State: there is serious discussion of European citizenship, for example (to start with a historically significant but comparatively mild displacement of the geographical locus of citizenship that scarcely alters its content), but there is also talk of cultural and ethnic citizenship (which really do imply different contents) and of global citizenship (whose content is very uncertain indeed); there is even talk, in a completely different vein, of corporate citizenship (which usually involves merely adding anodyne ethical constraints to the bottom-line imperative of simply making money). Meanwhile, Arjun Appadurai has observed that "we are in the process of moving to a global order in which the nation-state has become obsolete and other forms of allegiance and identity have taken its place,"[4] and although he may overstate the case for the State's obsolescence, he is right that "we need to think ourselves beyond the nation"[5] to fruitfully revise our notions of patriotism, allegiance, and citizenship. "Where soil and place were once the key to the linkage of territorial affiliation with state monopoly of the means of violence," Appadurai goes on to say, "key identities and identifications now only partially revolve around the realities and images of place."[6] Ultimately, Appadurai suggests, "the steady erosion of the capabilities of the nation-state to monopolize loyalty will encourage the spread of national forms that are largely divorced from territorial states"[7] so that as "bounded territories . . . give way to diasporic networks, nations to transnations," citizenship and patriotism could both "become plural, serial, contextual and mobile."[8] Nomad citizenship is designed to address precisely this growing placelessness and plurality of citizens' social affiliations.

More germane for our purposes is a long-standing ambivalence about the core meaning of the term and the kind and degree of active participation it entails, whose two poles Thomas Jefferson characterized in the following way:

> Men by their constitution are naturally divided into two parties. Firstly, those who fear and distrust the people, and wish to draw all powers from them into the hands of the higher classes. 2ndly, those who identify themselves with the people, have confidence in them, cherish and consider them as the most honest and safe, altho' not the most wise depository of the public interest.[9]

There is, then, what Terry Cooper identifies as a narrower, "legal" definition of citizenship centered on the State, which is designed by those who fear and distrust popular participation so as to limit democratic power and concentrate power instead in the hands of elites. And there is a more expansive, "ethical" version of citizenship (Cooper's term, again: often also referred to as *republican citizenship*) that encourages active involvement in social life and entails a larger scope of democratic participation within and perhaps even beyond the domain of the State. Nomad citizenship seeks to expand the scope of democratic participation (both intensively, as in small-group direct democracy, and extensively, as in various forms of mediated yet nonrepresentative indirect democracy supported by markets and the Internet). Owing to its more expansive construction of the field, nomad citizenship focuses less on passive rights, such as those granted to citizens by the State, and more on active engagement, on the affective dynamics of belonging and commitment to social groups of various kinds. Because it combines economic and political analysis with the psychodynamics of belonging, we will find that the "materialist psychiatry" Deleuze and Guattari developed under the name "schizoanalysis" is particularly well suited to the study of this aspect of citizenship, which I will call *affective citizenship*.[10] Belonging to a nuclear family and participating in capitalist markets turn out to share crucial dynamics, as we shall see, with being a citizen of a modern State—which argues for retaining the term *citizenship*.

In lengthy ruminations about the concept of the political, and in particular about Carl Schmitt's influential definition hinging on the State-drawn distinction between friend and enemy, Jacques Derrida raises similar questions about the terms *democracy* and *politics* in his attempt to rethink them as forms of friendship, well outside their habitual loci. "Would it still make sense to speak of democracy," he asks, "when it would no longer be a question . . . of country, nation, even State or citizen—in other words, *if at least one still keeps to the accepted use of this word*, when it would no longer be a political question?"[11] His answer to the question of whether to retain such terms even while radically displacing them is characteristically enigmatic, yet suggestive:

> There could be no choice: the decision would once again consist in deciding without excluding, in the invention of other names and other concepts, in moving out *beyond this* politics without ceasing to intervene therein to transform it.[12]

The point of retaining as point of reference a certain concept of the political—even that of Carl Schmitt—would be to intervene in the discourses and practices mobilizing that concept, precisely to transform it and them. Similarly, the purpose of retaining as point of reference the concept of citizenship is to transform it, in much the same way that Derrida proposes transforming politics and democracy, and indeed in the same general direction: his reconstructed, displaced, and expanded concept of friendship is akin to the concept of nomad citizenship under construction here.[13] The concept of free-market communism, meanwhile, serves as a crucial supplement to both Derrida's expansive friendship and nomad citizenship, for it handily deconstructs the notorious friend–enemy dichotomy central to State politics by means of the figure of the anonymous but mutually beneficial trading partner, who is neither friend nor enemy.

The second, more urgent reason for retaining the term *citizenship*, in line with the foregoing critique of the Schmittian definition of politics, is to break the State's despotic command over social belonging. To call the

State's dominion over sociality a monopoly is, admittedly, tendentious—but the tendency is a strong and dangerous one. The fact is that the State is the only modern instance of sociality that can—and does—demand the sacrifice of life in its name. (That radical fundamentalist religious groups have recently begun—or rather resumed—doing so as well is one index of their postmodernity.[14]) To name this lethal tendency of the modern capitalist State, and to characterize its tendency to devote itself to the destruction of life and the sacrifice of means of life, I construct the diagnostic concept of the Death-State in chapter 2. The tendency it names is the Intolerable Problem that provokes the construction of nomad citizenship in chapter 3 and of free-market communism in chapter 4. This is why the term *citizenship* must be retained: to disrupt and discard bad habits of thought—deeply rooted but Intolerably dangerous habits of thought, which are also bad habits of practice—and to *think the Problem of social belonging anew.*

The sense of urgency behind these concepts was brought to a head by the presidency of George W. Bush and, in particular, by the convergence of fundamentalist, national-supremacist, and fascist tendencies that characterize it.[15] Bush's claim as president to be the "decider" appears in this light to be an ironic—and no doubt unintentional—parody of Schmitt's theory of the sovereign decision as that which founds yet transcends the constitution of any established political order. Yet by declaring war on a permanent yet undefeatable enemy—"terrorism"—Bush has expanded the powers of the presidency and substantially transformed the American state. But at the same time, the Problems these concepts define go much deeper. The broad outlines of the Death-State, and especially its amalgamation of the State and the capitalist economy in a total war-machine, were already legible in the aftermath of World War II and were noted by figures as diverse as Georges Bataille, George Orwell, and Dwight Eisenhower—the general-turned-president who, in his final presidential address, coined the term *military–industrial complex* to designate two important components of the lethal synergy or resonance between economics and politics characterizing the Death-State. Schizoanalysis completes the characterization by adding a psychological register to the economic and the political, as we shall see in chapter 2.

Yet the Problems to which nomad citizenship and free-market communism respond lie deeper still. For these concepts ultimately target the two sustaining myths of modern society, both of which are based on the pious wish that modernity somehow replaced old-fashioned, "premodern" and compulsory, hierarchical social relations with voluntary, contractual ones. Nomad citizenship and free-market communism respond most profoundly, that is to say, to the myth of the social contract and the myth of the labor contract. They target the founding violence—which is also the enduring violence—at the heart of our political and economic systems: the formation and continuing concentration of sovereign State power; the formation and continuing expansion of private capital accumulation.[16] And they diagnose the myths of the social contract and the labor contract as screen narratives serving to conceal and whitewash the role that violence has played and continues to play in the constitution of modern forms of sociality. In one case, the violence is spectacularly noisy and direct—the modern State is indeed typically defined in terms of its absolute monopoly on legitimate or legitimated violence: on command, make war; disobey, and you answer to the police. In the other case, the violence is hidden, as it were, and indirect: Marx refers to the "silent compulsion of market relations" that makes the labor contract essentially involuntary; he also reveals that the "secret" of "so-called primitive accumulation" is that it more fundamentally means primitive destitution, that is, forcing people into abject dependence on capital for their very survival.[17]

Of course, nomad citizenship and free-market communism are by no means the only concepts critical of the modern liberal–capitalist State and the different kinds of violence it harbors at its core.[18] Philosophical concepts are not created out of thin air but instead draw components of concepts from other philosophers. For present purposes, Iris Marion Young and Pierre Rosanvallon, as well as Derrida, provide particularly productive points of departure. The alternative theory of justice propounded by Young (to which we return in chapter 3) aimed at simultaneously being critical of the State without becoming anarchist and being critical of liberal individualism without becoming communitarian. The concepts under construction here aim in a similar direction and to avoid the same pitfalls.[19] In reflections on the contemporary prospects for democracy, meanwhile, Rosanvallon promoted self-management (autogestion) as a critique of both liberal and Marxist political theory.[20] Liberal theory is inadequate to the modern State, according to Rosanvallon, because whereas the theory treats people as individuals, the modern State treats them as masses—and the practices of massification triumph easily and completely over theories of individualism. Marxist political theory, in turn, is inadequate because, in Rosanvallon's view, there simply isn't one—or there is only a negative, "revolutionary" one: there is in Marxist thought no positive conception of politics inasmuch as the ultimate goal of temporary, revolutionary politics is the "withering away of the state"—after which society is supposed to become transparent to itself. As the shortcomings of reigning liberal theory and practice become increasingly obvious and Intolerable, respectively, Rosanvallon suggests, self-management becomes the viable alternative both for the liberal present and for a "politics-free" Marxist future "after the revolution."

Many Interesting theories of economic democracy, like Rosanvallon's in this respect, either imply, propose, or presuppose the deconstruction of the modern boundary separating economics and politics.[21] They therefore chime with the expansive or nomadic thrust of Derrida's version of political friendship or friendly politics, alluded to earlier. Perhaps less friendly and/or more political than Derrida in this respect, I argue here in favor of categorically opposing Schmitt and for replacing his transcendent concept of the political, narrowly defined as determined externally and from on high by the State-declared opposition of friend and enemy, with an immanent concept of politics more broadly defined as emerging internally from social relations themselves, both within and beyond the scale of the nation-State. And free-market communism serves, as we have suggested, as an important supplement to nomad citizenship in this regard. A thoroughgoing aversion to transcendence is, of course, a key feature of Deleuze's philosophical stance, and immanence is a key component of most of his concepts. But for detailed analysis of the dynamics and virtues of group self-management as a crucial component of nomad citizenship, I draw extensively on the theories of the early-twentieth-century American management theorist Mary Parker Follett.[22] Many Deleuzian concepts—such as multiplicity, assemblage, immanence, and differentiation—can be readily understood in light of the central concept of *related difference* elaborated by Follett, which forms a cornerstone of the concept of affirmative nomadology constructed in chapter 1.

For nomadology to become affirmative, its concepts must be more than just critical responses to what is Intolerable in our sociohistorical milieu: they must be creative responses as well. "Those who criticize without creating," as Deleuze and Guattari insist in their final collaboration, "are the scourge of philosophy."[23] Furthermore, affirmative nomadology does not construe the sociohistorical milieu as totalized or homogeneous: it contains Intolerable elements, to be sure, but it just as surely contains elements that are tolerable, and even some that are laudable. The task of affirmative nomadology, and what makes it affirmative, is seeking out and highlighting actual instances of alternative, nonstate and noncapitalist forms of sociality to draw concepts from them, as "what belongs to political philosophy by right." On a scale larger than the nation-State, an emergent European citizenship could serve as such an instance; the European Union, however, lies far outside the scope of this book. On a smaller scale, Rosanvallon's self-managed cooperatives and Mary Parker Follett's neighborhood associations and flat-hierarchy business firms represent important instances of alternative organizations.

For our purposes, what is most important about these alternatives, beyond that they actually exist, is the *form of social relation* they epitomize: they are self-organizing. Here social order emerges immanently, or bottom up, rather than being imposed top down by a transcendent power from on high. The best illustration of immanent self-organization, as far as I know, is still jazz group improvisation, to which chapter 1 will add a number of others from a variety of fields (including science, games, and ethology); the concept of immanence they illustrate, in any case, is key to nomadism and nomadology, as first defined by Deleuze and Guattari.[24] Some of its roots lie in complexity theory and nonlinear mathematics, which have both formalized and reinforced long-standing impressions that order can and often does arise in systems spontaneously, without being imposed by some transcendent instance standing above or outside the system. Complexity theory supports both the nontotalized view of society and the nonlinear view of history informing nomadology.[25] The discovery of emergent self-organization seemed to belie the second law of thermodynamics, according to which entropy is supposed to increase—in any closed system operating close to equilibrium, that is. But the fields to which complexity theory was most dramatically applied were not closed systems and were nowhere near equilibrium: life on earth, for instance, receives practically immeasurable amounts of energy from the sun and thus represents a classic case of negentropy or syntropy rather than entropy. As Stuart Kauffmann (among others) has shown, starting from almost trivially simple mathematical models, spontaneous self-organization emerges in all kinds of systems, from inorganic molecule clusters to cells and organisms, to ecosystems, economies, and cultures.[26] Of course, debates about the sources or bases of social organization date back to the dawn of philosophy, but complexity theory gave new impetus and added credence to conceiving of various kinds of social order as immanently self-organizing, and this becomes a key component of the concept of nomad citizenship.

The main components of the concept of free-market communism, meanwhile, come from more disparate sources, starting with theories of the free market and Marxist theory itself. Drawing components from such ideologically opposed theories, the construction of the paradoxical concept of free-market communism will clearly have to be quite selective. But in fact, all concept construction is selective, as we shall see in chapter 1—and in two related senses. For one thing, each philosophical concept carefully selects which features of a Problematic sociohistorical state of affairs "belong to thought by right," and get mapped by the concept, and which features are thereby relegated to the status of mere historical facts.[27] The concept of the Death-State developed in chapter 2, for example, selects certain features of the Bush regime on which to concentrate and leaves other features behind in the historical record, as it were. And second, each philosophical concept carefully selects which features of other philosophical concepts it will draw on and adapt for its own purposes, leaving other components of that concept out of consideration altogether. For these reasons, affirmative nomadology's adaptation of components from other concepts will necessarily be highly selective, especially with respect to communism. Certain features of communism get selected to transform capitalist markets into truly free markets, as I suggested earlier. But it is equally the case that selected features of the free market will serve as means to realize—and indeed to transform and redefine our very conception of—communism.

One Important feature of communism, understood in this respect as a response to the Problems of alienation and possessive individualism generated by capitalism, is a renewed interest in community. With the accelerating destabilization of the ideal nation-State—both internally (increasing ethnic, religious, and cultural heterogeneity of its populations) and externally (decreasing sovereignty in the face of global interdependence and transnational capital)—much attention has been paid of late to questions of community and the forms of social belonging.[28] One concern has been how to negotiate (even conceptually, not to mention practically or institutionally) between the undesirable extremes of hyperindividualistic liberalism and hyperconformist communitarianism. In his recent *A Theory of Citizenship,* Herman van Gunsteren formulates the Problem clearly, in terms that resonate with Mary Parker Follett's interest in preserving and fostering "related difference" in neighborhood groups and business enterprises. How can we develop a concept of citizenship, he asks, "that acknowledges contemporary differences and focuses on the creative, positive task of citizenship—organizing those differences—rather than on the negative imposition of unity through uniformity?"[29] What are the prospects and means—other than by imposing unity through uniformity—of organizing differences in what van Gunsteren aptly calls *communities of fate,* which are practically the only kind of community that exists today? A community of fate is what Deleuze and Guattari would call a multiplicity or a nondenumerable set: a group that shares absolutely nothing but the minimal zero degree of relation, as expressed in the simple conjunctions *and, with,* and *among.* In van Gunsteren's terms, such a community is simply

> a given, in the sense that people find themselves involved in it without much forethought or choice, and in the sense that they cannot extricate themselves from it without paying a heavy price. . . . When individuals are so situated that they cannot avoid bumping into each other without giving up their ways of life and work, when they have to deal somehow with their differences, we speak of a "community of fate."[30]

Van Gunsteren goes on to define plurality as "differences among people who share a community of fate" and asserts that "*organiz[ing] plurality* is the primary task" of what he calls "neorepublican citizenship."[31] For our purposes, however, and as Mary Parker Follett clearly understood, plurality is not merely an inevitable *internal* feature of any given community of fate; it is itself the *condition* of communities of fate: there are many such communities, and every citizen belongs to any number of them. We therefore take van Gunsteren's image of "individuals so situated that they cannot avoid bumping into each other" metaphorically: there are more or less local communities of fate where people do indeed rub shoulders with one another, and other communities of fate that span the globe, and still others that are virtual communities. The Problem posed in different ways by van Gunsteren and Follett becomes for affirmative nomadology how to organize such a plurality of communities of fate immanently, that is, without imposing order from the top down and enforcing unity through uniformity: how to create a multiplicity of multiplicities. This is the Problem that the concept of free-market communism is designed to address.

In an idiom somewhat closer than van Gunsteren's and Follett's to Deleuze and Guattari's own, Jean-Luc Nancy has addressed similar questions about what he calls "community at loose ends" *(la communauté désoeuvrée)* through the concept of "literary communism."[32] In brief, communism for Nancy must be informed by literature rather than inspired by myth because myth unites communities by enforcing uniformity and allowing no "loose ends." Myth enforces community by stipulating what members must have in common; myth grounds their being-in-common. Literature, by contrast, ungrounds myth, so to speak. The literary being-in-common of community at or with loose ends is paradoxical: members have nothing essential in-common, only their contingent being-with one another. The communism of community at loose ends involves being-with multiple others rather than belonging-to a single united whole; it involves belonging without identity, belonging-with-(a)-difference. A community at loose ends, in other words, is a community of fate, or what Deleuze and Guattari would call an immanently composed multiplicity, assembled via the simple connective synthesis: and . . . and . . . and . . .

Yet there may be an important difference between Nancy and Deleuze and Guattari, as much as they might agree on the virtues of a literary, in-essential, or unfounded communism.[33] It is suggested by the standard and rather literal English rendition of Nancy's impossible-to-translate French title *(La Communauté désoeuvrée),* which is *The Inoperative Community*—but which could less charitably be translated as the "idle," "unemployed," or "unoccupied" community. For Nancy is intent on divorcing community from work *(oeuvre),* in the many senses of that term:

> community cannot pertain to the domain of the work [*oeuvre*]. . . .
> [To think of] community as a work . . . would suppose that the
> common being, as such, is objectifiable and producible (in places,
> persons, edifices, discourses, institutions, symbols: in sum, in
> subjects).[34]

Deleuze and Guattari, by contrast, prefer to emphasize production: a community, like any other assemblage, is produced—albeit not entirely in-tentionally and not even by human beings alone. A community for Deleuze and Guattari, to formulate it more precisely, is a machinic assemblage. Far from being "inoperative," it is the result of and a relay for mostly de-terminate (or at least partly determinable) material, natural, and social operations or processes. ("Nature = Industry, Nature = History," as they insist in *Anti-Oedipus*.[35]) Deleuze and Guattari might therefore demur at Nancy's suggestion that

> Being-*in*-common means . . . that being is nothing that we would
> possess as a common being, whilst notwithstanding we *are,* or that
> being is only common to us in the mode of being *shared/divided.*
> Not that a common substance is distributed amongst us, but that
> being is *only* shared *between* and *in* existents.[36]

And they would presumably want to emphasize instead that what the substance or being of human community is and has *in common* is simply life on planet earth. Communism in this context would imply reclaiming such being-in-common by restoring connections with life on what Deleuze and Guattari frequently call the "new earth"—connections that have been severed or expropriated by despotic gods, States, and capital in the service of power, infinite debt accumulation, and death, as we will see in chapters 2 and 4. It may be true that Deleuze and Guattari's frequent invocations of "life" and a "people-to-come" on a "new earth" risk mythologizing such figures (which certainly don't appear to be full-fledged concepts, in their strict definition of the term): affirmative nomadology avoids such mythologizing by indexing actual instances of nomadic social relations. Such differences in emphasis notwithstanding, affirmative nomadology shares with Nancy and Deleuze and Guattari an understanding of communism that poses the problem of community as a kind of being-with or a being-in-common that organizes multiple differences immanently, in various forms of nomad citizenship.

Beyond this interest in forms of community, the other aspect of communism that affirmative nomadology selects and construes as a response to the Problems of alienation and hyperindividualism is concern for the Common Good. Without a basis in some material process or institutional system, any invocation of the Common Good is bound to sound like false piety or moralizing cant. And indeed, in most systems associated with the Common Good—from the all-knowing philosopher-king of Plato's perfectly just republic to the party bureaucrats of Soviet-style State capitalism and the well-intentioned planners of recently existing socialism—someone decides what is Good from on high and imposes it top down on the members of society beneath. This is where the concept of the free market intervenes and intersects with certain components of communism. For it turns out that spontaneous order is not the only thing that can emerge unplanned from complex systems: something like spontaneous collective intelligence or distributed decision making can emerge from free markets as an unplanned consequence of the interactions of multiple agents, in much the same way. Of course, communism must intervene here, in turn, and modify certain features of the so-called free market: after all, a kind of distributed intelligence has been attributed to markets at least since the notorious invisible hand of Adam Smith, with results that bear no resemblance whatsoever to communism.[37] Construction of a viable concept of free-market communism will thus depend on spelling out the conditions—both positive and negative—under which truly free markets can be expected to generate an acceptable approximation of the Common Good immanently, from the bottom up.

On the basis of extensive historical studies, Fernand Braudel has proposed an Important distinction between markets and antimarkets that can serve as one point of departure.[38] Along similar lines, but on the basis of Marx's theoretical investigations, Deleuze and Guattari distinguished between the positive, economic component of markets and their negative, power component.[39] More specifically, James Surowiecki, in his recent work *The Wisdom of Crowds,* lays out the conditions under which large-scale interactive systems such as markets can produce surprising results in the domains of coordination and cooperation as well as cognition.[40] The prerequisites for the wisdom of crowds to emerge, as he shows, include diversity and independence of knowledge or opinion, decentralization of decisions, and some mechanism to aggregate multiple decisions to produce a result—prerequisites that truly free free markets often realize. Surowiecki's analysis thus provides important components of the concept of free-market communism, as we will see in chapter 4. For now, suffice it to mention the one minimum condition recognized by Surowiecki, Deleuze and Guattari, and Braudel alike: that all market agents be price takers rather than price makers, as economists are wont to say; or, in Braudelian terms, that the market remain free from the power of antimarket forces to control prices and thereby determine the fate of others—capital figuring, of course, among the most notorious of such antimarket forces, with the State a close second.[41]

This brings us to the final Important feature of communism selected by affirmative nomadology as a component of the concept of free-market communism—and which is no doubt its most Important feature: communism designates the end of capitalism. Conceptually, anyway, ending capitalism is the least of our Problems: without wage labor, there is no source of surplus-value—and capital accumulation comes to an end. The more Interesting Problems, as we will see in chapter 4, involve how to accomplish that end and what will then ensue. What forms of productive activity (other than wage labor), of community and political organization (other than the State and revolution), will emerge with the end of capitalism? Answers to such questions, of course, lie well beyond the scope of this book (and perhaps of any book). But we end by revisiting and modifying the concepts of revolution and the general strike—by repeating them, but with Important differences—to at least pose the questions anew and in as provocative and productive a way as possible. That is the purpose of creating a fourth, pragmatic concept, which, like the diagnostic concept of the Death-State, links philosophy with what lies outside it: this is the concept of the slow-motion general strike. Affirmative nomadology would hardly realize the utopian vocation of political philosophy if it didn't at least pose the question of how certain actually existing institutions and practices might get amplified and converge to foster large-scale social transformation for the better. An appendix spells out in further detail the utopian vocation of affirmative nomadology by contrasting it with better-known dialectical views.

I mentioned earlier that philosophical concepts don't get created out of thin air but adapt components of concepts from other philosophers for new uses. The concept and practice of affirmative nomadology created and exercised in what follows obviously owe a great deal to the theory of nomadology presented in *A Thousand Plateaus*. But affirmative nomadology also draws extensively on the theory of schizoanalysis presented in *Anti-Oedipus*, particularly in chapter 2. (Deleuze's book *Foucault* and Deleuze and Guattari's final collaboration, *What Is Philosophy?*, are also important sources.[42]) One of the subsidiary philosophical aims of the book, then—beyond simply acknowledging such debts to *Capitalism and Schizophrenia*—is to explore the relations between schizoanalysis and nomadology as well as to explain how concepts from both of them get modified in the creation of affirmative nomadology. Schizoanalysis and nomadology are not exactly the same thing, but they are by no means incompatible, either; nomadology does not simply supersede schizoanalysis. It is true that on the occasion of an interview (1973) shortly after the publication of *Anti-Oedipus*, Deleuze spoke about renouncing the term *schizoanalysis*; this was done, he explains, mostly to focus his critique on the institutions rather than the theory of psychoanalysis. But he also explained that he and Guattari henceforth wanted to avoid privileging the discourse of schizophrenia, when so many other discourses (he mentions homosexuality and perversion, among other "marginal discourses") had the same potential as schizophrenia for "graft[ing] themselves onto a war-machine that won't reproduce a State or Party apparatus."[43] Indeed, the war-machine is a crucial component of the concept of nomadology, as we show at the end of chapter 1. It subsumes not only the concepts of socius and schizophrenia from schizoanalysis but also the concepts of subject-group and subjected group from Sartre (which were themselves adapted by schizoanalysis to mediate, as it were, between schizophrenia and socius).[44] That does not mean that nomadology simply replaces schizoanalysis, however: on one occasion in *A Thousand Plateaus*, the two are presented as practically synonymous—albeit in a long list of the "various names" of a single discipline supposedly invented by a fictional conceptual persona named "Professor Challenger" that also includes "rhizomatics, stratoanalysis, . . . micropolitics, pragmatics, [and] the science of multiplicities."[45] But *schizoanalysis* is usually presented in the second volume of *Capitalism and Schizophrenia* as a synonym for *pragmatics*.[46] In any case, schizoanalysis is invaluable here for its contribution to diagnosing the Death-State by showing how the psychodynamics of Death-State citizenship relate to the political dynamics of the State and the economic dynamics of capital.

Affirmative nomadology does not just adapt concepts from schizoanalysis and nomadology, however: it takes up and modifies concepts from other thinkers as well—notably Freud and Marx. The construction of the concept of affirmative nomadology thus entails a set of displacements within established theories leading from major to minor, from State-centric to nomadic thought. The first of four such displacements, and the most general, is already implied in the paradoxical term *nomad citizenship*. The point of the concept, as we have already suggested, is to break the State's monopoly on citizenship and redistribute social belonging among other groups and other scales and forms of group organization. Through such a displacement, the actual multiplicity of minor group allegiances in modern societies is recognized and fostered, while the lethal master-allegiance claimed by the State is denied.[47]

The second theoretical displacement affects psychoanalysis and is already suggested by the title of *Anti-Oedipus,* although Deleuze and Guattari themselves do not make it explicit. This displacement shifts the theoretical focus of schizoanalysis as a component of affirmative nomadology from castration anxiety to separation anxiety and from the Oedipal field to pre-Oedipal relations. Whereas Freudian theory centered on the figure of the Father (and Lacanian theory on the figure of the Phallus), schizoanalysis shifts its focus to the figure of the Mother. Instead of considering the "dark continent" of woman in light of the Oedipus complex, schizoanalysis treats Oedipal dynamics as an epiphenomenon peculiar to a historically specific institutional arrangement: the nuclear family under capitalism.[48] Pre-Oedipal dynamics remain the fundamental ones. And indeed, the kinds of group dynamics highlighted by the concept of nomad citizenship are all fundamentally anti-Oedipal, if not explicitly feminist, starting with the dynamics analyzed by Mary Parker Follett herself. It is probably no accident that outside the field of management theory itself, it is feminists who have most readily understood the importance of Follett's theoretical contributions.[49]

The third displacement targets economic theory, including most variants of Marxist theory. It shifts the focus of attention away from the development of productive forces as a means of overcoming scarcity and refocuses it on the development of the division of labor—also necessarily understood as the social articulation of labor—as both a means and a result of socializing production. Historically, the division-articulation of labor has taken a quantum leap forward in connection with each of two institutions: once with the development of market exchange itself, then again with the expansion, distortion, and acceleration of market dynamics by industrial capitalism. Market economies and industrial capitalism thus function as what I have elsewhere called *difference-engines* and take their place alongside the other difference-engines highlighted by Deleuze in his career-long elaboration of a materialist philosophy of difference—including the evolution of life and the semiotic expression of sense.[50] If there is a motor of history, on this view, it would not be class struggle or the development of productive forces but the progressive differentiation of labor articulated into increasingly complex social assemblages or multiplicities—the world-historical and global development of what Mary Parker Follett called *related difference*. In the same vein, the socialization of production would historically count for more than private accumulation. Indeed, on this view, capital is not only a social relation rather than a thing, it is also less a social relation than a pure limit: private accumulation as a limit and obstacle to further socialization of production. And the principal Problem posed by capitalism is that, far from ever reaching its own limit, capital continually displaces it, lurching from crisis to crisis in a history without end. Yet capitalist history—or rather capitalist historicity—is not the only form of historicity in history: there are others, and so one articulation of the Problem of capitalism will be to conceive and practice ways to starve its peculiar form of historicity in favor of others.

The fourth theoretical displacement also targets economic theory, including dominant variants of Marx's own. But it takes as point of departure Marx's recognition that the secret of primitive accumulation is that it is fundamentally a process of destitution—a process that has continuing accumulation as an important by-product, and subsequently as its very object and aim. This is not to deny the centrality of accumulation to capital and capitalism but rather to insist that capital accumulation cannot occur without the initial establishment and subsequent constant expansion of a generalized dependence on capital for people's survival—and hence to displace the theoretical and practical emphasis from the aim and result of the process to its fundamental precondition. This displacement thus ultimately shifts the target of revolutionary strategy away from privately accumulated capital—and hence away from class struggle conceived as the expropriation of the expropriators and all that they have expropriated—to refocus it on the restoration and creation of the Commons as publicly or commonly available means of life. Communism is the antithesis of capitalism, in this light, inasmuch as it replaces abject dependence on capital with free public access to the Commons or what is in-common.

The third and fourth displacements are obviously related, and taken together, they yield what I call a *minor* or *nomad* reading of Marx—a minor marxism, if you will, to contrast with the major Marxism (one could even say the State Marxism, or the State form of Marxism[51]) promulgated by Communist parties and communist States around the world over the last century or so. But even more Important, to my mind, is the perhaps not-so-obvious relation between these displacements and the second one, which is addressed—nominally at least—to psychoanalytic theory. The main effect of that displacement, once again, is to transvalue the figure of the Mother in relation to that of the Father—that is, to shift theoretical attention away from castration, prohibition, obedience, individuation, and the exercise of power, as a result of refocusing it on connection, sustenance, cooperation, and the cultivation of freedom. As we will see in chapter 2, there is a world of difference between dependence on the Mother, on community, and on the earth, on one hand, and abject dependence on the Father-figure, on the State, and on capital, on the other—and, if I may say so, they are the *same difference*: abject dependence must be distinguished categorically from reciprocal interdependence in all three spheres. What affirmative nomadology adapts from schizoanalysis, in other words, is the harrowing realization that abject dependency underlies, links together, and intensifies the mutually reinforcing noxious effects of the nuclear family, the State, and capital. This is the other secret of primitive accumulation, hinted at by Marx in his lurid descriptions of the process toward the end of *Capital*, volume 1, then elaborated on by Rosa Luxemburg, but only fully developed in recent work by feminists such as Maria Mies and Sylvia Federici on the dependence of accumulation on patriarchy: the accumulation of capital requires not only the destitution of the poor in the marketplace but also the subordination of women in the domestic sphere and the subordination or enslavement of indigenous peoples around the globe.[52] Capital accumulation becomes possible, in other words, not only because of the reduction of wage levels by job-market competition among destitute workers but also because of completely unremunerated labor performed by those workers' wives at home and by slaves and other workers in the colonies.

If the third and fourth theoretical displacements yield a kind of minor marxism, the four displacements taken together yield something like a minor feminism or a feminist nomadology. Affirmative nomadology is, to be sure, adapted from the work of Deleuze and Guattari, but it is informed through and through by the perspectives of Mies and Federici and the work of Mary Parker Follett, Jane Jacobs, Iris Marion Young, Rosa Luxemburg, and J. K. Gibson-Graham, among others. I chose these women's works—or rather they chose me, forced and helped me to think—because their work offers means with which to address the Problems confronting us, both sociohistorical and philosophical, in the most provocative and productive ways. The only thing minor about the feminism of affirmative nomadology, I hasten to add, is that, like all other conceptual components adapted for use here, they are mobilized not to erect some general theory but to address a specific set of Problems. It will be up to others to further develop a feminist nomadology, should the concept prove to be of sufficient Interest.[53]

Following the definition of a minor science, affirmative nomadology is constructed in chapter 1 as a form of problem posing rather than problem solving—the point of creating concepts in philosophy being to articulate Problems as productively as possible, not to pretend or claim to have solved them.[54] The Problem of the Death-State is posed in chapter 2, and the concepts of nomad citizenship and free-market communism are then developed in chapters 3 and 4 as ways to address and further articulate the Problem. Ultimately, for these concepts to be of any real Interest or Importance, they must inform or suggest an open set of practical measures with which to experiment. Like minor science, political philosophy depends on what lies outside philosophy, not only for the specific Problems it forces us to confront by creating concepts to begin with but also for the "collective, non-scientific activities" by which to gauge the actual value of the concepts created as a result.[55] While the diagnostic concept of the Death-State reveals what is most Intolerable about U.S. citizenship at the dawn of the twenty-first century, and the paradoxical concepts of nomad citizenship and free-market communism force us to rethink the dynamics of political and economic participation beyond the liberal–democratic social contract and the capitalist labor contract, the pragmatic concept of the slow-motion general strike proposes a new, minor form for the struggle with capitalism. Political philosophy does not legislate solutions to the Problems it addresses but rather articulates them in ways that suggest avenues for practical experimentation outside philosophy. Theory, as Deleuze once famously said, serves as a kind of "relay [from] one praxis to another"[56]—the ultimate aim of political philosophy, and hence of affirmative nomadology, still being not merely to interpret the world but to change it.

CHAPTER ONE

From Political Philosophy to Affirmative Nomadology

If philosophy is the creation of concepts, then how and why does this creation occur? And when does it become political—when does philosophy become political philosophy? An understanding of why concept creation occurs and of the conditions under which it becomes political will enable us to examine how concepts are created in and by political philosophy. We will then examine the concept of nomadism developed by Deleuze and Guattari in the "Treatise on Nomadology" and the principles of nomadology itself.

Why Create Concepts?

"Subject and object give a poor approximation of thought," Deleuze and Guattari proclaim in their final collaboration, *What Is Philosophy?*[1] Instead, thought is something that happens to thinkers, something that befalls them: philosophers are subject *to* thought rather than subjects *of* thought. And although the provocation of thought does lead to the creation of concepts, these concepts, in turn, create (rather than reflect) their objects, and these objects are objects of thought (virtual objects), not objects one would find in the real world. To insist that philosophical thought is in an important sense asubjective is not to deny the importance of great philosophers, but the names Spinoza, Nietzsche, and others come to designate in philosophy distinctive bodies of concepts rather than flesh-and-blood historical personages. As philosopher, Deleuze insists, "I am no longer myself but thought's aptitude for finding itself and spreading across a plane that passes through me at several places."[2] Yet if philosophical thought is not subjective, not the accomplishment of philosopher-subjects but something that happens to them, neither is it objective or historical. Philosophers are not spokespersons or ventriloquists for their age: the creation of concepts takes place outside of or rather orthogonal to historical time, by resisting the present: "to create is to resist."[3] In explicit contrast with historicists like Hegel and Heidegger, "inasmuch as they posit history as a form of interiority in which the concept necessarily develops or unveils its destiny,"[4] Deleuze and Guattari propose a "geophilosophy" (following Braudel's notion of geohistory[5]): philosophical thought may have historical preconditions, but thought becomes philosophical by extracting itself from history and by extracting philosophical concepts from historical states of affairs, as we shall see.[6]

If not as an expression of the philosophical subject, nor as a reflection of a sociohistorical object or epoch, why does philosophy create concepts? In the most general terms, the circumstance that provokes thought is chaos, the infinity of determinations that compose the complexity of the cosmos.[7] To deal with chaos, philosophical thought invents what Deleuze and Guattari call a "plane of immanence": this plane "sections" chaos (much as a plane sections a cone) and thereby reduces its complexity by considering it from a certain angle (or perspective, as Nietzsche might put it); it is on this plane that concepts will be created.[8] Chaos harbors many potential planes of immanence—infinitely many, in fact; all great philosophers have invented one (or more), but that still leaves infinitely many more to be invented. The plane of immanence combines powers of being and powers of thinking (following Spinoza's extension and thought[9]), and it is their coexistence that enables thought to get a grasp of being.[10] But each plane of immanence is itself infinitely complex (comprising an infinity of determinations)—even though it is only one section of chaos—and hence its powers of thought move at infinite speed. Indeed, thought must move at infinite speed to prevent the emergence of transcendence[11] because stopping the infinite play of determinations (principle of the plane's very immanence) at any one point of the plane would establish that point as its center.[12]

Another key feature of the plane of immanence is that as a particular section of chaos, it inevitably has a specific orientation, some principle of selectivity by which it reduces the infinity of chaos to something concepts can grasp, even if that principle becomes visible as such only after the concepts have been created. Deleuze and Guattari call such an orientation the "image of thought" implicated in a plane of immanence:[13] it provides a basic *why* for conceptual creation, a sense of what thinking is for to begin with—recollecting the Truth for Plato, correcting sense-evidence for Descartes, exercising will-to-power for Nietzsche, and so on—even before concepts themselves get created. Finally, Deleuze and Guattari maintain that concepts are created on the plane of immanence by means of what they call *conceptual personae*.[14] In line with their desubjectification of philosophy, Deleuze and Guattari suggest that it is these conceptual personae that actually do the thinking for the philosopher:

> The conceptual persona is not the philosopher's representative but rather, the reverse: the philosopher is only the envelope of his principal conceptual persona and of all the other personae who are the intercessors, the real subjects of his philosophy. Conceptual personae are the philosopher's "heteronyms," and the philosopher's name is the simple pseudonym of his personae.[15]

In some cases, a philosopher's conceptual personae are obvious—Socrates and the philosopher-king for Plato; Dionysus, but also the priest and others, for Nietzsche—sometimes they are not. But all philosophy thinks through conceptual personae who are distinct from their authors, just as narrators are distinct from their literary authors. For Deleuze and Guattari, to take a prime example from *Anti-Oedipus,* the schizophrenic becomes "a conceptual persona who lives intensely within the thinker and forces him to think."[16]

What is it that befalls or happens to philosophers that forces them to think? What specific circumstances, aside from mere chaos, provoke the creation of concepts by conceptual personae on a plane of immanence? In the course of his career, Deleuze has given three kinds of answer to this question. In his early works, it is paradox that provokes thought: "Philosophy is revealed not by good sense but by paradox," says Deleuze in *Difference and Repetition.* "Paradox is the pathos or passion of philosophy."[17] *The Logic of Sense,* in turn, comprises in its entirety "a series of paradoxes which form the theory of sense."[18] Here the provocation to thought is as it were internal to thought itself: logical paradoxes provide the irritants that shake the brain out of its habitual slumber and force it to think. The second kind of provocation consists of topics or problems within philosophy (no longer limited to logical contradictions or paradoxes) that, in the estimation of a creative philosopher, have been poorly conceived and hence demand to be reconceived: "in philosophy, concepts are only created as a function of problems which are thought to be badly understood or badly posed."[19] In the later collaborations with Guattari (and perhaps because of that collaboration), the locus of the stimulus to thought shifts steadily outside of philosophy and eventually even outside of thought.

The third kind of provocation, which most interests us here, arises from the connection between philosophy and its sociohistorical context; here the problems are not strictly speaking or originally philosophical, but they nonetheless provoke philosophical thought to furnish solutions to, or rather new and improved articulations of, those problems—articulations that are indeed philosophical. In this connection, it is possible to argue that there is no "history of philosophy" per se, that philosophy has no history internal to itself, but that its evolution depends on and derives from the transformation of the problems to which it responds. As Deleuze and Guattari put it in *What Is Philosophy?*, "human history and the history of philosophy do not have the same rhythm."[20] How is it possible to be a Platonist or a Kantian today? Why didn't Stoic philosophy die with the Stoics themselves or with the passing of their epoch? Is it because we face some of the same problems they did? Or is it because we can reshape their concepts to respond to new problems of our own?

> If one can still be a Platonist, Cartesian, or Kantian today, it is because one is justified in thinking that their concepts can be reactivated in our problems and inspire those concepts that need to be created. What is the best way to follow the great philosophers? Is it to repeat what they said or *to do what they did*, that is, create concepts for problems that necessarily change?[21]

In this instance, philosophy does not respond to problems of "its own" but to problems presented to it or forced on it by its real-world milieu. And it is this kind of connection, between philosophy and sociohistorical context, that Deleuze and Guattari call *political philosophy* or *utopia*: "utopia is *what links* philosophy with its own epoch. . . . Utopia . . . designates *that conjunction of philosophy, or of the concept, with the present milieu—* political philosophy."[22] So we see that philosophy creates concepts in response to internal as well as external problems, and when those problems are external to philosophy, when they put philosophy in contact with its real-world milieu, philosophy becomes political philosophy.

But here it is important to pause and evaluate the terms in which Deleuze and Guattari cast the relation of the concept with the present milieu in their definition of political philosophy. Is this relation construed as positive or negative? For the most part, Deleuze and Guattari discuss this relation in negative terms—despite the positive connotations of the term *utopia*, which they use synonymously with political philosophy.[23] Thus "it is with utopia that philosophy becomes political and takes the criticism of its own time to its highest point";[24] or again, "etymologically [utopia] stands for absolute deterritorialization but always at the critical point at which it is connected with the present relative milieu, and especially with the forces stifled by this milieu."[25] Even worse, "we continue to undergo shameful compromises with [the present time]. This feeling of shame is one of philosophy's most powerful motifs";[26] and again, "books of philosophy and works of art contain their sum of unimaginable sufferings. . . . They have *resistance* in common—their resistance to death, to servitude, to the intolerable, to shame, and to the present."[27] And finally, they "posit revolution as plane of immanence, but to the extent that [its] features connect up with what is real here and now in the struggle against capitalism."[28] Compromise, critique, shame, suffering, resistance, the struggle against capitalism: such terms betray an overwhelmingly negative relation between philosophy and the real-world milieu that risks making political philosophy a purely *reactive* enterprise.[29]

It is not a question here of denying the validity of a critical political philosophy: critique is not only important, it is necessary. But it is also important to prevent the wholesale reduction of political philosophy to its negative pole and to reassert the legitimacy and, indeed, priority of a positive political philosophy. As Deleuze argues in his book on Nietzsche, active forces should always take priority over reactive ones.[30] So it is a matter of restoring the positive pole of political philosophy to its rightful place in relation to compromise, shame, suffering, and all the rest—a matter of finding alternatives to capitalism rather than struggling against, critiquing, or resisting it. Fortunately, Deleuze and Guattari themselves provide means for doing so.

For Deleuze and Guattari suggest that philosophy has truly flourished in two specific historical epochs, that it emerged and reemerged in connection with two distinctive social milieus: the Greek city-State and the world market.[31] In both cases, what is especially propitious for philosophical thought is *"the connection of an absolute plane of immanence with a relative social milieu that also functions through immanence."*[32] The philosophical plane, as we have seen, is characterized by absolute immanence as long as thought proceeds at infinite speed and thereby prevents transcendence. But a social milieu can also be characterized by a degree of immanence, when social composition prevents absolute authority from imposing itself in a top-down fashion and shows strong tendencies toward self-organization instead. The social milieu of the Greek city-State was characterized by relative immanence inasmuch as the agora brought together citizens as friends and rivals, among whom there was (in principle) no preestablished social hierarchy and hence no divinely or other transcendent authority figure; authority was to arise immanently from discussion itself. Here, we could say, immanence was constructed *politically*. The social milieu of world capitalism is characterized, at least in part, by deterritorialization and the decoding that accompanies it, which subordinate meaning to the abstract calculus of market exchange and hence dissolve or subvert any and all social authority. Here, we would then say, immanence is constructed *economically*. But it is also true that world capitalism is characterized by reterritorialization, particularly in the operations of the nation-State; hence Deleuze and Guattari's struggle to keep philosophical (or "nomad") thought free from capture by State-supported and State-supportive thought in its many forms (including Platonism, Hegelianism, etc.). For now, what matters is the kind of connection between thought and context that Deleuze and Guattari are proposing. Generally speaking, high-speed philosophy as absolute immanence finds fertile ground in milieus that themselves have strong (though always relative) tendencies toward immanent self-organization, whether based politically on the agora or economically on the market. The question then becomes, what kind of relation obtains between the absolute plane of immanence of philosophical thought and each of these relative social milieus: the city-State and the world market?

There is a crucial asymmetry between these two historical moments, especially regarding the role played by philosophy. The Greek city-State provided a deterritorialized space and the opportunity for philosophical thought to take root among its citizens. In this context, philosophy's task was to develop concepts and seek (if not attain) agreement as to the content of those concepts ("the Good," "Justice," etc.). Two things must be said about this propitious milieu. The first is that, despite a considerable and indeed essential degree of immanence in philosophical discussion itself, the Greek agora was a severely controlled, reterritorialized space where participation in discussion was restricted to elite citizens, that is, to adult male heads of household; women and other others (barbarians, slaves) were strictly excluded. The second has to do with the perhaps paradoxical relation in ancient Greece between immanence and abstraction, two key elements in the creation of philosophical concepts.

As the work of Jean-Joseph Goux and Alfred Sohn-Rethel has shown, the degree and kind of abstraction characteristic of Greek philosophy are closely related to the emerging prevalence of coined money, which embodies a similar kind of abstraction.[33] Important differences notwithstanding, money enables and then reflects a comparison between two different products that are deemed equivalent (e.g., if both are worth a dollar), in much the same way that a word or concept enables and then reflects a comparison between two discrete objects that are deemed identical (e.g., if both are trees). In both cases, despite the undeniable advantages of abstraction, the risk of reification or fetishization haunts the act of comparison through the very materialization (in coin or word) of the result of the comparison itself.[34] A minted coin bearing the image of a god or king appears to be the source and standard of equivalence and value rather than a token for acts of exchange. A minted word inscribed on a tablet or papyrus appears to be the source and standard of resemblances and meaning rather than a token for discussion. Plato does not merely succumb to such fetishization: he actively promotes it. The incarnation of exchange activity in money makes it appear as though its value transcends and measures the objects exchanged, just as the Platonic Forms make it appear as though meaning as eternal essence transcends and defines from on high the objects named. The Platonic theory of Forms celebrates the reification and deification of a transcendent standard of judgment, over and against the play of democratic philosophical discussion in the agora. It marks the emergence of the major or State form of philosophy against which Deleuze struggles throughout his work. The singularity of the Greek agora is that it combined powers of abstraction, through the persistent search for meaning agreed on among equals, with absolute immanence—inasmuch as the citizens accepted no authority over themselves or one another and the search had no end. This is the milieu in which the creation of concepts appears as the task proper to philosophy for the first time.

Today, however, philosophy is practically smothered under a plethora of concepts inherited from centuries of philosophical endeavor; the world market as locus of deterritorialization, meanwhile, provides nothing like an agora in which the value of these concepts could be immanently debated and assessed. Nevertheless, the task of most Western philosophy, following the Greek model, became settling issues, answering questions, making rational judgments, providing problems with conceptual solutions that would then be executed (usually by others) in the real-world milieu. The image of thought derived from Greek philosophy lost touch with philosophy's real conditions of existence.

Hence Deleuze and Guattari insist that the task of philosophy today in relation to the milieu of immanence provided by the world market is very different. For one thing, although many remain fixated on the classical image of the philosophical and urge its resuscitation, a public sphere for the reasoned discussion of political issues like the classical agora no longer exists: political discussion among equals has given way to mere policy discussion among professional politicians and bureaucrats, on one hand, and to sound-bite conventional wisdom broadcast to the masses by monopoly media conglomerates, on the other. Recently, the Internet has become a platform for much discussion, but it does not constitute a public sphere: not only are citizens without computer access excluded to begin with, but even those who are able to participate subdivide into more or less self-contained niche groups that communicate only rarely with one another and never with the whole—because such a whole does not exist. As Deleuze and Guattari put it,

> as for us, we possess concepts—after so many centuries of Western thought we think we possess them—but we hardly know where to put them because we lack a genuine plane. . . . We today possess concepts, but the Greeks did not yet possess them; they possessed the plane that we no longer possess.[35]

In this context, the point of philosophy is not to settle issues but rather to unsettle our stultified habits of thought, which change far more slowly than the conditions produced by high-speed capitalism to which they are supposed to respond; the point is not to provide solutions to problems for others to execute but to offer novel diagnoses or articulations of problems and to encourage experimentation with various solutions to them. Philosophical thought thus serves, as we have said, as a kind of relay between one practical orientation toward the real-world milieu and what may become a new, more productive orientation.[36] Moreover, the proof of such thought experiments can no longer come from within philosophy itself. Philosophy must connect with nonphilosophy; thought must find what Deleuze and Guattari somewhat enigmatically call a "people to come," and it is they who determine the results of a philosophical thought experiment through actual experimentation in real life.[37] Citizenship in this kind of philosophical endeavor is poles apart from the reterritorialized elite citizenship of the ancient Greek city-State: it is radically indeterminate, spatially unbounded, and open to whoever can make use of philosophical thought to generate and experiment with what Deleuze and Guattari call new "possibilities of life."[38] Political philosophy in the deterritorialized social milieu of the world market thus calls for a correspondingly deterritorialized form of citizenship, nomad citizenship, just as its plane of immanence calls for a form of distributed decision making, such as free-market communism.

How to Create Concepts

We have seen that each philosophy proceeds by way of an image of thought, a sense of what thinking is for, and by way of conceptual personae (such as the nomad citizen) that in effect do the thinking on behalf of the philosopher and are responsible for the creation of philosophical concepts.

We have also seen that philosophical concepts today are inherently problematic: they seek to destabilize rather than stabilize our understanding of the world, and when they are political concepts, they offer novel articulations or diagnoses of real-world problems rather than legislate solutions to them. The construction of philosophical concepts must therefore be carefully distinguished from the procedures that create scientific concepts, which do indeed seek to stabilize our understanding of the world (or of discrete portions of it): the *diagnostic* relation of philosophical concepts to the real-world milieu is very different from the *representational* relation of scientific concepts to it.

But first it is important to note that philosophy, and even political philosophy, draws on resources from within philosophy itself, even if only to rearrange and transform them in light of the new problematics it articulates. One of the things that is so distinctive about Deleuze is the way he has drawn on a vast repertoire of concepts from philosophers such as Bergson, Kant, Marx, Nietzsche, and Spinoza (to mention just a few) in developing his own philosophical perspective. Guattari, in a similar vein, contributes concepts adapted from Hjelmslev, Lacan, and Marx (among others), which then get retooled for use in conjunction with Deleuze's repertoire. As we shall see in the next section, the concept of nomadism developed by Deleuze and Guattari owes at least as much to internal references to the concept of *nomos* within Greek philosophy as it does to external references to nomadic peoples. But it is never a question of remaining faithful to this or that predecessor: old concepts had other problems to solve or diagnose, even if certain of their components can be salvaged and put to use in new ways. Deleuze and Guattari thus always draw selectively on the philosophical tradition, combining components from old concepts into new concepts created "for problems that necessarily change."[39]

Schizophrenia is certainly one of the most dramatic—and widely misunderstood—of the concepts they have adapted for diagnosing some of the problems and prospects presented by advanced capitalism. Borrowed from Lacan, where it designates a radically indeterminate mode of semiosis, a metonymy of desire free from overcoding by the Symbolic Order, it gets combined with Marx's analysis of the cash nexus of the market, which "strips of its halo" any and all socially authorized meaning. On this view (as presented in *Anti-Oedipus*), if the Symbolic Order is vacant, it is because capital and finance calculations have replaced authority and meaning as the ground of the social bond, leaving meaning and subjectivity to float free, except where capital ties them down temporarily to local regimes of production and consumption in its pursuit of surplus value. The schizophrenic thus subsumes the proletariat as the hero of a drama in which the prospect of free-form libidinal production and freedom from socially imposed meaning and representation supplements the promise of free labor power and freedom from necessity as objectives for an ironic universal history. This "philosophical" schizophrenic, the schizophrenic as conceptual persona, let me say in passing, does not represent psychiatric-ward patients at all: combining selected features of schizophrenia into a new philosophical concept also entails leaving selected features out.

The same must be said of the references philosophy makes to any real-world states of affairs lying outside it: external reference in the creation of concepts is also always selective, though the principle of selectivity in philosophy differs significantly from that of science, which, of course, also makes reference to the real world. Deleuze and Guattari are therefore very careful to distinguish a properly philosophical relation between concept and context from the better-known scientific relation. Already in *A Thousand Plateaus*, they are categorical about the distinction: "nowhere do we claim for our concepts the title of science."[40] And they also devote a good part of *What Is Philosophy?* to rigorously distinguishing philosophical concepts from scientific ones.[41] Unlike both the human and the natural sciences, which are representative, philosophy is creative, serving, as we have said, as a kind of relay between one practical orientation to the world and another, new (and, it is hoped, improved) one. Philosophy responds to Problems that arise when a given mode of existence or practical orientation no longer suffices. Such Problems are real enough, but they are not reducible to reality. The purpose of philosophy is not to represent the world but to create concepts, and these concepts serve not to accurately replicate in discourse specific segments of the world as it really is (as science does) but to diagnose Problems and propose articulations of and/or solutions to them, to offer new and different perspectives on or orientations toward the world.[42] Take, for example, the Problem facing Greek society, as Plato construes it: emergent democracy fosters free speech, and through its exercise, sophists threaten to undermine hierarchical social order. His solution is the conceptual persona called "Socrates," who will invent a practice of the dialectic to engage with and "correct" immanent public opinion in the interests of a transcendent Truth, becoming thereby a cornerstone of State philosophy (and hence a constant target of Deleuze and Guattari's nomad thought). We have, on one hand, a prodigious creation of concepts (the Socratic dialectic, the Ideal Forms, etc.) and of conceptual personae (not just the figure of Socrates but also the philosopher-king, the guardians, and others). We have, on the other hand, numerous rhizomatic points of contact with the real: nascent democracy, the agora, the sophists, Socrates himself, and so on. The conceptual persona "Socrates" is indeed derived from Socrates the person and his particular social milieu, but the conceptual persona does not represent him or that milieu. Even if there are features of the historical milieu that resemble concept formations in philosophy (features such as the real-life sophists and Socrates), the "corresponding" conceptual persona or philosophical concept (e.g., Socrates or the dialectic) *does not represent* those psychosocial types: "conceptual personae are irreducible to *psychosocial types*. . . . Nietzsche's Dionysus is no more the mythical Dionysus than Plato's Socrates is the historical Socrates."[43] In the same vein, Deleuze and Guattari insist in *Anti-Oedipus* that "they have never seen a schizophrenic"—even though the schizophrenic as conceptual persona is, in a sense, the very hero of the book (though not its only conceptual persona).[44] The point is that the conceptual persona of the schizophrenic is a completely different kind of entity from the flesh-and-blood schizophrenic: "in one case the schizophrenic is a conceptual persona who lives intensely within the thinker and forces him to think, whereas in the other the schizophrenic is a psychosocial type who represses the living being and robs him of his thought."[45]

So the connection between philosophy and its sociohistorical milieu is essentially diagnostic rather than representative-scientific: "all concepts are connected to problems without which they would have no meaning and which can themselves only be isolated or understood [as problems] as their solution emerges."[46] Sciences aim to grasp states of affairs as they are; the point is to get reality right, to settle on a correct understanding of the world. Philosophy aims never to settle but on the contrary always to unsettle and to transform our understanding of certain Problems because they are thought to have been badly posed, or not posed at all, by previous thinkers and/or because the Problems are historically new or have changed so radically over time as to render previous responses inadequate. Hence Deleuze and Guattari insist that philosophy for them "does not consist in knowing and is not inspired by truth. Rather it is categories like Interesting, Remarkable, or Important that determine [its] success or failure."[47] In the same vein, they distinguish at the beginning of *A Thousand Plateaus*[48] between scientific tracing and philosophical mapping: a tracing (or a photograph) simply captures or reproduces reality as it is; mapping selects and extracts certain features because it entails a certain orientation toward (or perspective on) reality. A map showing the location of freeway entrances but not school buildings is no more or less accurate than one showing the location of schools but not freeways, and neither one of them is completely accurate: neither one includes all the facts. Their special value as maps depends on the Problem at hand—whether getting on a freeway or finding a school—and then, of course, but only then, does it depend on whether they get those locations right. And even then, actually getting to the school or onto the freeway requires more than just the map itself: the actual solution to the Problem involves social practices (physiological capacities and/or technologies such as walking or driving a car) that lie outside philosophy itself. This is the sense in which philosophy articulates a Problem in such a way as to orient or improve a given social practice, which may in turn provide a solution (although it may not: philosophy itself cannot determine its own success; it can only propose experiments). In any case, the creation of concepts is thus crucially selective as well as (or as part of being) diagnostic; thought selects out from states of affairs "what belongs to philosophy by right."[49] And in extracting a philosophical concept from a historical state of affairs, thought chooses certain determinations as "Interesting, Remarkable or Important" and "relegates other determinations to the status of mere facts, characteristics of states of affairs, or lived contents."[50] The concept of schizophrenia, for instance, gets created through the extraction of selected features from a historical state of affairs characterized by the spread of the market, the predominance of capital over social relations, and the subversion of meaning by calculation (among other things) and the relegation of other features (such as reference to psychiatric patients) to the status of irrelevant empirical fact.

Finally, though both philosophy and science wrest order from chaos, they do so through two procedures in which the relation between the virtual and the actual differs crucially.[51] Whatever is and whatever happens come into being, according to Deleuze and Guattari, by passing from a state of virtuality to actuality. The virtual, Deleuze says, is real without being actual and ideal without being abstract.[52] It has the reality of a structure of determinations that simultaneously enables and sets limits to what can come into existence, what can become actual. The structure of the English language (what Saussure called *langue*), for example, is real without being actual: it nowhere exists in actual form but nonetheless determines what can be actualized as English-language statements. It is ideal in that it serves as a set of formal rules for which actual statements can provide content, yet it is not abstract because it is merely the contingent residue or sediment left by previous utterances in the language. Now at the absolute limit, virtuality is characterized by an infinity of determinations: chaos. Philosophy and science have distinctive means of grasping and managing the relations between virtuality and actuality for their respective purposes. Where philosophy sections chaos, as we have seen, using a plane of immanence and concepts, science sections chaos using what Deleuze and Guattari call a plane of reference and functions. Science employs functions and the plane of reference to limit chaos, to reduce and slow down the infinity of determinations constituting virtual chaos, so as ultimately to produce a freeze-frame in which the actualization of virtual determinations in a specific state of affairs can be seized, understood, and predicted.[53] The passage from chaotic virtuality to actuality is traced by science through the ascription of limits and coordinates on the plane of reference and by what Deleuze and Guattari call the "de-potentiation" of the infinity of chaos.[54] A familiar instance of this depotentiation of chaos is the control of variables in some kinds of scientific experiments. A whole host of determinations is held constant so that the effects on the object of study (the dependent variable) of carefully varying just one factor (the independent variable) can be ascertained. In this way, the chaotic virtual gets progressively deprived of determinations (through the control and isolation of variables) until the point at which actual behavior appears to "obey" natural laws (through what Deleuze calls bare repetition of the same[55]). Science turns its back on chaos, as it were, and thins out virtuality to the point that there appears to be nothing between the absolute chaos it leaves behind and the absolute natural law that is its end and goal. Philosophy, by contrast, turns away from actuality to *give consistency* to virtuality by extracting from actual states of affairs the selected determinations constitutive of and mapped by its concepts. Philosophical concepts do not represent the actual states of affairs from which they are extracted but rather give consistency to the virtuality from which those states of affairs arose or were actualized. Philosophy thus counteractualizes actuality and repotentiates virtuality, restoring the latter's motility and, perhaps most important, its potential to be actualized differently (through what Deleuze calls "clothed," i.e., differential or creative repetition[56]). Where science captures or traces reality itself (or segments of actuality on various planes of reference), philosophy maps the virtual or rather maps diverse sections of virtuality on its various planes of immanence.

Political philosophy creates concepts, then, in response to Problems presented to it by its real-world milieu. Constructing a plane of immanence according to its own particular image of thought, its motive force for thinking, a philosophy gives consistency to the virtual by extracting from real-world states of affairs certain features that it considers most Important or Significant, given the Problem it is addressing, and by combining these features with components drawn from concepts developed by other thinkers to create a new concept. By thus counteractualizing actuality, the concept maps the virtual from which it arose and thereby reveals the real potential it harbors. Conceptual personae embody what Deleuze and Guattari, following Nietzsche, call "modes of existence" or possibilities of life,[57] incarnating not a mere theoretical possibility but real potential to live otherwise, a potential that is harbored in the virtual structure and revealed by being extracted by the concept from actual states of affairs. The concept of schizophrenia, for example, counteractualizes the psychiatric patient, disclosing in the virtual structure and dynamics of market deterritorialization the revolutionary potential for freedom from representation as well as from exploitation. So the schizophrenic as conceptual persona embodies a real potential for a libidinal mode of existence beyond the constraints of capitalism and the State. What real potential does the nomad personify?

The Concept of Nomadism

Despite the familiar connotations of the term, it is important not to equate the concept of nomadism with nomadic peoples. This is not to say that nomadism has nothing whatsoever to do with nomadic peoples, for it does. But nomadism for Deleuze and Guattari means something other and more than the mobility of itinerant peoples. For although there are some external references to nomadic peoples to be found in the "Treatise on Nomadology," in which Deleuze and Guattari discuss nomadism most directly and extensively, internal references to the Greek term *nomos* are far more central. And this term itself refers to a set of distinct concepts with which it is most often associated or compared in Greek philosophy: *physis, logos,* and *polis.* Each of these internal references to conceptual differences within Greek philosophy—*nomos–physis, nomos–logos, nomos–polis*—contributes components to the concept of nomadism in Deleuze and Guattari's philosophy. After reviewing these internal references, we will extract additional conceptual components from external references to various forms of science and music to arrive at a broader understanding of nomadism as a distinctive and widespread form of social practice.

In opposition to *polis, nomos* refers to space outside of city walls, a space not subject to the laws and mode of organization of the State (or city-State). It is in opposition to *polis* that the term *nomos* generates the sense of nomadism as a way of occupying space that is characteristic of nomadic peoples and a key component of Deleuze and Guattari's concept. Early in the "Treatise on Nomadology," they draw on game theory and the contrast between Go and chess to explain the difference between nomadic or "smooth" space and the "striated" space of the State.[58] Both the chessboard and the Go board are composed of a square grid and thus appear striated, but in chess, battle lines are drawn by the placement of pieces in two sets of rows at the very start of the game, imposing a distinct directionality on the space of the board for most of the game (except, in some cases, for the end game). In Go, however, pieces are placed one at a time starting on an empty board so that there is no inherent directionality involved; indeed, the entire topography of Go emerges from the ongoing placement of pieces rather than from preexisting battle lines. Chess space is also striated by the intrinsic qualities of the pieces themselves, each of which has a characteristic kind of "move" and thus controls or threatens certain rows, files, or squares of the board from its given or acquired location. Go pieces, by contrast, are absolutely indistinguishable from one another and have no intrinsic qualities, their strategic value being determined solely by their extrinsic position relative to the shifting constellation of other pieces on the board. Whereas the striated space of the chessboard is determined both by the initial position and the assigned capabilities of the pieces, the smooth space of the Go board starts off utterly indeterminate and only acquires a specific shape through the gradual placement of interchangeable pieces. The distribution of pieces on the Go board is like the distribution of animals in open pasture, who occupy the space without any preassigned directions or partitions; indeed, one of the roots of *nomos, nemo,* means "to put out to pasture" (well before *nomos* became, in some Greek texts, a synonym for "custom" and, eventually, "law"[59]). This component of the concept of nomadism thus derives ultimately from open pastureland outside city walls and particularly from a nondirectional and nonpartitioned way of occupying such space, in contrast to the space of the city, with its walls, streets, private property rights, and laws.

Far more often in Greek philosophy, *nomos* is opposed to *physis.* In this context, it refers to the domain of human culture as distinguished from that of nature. Thus, in a conceptual topography, the realm of *nomos* would lie somewhere between the unruly realm of nature or wilderness *(physis),* on one hand, and the enclosed and strictly regulated space of the city or the State *(polis),* on the other. The third sense of *nomos,* which arises in contradistinction with *logos,* appears at first glance to confirm such a topography, inasmuch as it can be related directly to the space of the city *(polis)*: for *logos* refers to the law of the city-State as well as more generally to reason and discourse with which such law is associated. In this context, *nomos* might translate as informal "custom" or even "rule of thumb" in contrast with formal "law": customary rules *(nomos)* govern group behavior without being deliberately legislated for the group or explicitly re-presented to it in the form of law *(logos).* But with the conquest of nature by Western reason and the discourse of science, the topography breaks down: for the term *law* henceforth applies not only to the city and the organization of social relations but also to nature and the functioning of matter, energy, and life. Yet customary rules of thumb are unlike either the laws formally legislated to govern the behavior of social subjects or the laws "discovered" to govern the behavior of natural objects. Indeed, the very etymology of *rule of thumb* nicely expresses the difference between *nomos* as an embodied mode of measurement and an approximating form of knowledge or practice, on one hand, and *logos* as a formal system of abstract measurement, exact observation, logical theorization, and empirical verification, on the other. It is sometimes said that a true community "follows more rules than it knows" because such rules form part of the unconsciously accepted culture or collective habits of the community and do not require explicit formulation or enforcement in the form of a legal and juridical system; this difference is eloquently conveyed by the palpable disparity between the expressions "following rules" and "obeying laws." The *nomos–logos* opposition thus underlies the distinction Deleuze and Guattari propose in the "Treatise on Nomadology" between *minor* or *nomad science* and what they call *royal* or *State science*.

Nomad Science

Much could be said about the distinction Deleuze and Guattari propose between these two versions of science; for our purposes, two points are essential. One is the difference between the principles of "following" and "reproducing" that characterize the two kinds of science; the other involves the social consequences that follow from them. But first, it is important to note that the distinction presented here (derived from *A Thousand Plateaus*) between two kinds of science seriously complicates the stark distinction between science and philosophy discussed earlier (and derived from *What Is Philosophy?*). The fact is that Deleuze and Guattari were very well versed and extremely interested in developments in contemporary science inspired by nonlinear mathematics and complexity theory, as I mentioned earlier.[60] Compared to classical mechanics, for example (which may represent the epitome of controlled-variable empirical science), many contemporary sciences pay far more attention to the conditions of emergence of their objects of study, to the virtual intensive processes that give rise to actual objects. There is therefore considerable overlap between the contributions of these sciences and what Jeffrey Bell has called Deleuze's "historical ontology"—the view he derives from Bergson and Leibniz (among others), according to which each and every thing is understood to be simply the result (the "contraction") of its virtual conditions of actualization or emergence.[61] Ultimately, however, the main thrust of Deleuze and Guattari's philosophy is not ontological: it is political. The point of doing philosophy is not to arrive at even the best possible understanding of the nature of being: they presuppose an ontology compatible with contemporary math and science to do political philosophy—to articulate Problems posed by contemporary social life in the hope of provoking the discovery of practical solutions to them or, at least, better ways of addressing them. One of those Problems has to with the nature of science itself, prompting the elaboration of the heuristic distinction between State and nomad science with which we are concerned here.

State or royal science proceeds by extracting invariant (universal) laws from the variations of matter, in line with the binary opposition of form and matter: matter is inherently variable but is supposed to obey formal laws that are universal. Reproducing the results of a successful experiment is crucial to establishing the veracity and universality of the hypothesized law that the experiment was designed to test. Nomad science, by contrast, proceeds not by extracting a constant but by following the variations or singularities of matter. Its operations are better mapped by the fourfold Hjelmslevian distinction between content and expression—each of which involves both form and substance—rather than the binary opposition of form and matter.[62] To illustrate this difference, we can take a piece of wood. Royal science will want it milled to established specifications—as a two-by-four, for instance—so it can be used in building construction whose designs are based on the availability of lumber conforming to certain predictable constants (size, regularity of grain, strength, surface appearance, etc.). Any knots that occur are considered mere imperfections and may indeed lower the quality rating of the piece of wood as construction lumber or preclude its use altogether. An artisan or sculptor, standing in here for the nomad scientist, will assess the piece of wood very differently. For the sculptor, knots and grain irregularities appear as singularities, features that inhere in the wood-matter as its unique form of content. And in the sculptor's hands, each singularity can become a substance of expression: a knot may become the eye of a fish; a grain pattern, the waves of the sea; or something else entirely: the content–expression relation here is one of contingency, not necessity.[63] The material singularity of the piece of wood thereby comes to embody in the sculptor's hands what Deleuze and Guattari in *What Is Philosophy?* call a *sensation*.[64] In the sensations embodied in works of art, content and form, the raw material and artistic composition, become indiscernible; it becomes impossible to determine whether the wood grain itself suggests ocean waves or whether the image of ocean waves enables us to see the wood grain in this way: "the plane of the material [the wood grain] ascends irresistibly and invades the plane of composition of the sensations themselves [the work of art] to the point of being part of them or indiscernible from them."[65] Instead of a pregiven form being unilaterally imposed on completely indeterminate or inert matter, artistic sensations arise in between, in what Hjelmslev calls the *reciprocal determination of expression and content.*

This illustration may appear to be far from scientific, but there are fields within science—of which we are becoming increasingly aware, although some were already known to the Greeks—where singularities rather than constants abound. Fluid dynamics is perhaps the best known of these fields: it is impossible to predict exactly where an accelerating liquid will swerve, or even to which side of a moving stream an eddy will form; there are no constant laws for these phenomena. Royal science was in fact constituted in part by the rejection of fluid dynamics (which were considered a special case, an exception to the laws of nature) in favor of solids;[66] but even for solids, gravitational dynamics are only rigorously predictable between two bodies: the effects of gravity on three or more bodies of roughly equal mass and in close proximity become as unpredictable as a liquid whorl.

This is not the place for an extended discussion of complexity theory and nonlinear mathematics, which lie well beyond the scope of this book. A more familiar illustration of nomad science, however, is available in evolutionary biology. Crucially, evolutionary science cannot predict evolution or reproduce it experimentally; what it does instead is follow its development. (It is no less a science for this.) To put the point another way, there are no universal laws enabling us to predict how evolution will occur, only patterns of what has happened. Even the original notion of "survival of the fittest" has given way more recently to the notion of "survival of the sufficiently fit": not only is random mutation (by definition) not predictable or reproducible, but neither is the interaction of a mutation with its environment. Rewind and rerun evolution a hundred times, as the scientific wisdom now has it, and even if you could reproduce the same mutations, you might get up to a hundred different results.[67] Evolution is thus a matter of what Deleuze and Guattari call *itineration* rather than *iteration* or reproduction according to universal law: it traces a path that can be followed but not predicted.[68]

Turning now to the social consequences of the distinction between State and nomad science, Deleuze and Guattari insist that "nomad science doesn't lead science in the direction of power, or even of autonomous development"[69]—by which they mean autonomous from other social practices. And this difference involves, among other things, the relations of sciences to work: "nomad science does not have the same relation to work as royal science."[70] Useful here is the distinction (which Deleuze and Guattari don't themselves invoke) between the technical division of labor and the political division of labor. The technical division of labor arises from the level of complexity of tasks, skills, and knowledges involved in a given process of production, but it does not necessarily entail any hierarchy of status or power among specialists participating in the process. The political division of labor, by contrast, although it often overlaps with a technical division of labor, involves distinctions of prestige or power that have nothing intrinsically to do with the skills exercised or level of participation in the process.[71] Most notable is the political division between intellectual and manual labor, which is an essential feature of royal or State science, according to Deleuze and Guattari:

> Royal science operates a "disqualification" of manual labor, a "de-skilling." . . . Without conferring on "intellectuals" any real, autonomous power, royal science nonetheless empowers them relatively by withdrawing all autonomy and power from laborers [formerly artisans] who now do nothing more than reproduce or execute the plans formulated by the "intellectuals" [technocrats and managers].[72]

Owing to the power of royal science to extract abstract concepts from the concrete operations of productive practice, conception and execution become distinct activities, and each gets assigned to a distinct status group.[73] Francis Bacon's program for the development of early modern science illustrates this process perfectly: he charged agents of the Royal Academy with the task of visiting local workshops to extract whatever knowledges were in practice there, and then bringing them back to the academy, where they would be elaborated into formal scientific knowledge, only to be eventually reapplied to the production process in the form of technology, thereby liquidating the autonomy of the workers and subjecting them to technicomanagerial control.[74]

It is significant that this is not a directly or obviously political form of control: it stems instead from a form of the division of labor which, howsoever "natural" or necessary it has come to seem as the gap between conception and execution has widened with the ever-increasing application of technology, nonetheless operates normatively to subordinate manual to intellectual labor. As Deleuze and Guattari insist, "if the State always tends to repress minor and nomad sciences, it's not because they lack accuracy or precision, but because they entail a division of labor opposed to that of State norms."[75] To the (royal) conception of science that sees universal laws as distinct from yet applicable to inert matter corresponds a conception of society as being composed of inert subjects susceptible and, indeed, bound to the application of universal laws by the State.[76] From this,

Deleuze and Guattari will conclude that *"the manner in which a science, or a conception of science, contributes to the organization of the social field, and in particular [the way in which it] induces a certain division of labor [intellectual–manual] forms an intrinsic part of that science itself."*[77] I want to argue the same thing about music, where the implications for differing forms of social organization are somewhat clearer: the manner in which a conception or practice of music contributes to the organization of the social field is, for our purposes, an intrinsic part of the music itself.

Nomad Music

Jazz is not the only instance in the field of "play"—playing music, playing sports, playing games—that can be characterized as nomadic.[78] Deleuze and Guattari themselves analyze the formal differences between Go and chess, as we have seen: the one involves a multiplicity of interchangeable pieces operating in an open or *smooth* space, the other a hierarchy of distinct pieces operating in a closed and *striated* space.[79] A similar argument can be made regarding the formal differences between soccer and (North American) football.[80] The playing field in soccer is certainly not as open a space as a Go board: the soccer field has a binary directional orientation and two fixed attractors, the goals, whereas the Go board has no fixed spatial orientation whatsoever. But the soccer field is considerably less striated than the football field, which, in addition to having goals (of two kinds: an end zone and goalposts), is so striated that every yard line is marked. The degree of distinction and hierarchy among soccer players is also considerably less than among football players. Soccer players (particularly the goalie) are not as interchangeable as Go pieces, but offensive and defensive players alternate roles far more fluidly in soccer than in football, which stops the action and substitutes entire teams in changing from offense to defense and back. In soccer, offensive players play defense and defensive players play offense (and score goals) far more routinely than in football, where such role changes are exceptional and very short-lived (never lasting more than one play in a row). Soccer teams also exhibit almost no internal hierarchy, whereas football teams are rigidly hierarchized, with linesmen doing the grunt work (the manual labor, as it were) and quarterbacks calling the plays (the "intellectual labor"). In some cases, it is the coach rather than the quarterback who calls the plays; in soccer, coaches play a far smaller role, especially during game time. In a sense, football evidences a clear political division of labor along with an extensive technical division of labor; soccer has a much less pronounced technical division of labor and no political division of labor to speak of.[81]

Returning now to the field of music, I want to argue that jazz resembles soccer more closely than football and that football—ironically enough, given their difference in prestige value—resembles classical music more closely than jazz. Two general points, however, should already be clear from what we have said about the way Deleuze and Guattari characterize nomadism and nomad science. For one thing, improvisational jazz, like nomad science, repudiates reproducing in favor of following or, indeed, creating. Whereas a classical symphony orchestra, for the most part, merely reproduces in performance what the composer has already created and written down in the score, jazz bands intentionally depart from what is already known in order to improvise and create something new—not just once (namely, at the moment of composition) but every time they play.[82] John Coltrane will take a familiar tune—"My Favorite Things" from *Mary Poppins,* for example—and put it to flight, adding (and subtracting) notes, changing the melody and tempo, and the resulting improvisation will be different every time he plays it. Improvisational jazz thus epitomizes what Deleuze and Guattari call *free action*[83]—action not programmed in advance, not devoted to any ulterior aim other than maximizing creative difference in repetition. Even when working from a chord chart, for example, jazz improvisation is far more itinerative than iterative: solos can vary in length, there is not necessarily a set order as to who takes one when, a clever soloist can change keys or tempo unexpectedly and challenge the others to follow her lead, and so on.

And this brings us to the second point: in jazz improvisation, there is no need for a band leader (even if soloists sometimes serve such a function temporarily and get the band to follow them in a spontaneous key or tempo change), whereas classical symphony orchestras always have a conductor as well as a composer. Elias Canetti, in *Crowds and Power,* provides a succinct analysis of the orchestra conductor.[84] Like Deleuze and Guattari, Canetti is interested at least as much in the manner in which a symphony orchestra performance contributes to the organization of the social field as he is in the music actually produced:

> Someone who knew nothing about power could discover all of its attributes, one after another, by careful observation of a conductor. The reason why this has never been done is obvious: the music the conductor evokes is thought to be the only thing that counts. . . . The idea of his activity having another, non-musical meaning never enters his head.[85]

Canetti goes on to describe this nonmusical aspect of the conductor's role in terms that make its pertinence to social organization patently clear: the conductor "has the power of life and death over the voices of the instruments"; "their diversity stands for the diversity of mankind"; "the voices of the instruments are opinions and convictions on which [the conductor] keeps a close watch"; "he is omniscient, for, while they have only their part in front of them, he has the whole score"; "he is the living embodiment of law"; "the code of laws is in his hand, in the form of the score":[86]

> The conductor wields this kind of absolute power not just over the orchestra, but over the audience, too: the immobility of the audience is as much part of the conductor's design as the obedience of the orchestra. They are under a compulsion to keep still. . . . The presence of the players disturbs no-one; indeed they are scarcely noticed. Then the conductor appears and everyone becomes still. . . . While he is conducting no-one may move, and as soon as he finishes they must applaud.[87]

Most important for our purposes, however, is the nature of the compact between conductor and orchestra members themselves. He holds symbolic life-or-death power over their voices; without him, they are nothing: "the willingness of [orchestra] members to obey him makes it possible for the conductor to transform them into a unit, which he then embodies."[88] As in football, the classical symphony orchestra requires a transcendent instance of command in the figure of the conductor to guarantee coordination, whereas coordination arises more spontaneously and in a manner immanent to the group activity in soccer and jazz. This does not mean that power relations are completely absent from jazz groups. Miles Davis was reputed to have been somewhat of a tyrant as a band leader—although this did not prevent most of the best musicians of his time from wanting to play with him. But whatever power relations exist within the jazz group are interpersonal and fluid, susceptible to modulations and reversals, whereas the power relations in classical music are institutional, fixed, and irreversible: the composer composes, the conductor conducts, the musicians merely perform. Football and classical music, in other words, are like State science in that they entail a social division of labor whereby some merely execute discrete parts of what others (coaches and composers, quarterbacks and conductors) conceive and command; coaches develop elaborate compendia of plays (sometimes stretching to hundreds of pages), of which players are then called on to execute their individual parts under the direction of the quarterback, in much the same way that orchestra members execute their parts of the musical score under the direction of the conductor.[89] There's almost none of that to speak of in soccer and improvisational jazz.

Finally, jazz improvisation illustrates the third key feature of nomadism, which distinguishes what Deleuze and Guattari (following Simondon) call *hylomorphic organization* from nomadic composition. Not only does jazz improvisation operate by creative itineration (or following) rather than reproductive repetition (of a precomposed score or of a supposed law of nature), as we have seen, it also follows singularities of sound matter just as nomad science follows singularities of physical or biological matter. Thus a false—or rather an *unexpected*—note played in the course of jazz improvisation is not necessarily a mistake, as it would certainly be in a performance of classical music; instead it can be incorporated as a singularity into the flow of the music and become part of the piece being improvised by the group. Classical music abhors contingency of this kind; jazz improvisation thrives on it. If a saxophone suddenly squawks in the middle of a symphony, it's a mistake; if a saxophone squawks in the course of a jazz performance, that can become part of the performance, part of the improvisation. Indeed, when improvising musicians are really in the groove, there *is* no such thing as a wrong note: even accidents get incorporated into the creative process and become part of the improvisation. Dave Brubeck's bass player once played an E in a piece that was being played in a key for which it was totally unexpected, but the famous pianist subsequently picked up on it, repeated it, and then used it to actually transpose the piece into a different key altogether, while performing it. (This is also an example of the reversible power relations in jazz bands mentioned earlier.) In a classical performance, by contrast, an unexpected note is simply a wrong note—and a horror to be avoided at all costs. Rather than merely reproduce a preexisting score, then, jazz musicians follow a process of creation of which they are part yet which they don't entirely control: jazz as a process of itineration thus traces a path than can be followed but not predicted. And in fact, cutting-edge jazz improvisation involves maximizing the incorporation of singularities on the part of all group members, yet without allowing contingency to overwhelm coherence to the point of chaos or cacophony. This is very different from the hylomorphic imposition of a created form onto inert or passive matter. In jazz improvisation, neither the flow of notes nor the musicians are passive: they are engaged, instead, in a process of spontaneous self-organization, in which a unique musical coherence emerges contingently, a coherence that is not imposed by an orchestra conductor nor by a precomposed score but arises immanently from the creative activity of the group. The jazz band follows immanent rules *(nomoi)* that remain implicit, instead of obeying explicit laws *(logoi)* formulated or imposed by a transcendent instance of command such as a composer or a conductor.[90]

The concept of nomadism, in sum, hinges on the notion that *the manner in which forms of human activity contribute to the organization of the social field, and in particular, the way in which they induce a certain division of labor or not (political vs. technical, intellectual vs. manual), constitutes an intrinsic part of that activity itself.* Nomadism thus designates forms of human activity where the social field remains a smooth space; where modes and principles of social organization arise immanently from group activity itself, instead of being imposed by a transcendent instance from above; where itinerant following of singularities and group creation prevails over the reproduction and/or imposition of preexisting forms and the issuing and obeying of commands. It should be understood that this is a heuristic distinction: few real instances of human activity will appear purely immanent or purely transcendent. But it is the components of this concept that guide nomadology in mapping various instances of nomadism and assessing their potential for creative repetition, mutually reinforcing intersections and social transformation.

Affirmative Nomadology

The subtitle of the "Treatise on Nomadology" is "The War Machine." Yet everything we have said about nomad science, nomad music, and nomadism in general appears to have little to do with war-machines. Given the subtitle of Deleuze and Guattari's nomadology plateau, and even though I use *nomadology* more often than *war-machine*, it is important to understand the relation and distinction between nomadology in general and the war-machine as a particular kind of nomadism. Deleuze and Guattari themselves admit that what they call the war-machine only has war as its object under certain conditions.[91] And just as they insist that the war-machine and war do not coincide—that the relation between the two is "synthetic" (in the Kantian sense of the term[92])—I want to insist that nomadism and the war-machine do not coincide, that the war-machine was indeed "the invention of the nomad,"[93] but it is only one among many. In a similar vein, it is important not to limit the concept of nomadism to nomadic peoples, as we have already seen: the nomad science developed in the course of the "Treatise on Nomadology" does not belong exclusively or even primarily to nomadic peoples; the same is true for nomad games such as Go in contrast to chess, or soccer in contrast to football; and the same holds for nomad music, for jazz improvisation in contrast to classical music. Yet the war-machine is a crucial addition to the conceptual repertoire of the second volume of *Capitalism and Schizophrenia* and merits serious consideration.

Whereas *Anti-Oedipus* had deployed the term *socius* to designate the basis or focus of social organization at the level of the social–libidinal mode production (the savage, despotic, capitalist modes of production; with the earth, the despot, capital, as socius), *A Thousand Plateaus* replaces *socius* with a far richer and finer set of analytic tools, including strata, types of capture, regimes of signs and faciality, and war-machines. At the same time, the psychoanalytic terminology of schizoanalysis gives way to the language of set theory in nomadology: nomad social organization in smooth space involves nondenumerable sets, as we will see in chapter 4. If, for nomadology, the concept of strata supplements earlier discussions of territories, and regimes of signs and faciality supplement those of codes, the concept of war-machine focuses on group dynamics and various forms of social organization itself, well beneath the level of (or within) the mode of production. Though the concept's consistency derives from this focus on forms of sociality, its scope of variation is wide: "the first theoretical element of importance," Deleuze and Guattari insist, "is the fact that the war machine has many varied meanings."[94] There are in fact no fewer than six very different variants of the war-machine in *A Thousand Plateaus,* among which it is crucial to make careful distinctions. (Purely for convenience of exposition, I number them in an order approximating a timeline; they by no means obey a linear historical progression, however, as we will see.) Moreover, in addition to ascertaining the different variants of a concept, it is important to identify its four key components. For the concept of war-machine, these include aim, object, space (smooth vs. striated), and form of sociality (ultimately hinging on the distinction between denumerable and nondenumerable sets).

Two of the six war-machine variants belong exclusively to nomad groups. The first barely merits the name "war-machine," inasmuch as it does not have war as its object at all: its essence is a rhizomatic or nomadic form of social relations operating in smooth space,[95] and its objectives can be as varied as "building bridges or cathedrals or rendering judgments or making music or instituting a science, a technology."[96] Nomadic bands only begin to justify the name "war-machine" in its second variant, for here they can indeed take on war itself as their object—in opposition to the State, with the aim of protecting or rescuing their smooth space from State striation. This is essentially a tactical war (in de Certeau's sense[97]), fought against the State's strategic aim of incorporating all available "open" space into its territory. The sixth variant is the war-machine of "revolutionary movement . . . the becoming-minoritarian of everybody/everything,"[98] whose ultimate aim is to render all social relations nomadic. Here the schizoanalytic opposition between schizophrenia and paranoia, between the molecular and the molar, reappears in only slightly different terms: "Every struggle . . . constructs *revolutionary connections* in opposition to the *conjugations of the [capitalist] axiomatic.*"[99] The third, fourth, and fifth variants involve the appropriation of war-machines by the State, and vice versa, and require closer examination.

The third variant of the war-machine involves its appropriation by the State as a means to serve the State's essentially political ends: the aim of striating, securing, and expanding territory. The State war-machine always has war as its exclusive object (it must constantly protect, if not expand, its territory), yet it remains subordinate to the State's political aim: in this context, war is merely "the continuation of politics by other means,"[100] and it is still only limited war. The fourth variant of the war-machine, which is fascism, serves for Deleuze and Guattari as a transition from the third war-machine to the fifth: fascism is what transformed limited war into total war, paving the way for the totalizing war-machine of global capitalism. The fifth variant of the war-machine—global capitalism—has escaped the grasp of the State and now envelops it, with the State becoming merely a variable model of realization for capitalist axiomatization. Here capital accumulation as the aim of the war-machine exceeds the control of the State and pervades society totally (i.e., extensively as well as intensively, via globalization as well as real subsumption, as we will see in chapter 4), with its economic imperatives subordinating political ends, without, of course, doing away with politics altogether. State politics and diplomacy, even war itself, are now merely the continuation of capital accumulation by other means, as it were. The object of the global–capitalist war-machine, according to Deleuze and Guattari, is no longer hot war (as means to an end furnished by the State) but capital accumulation itself, which, at the time they wrote, took the form of a cold war of deterrence in which the State-administered welfare system and military–industrial complex were no more than political means serving ultimately economic ends (capital accumulation).[101] But it has taken a variety of different forms since.

Of course, this neat conceptual categorization inevitably belies the complexity of actual historical states of affairs, particularly regarding the relations between the State and global capitalism, between politics and economics as ends and means, and between war-machines and war itself. We will return to consider this issue in some detail at the end of chapter 2. For now, suffice it to say that Deleuze and Guattari are forthright about the dual nature of the war-machine, acknowledging at the end of the "Treatise on Nomadology" that there are in fact "two kinds of war machine,"[102] those with war as object and those without.

Ultimately, the decisive reason for distinguishing nomadism in general from the war-machine in the development of an affirmative nomadology is that the war-machine represents the *reactive* component of nomadism. Just as we insisted earlier on the importance of distinguishing a creative positive political philosophy from a reactive, purely critical one, it is crucial to distinguish creative nomadism and affirmative nomadology from the war-machine. For it is *opposition,* in fact, that transforms nomadism into a war-waging war-machine in the first place, by assigning it the State as enemy or obstacle and war as (synthetic) object. And even the global–capitalist war-machine, despite appearances, is reactive in its drive to capture lines-of-flight, as we shall see in chapter 4: resistance, Deleuze insists, always comes first.[103] It should go without saying that the reactive aspects of a phenomenon are to be considered secondary to its positive or affirmative aspects—yet Deleuze and Guattari say this here (in *A Thousand Plateaus*) only in reference to Foucault's work, not their own.[104] In any case, what is essential is to determine what the affirmative aspect of nomadism is, and here, once again, Deleuze and Guattari are perfectly clear: "the war machine was the invention [*par excellence*] of the nomad because it is *in its essence* the constitutive element of smooth space, the occupation of this space, displacement within this space, *and the corresponding composition of people: this is its sole and veritable positive object (nomos).*"[105] In the same vein, Deleuze and Guattari assert at the conclusion of the "Treatise," and concerning precisely the supplementarity of war in relation to nomadism itself, that if nomads wage war, they do so "*only on the condition that they simultaneously create something else,* if only new nonorganic social relations."[106] Nomadism thus has as its primary and positive object not war but rather a distinctive alternative form of organization of social relations operating in smooth space. Hence the importance of mapping positive (creative, nonreactive) instances of nomadism such as nomad science and nomad music for the project of an affirmative nomadology.

But the point is not simply to multiply models of nomadism such as nomad science, nomad games, and nomad music: Deleuze and Guattari warn against this near the end of the last plateau of their book[107]—albeit after having listed at least six models of smooth and striated space. But they are right: it is not a question of simply *adopting* this or that model of nomadism but of examining various instances of nomadism to *adapt* them to diverse circumstances, that is to say, of examining instances of nomadism to extract from them principles that can be adapted for use in other domains. Nomadology's characteristic and proper activity, Deleuze and Guattari insist, is "that of relaying, even with modest means—not that of the architectonic model or the monument. An ambulant people of relayers, rather than a model society."[108] The utopian function of concepts in political philosophy, as we have said, is not to legislate action according to some ideal model worked out in advance but to extract principles from actually existing instances of, for example, nomadism; to map their virtual potential as alternatives to the norms of capitalism and the State; and to assess the prospects of adapting those principles via experimentation to other domains of activity. Nomadology, to borrow a phrase from Deleuze and Guattari, "turn[s] the thinker into a sort of surfer as conceptual persona":[109] the nomad thinker rides the energy of an existing alternative social movement the way surfers ride the energy of an ocean wave, giving it dramatic expression and hopefully relaying it to others moving in similar directions.[110] So for affirmative nomadology, the positive or utopian force of a philosophical concept has three aspects: (1) its capacity to intervene in and transform our habitual modes of thinking, desiring, and acting; (2) its capacity to detect and draw attention to viable and *actually existing* alternatives to State and capitalist norms; and (3) its capacity to give expression to alternative becomings and social movements in order to strengthen them, broaden them, and even extend them to other social fields and to connect them with other movements to promote widespread social change.

If nomadology as political philosophy is able to connect to its social milieu in this way, it is not only because there are "unimaginable sufferings" and "shameful compromises" to react or respond to but also because there are outside "forces stifled by [their] milieu" whose energy and properties of immanent self-organization can be relayed into philosophy, accelerated and magnified by the absolute deterritorialization of thought and then relayed back out to other social movements. The most propitious of these outside forces are those informed or produced by the relative deterritorialization of their social milieu: for ancient Greek philosophy, as we have seen, this was the agora as a free space of discussion among equals (friends and rivals); for us today, the world market—"the only thing that is universal in capitalism"[111]—offers the greatest degree of relative deterritorialization. But thought seems hard-pressed to gain a footing, carve out a space for discussion, or find any friends there. So most philosophy today reterritorializes instead on "the modern democratic state and [on] human rights"—or rather, since "there is no universal democratic state," philosophy gets "reterritorialized on a [particular] national state [and on]

. . . its way of expressing human rights and outlining the modern society of brothers"[112] as a substitute for the agora of friends and rivals. This represents a double betrayal of philosophy. Not only does it abandon universality in favor of the narrowly opinionated "nationalitarianisms"[113] of this or that particular nation-state; it also connects thought not to the most deterritorialized element of its milieu—the world market—but to one of the most reterritorialized elements: the State, archenemy of nomad philosophy since Plato.

"*Philosophy is reterritorialized three times,*" Deleuze and Guattari conclude: "on the Greeks in the past, on the democratic State in the present, and on the new people and earth in the future."[114] But they say very little about this "people to come" and this "new earth"—and even less about the connection between these enigmatic figures and the radical deterritorialization of the world market. Can something like the ancient Greek society of friends get "reactivated in our problems and inspire . . . concepts that need to be created"[115]—such as the concept of nomad citizenship? Can virtual communities and anonymous trading networks institute forms of distributed decision making and collective intelligence, establishing and occupying a new earth on the self-organizing plane of a world market free from capitalism's infinite debt? Later chapters will return to explore these questions further than the enigmatic (and perhaps mythical) figures of a "people to come" and a "new earth" allow. About the deficiencies of the democratic State and human rights as a philosophical territory, meanwhile, Deleuze and Guattari are anything but enigmatic: "rights save neither men nor a philosophy that is reterritorialized on the democratic State," Deleuze and Guattari conclude in *What Is Philosophy?*, and "human rights will not make us bless capitalism."[116] This is largely because national states tend to lose their transcendent sovereignty the more they become, in Deleuze and Guattari's terms, mere "models of realization" for the immanent axioms of capital. "What social democracy has not given the order to fire when the poor come out of their . . . ghetto?" they pointedly ask.[117] Yet this tendency to axiomatize the State is complicated by a countertendency to reassert its despotic sovereignty. To see why this is so, and how it bears on questions of affective citizenship, the next chapter develops the diagnostic concept of the Death-State.

CHAPTER TWO

Death-State Citizenship

In developing the concept of the Death-State, I draw on both volumes of *Capitalism and Schizophrenia,* even though they contain significantly different treatments of the State.[1] In *Anti-Oedipus,* analysis of the State plays a key role in the genealogy of the Oedipus complex, by means of which schizoanalysis is generated from the critique of psychoanalysis. But in the first volume, the category of the State remains abstract: Deleuze and Guattari even invoke the notion of an *Urstaat*[2] to emphasize that they are defining an ideal type, an abstract form of social organization. In *A Thousand Plateaus,* by contrast, the analysis is far more complex. The State now appears as an apparatus of capture for forces originating outside it and as a resonance machine for aligning multiple centers of power on its own centered structure. In both cases, contrasts between a despotic or sovereign, overcoding State and the biopolitical or axiomatizing State associated with capitalism are crucial and bear closer examination.

For schizoanalysis, the despotic State provides the model of power relations. Rather than evolving from pre-State forms of social organization, it emerges all at once ("at a single stroke") with the conquest of one people by another.[3] The conquerors overcode all preexistent relations and meanings via imperial decree to realign all obedience and debt obligations on their own leader or god. The form of power exercised under despotism includes what Foucault has called sovereign power: it entails the sovereign's right to take life and to levy taxes. With the advent of capitalism, however, the status of the State changes: the despotic State becomes a "civilized" or liberal State, and as economics separates out from politics (construed in a narrow sense), the economic debt obligations formerly owed to the despot don't disappear but transfer to capital.[4] As rights gradually redistribute from the sovereign to society at large, meanwhile, citizens gain the right to assert their rights even against the State, and political obedience in the strict, despotic sense disappears from the social field: labor is "free" and supposedly contractual, not bound by fealty; citizens are "free" and supposedly consent to be governed and to obey.[5] The form of power, meanwhile, changes from sovereign to biopower: instead of taking life and taxing production at a distance, biopower devotes itself to enhancing life and intervenes in all facets of human life, from the most public to the most intimate, to make it healthier and more productive. The State adds what Foucault calls the "art of government" (or the "conduct of conduct") to its concerns and practices: it increasingly intercedes in the lives of its citizens to conduct and improve their conduct rather than merely extracting from afar whatever surpluses happen to be available. Furthermore, to return to the schizoanalytic idiom, the social field is now organized not by codes or overcodes of interpersonal and political responsibility but by the decoded, quantitative calculus of the market: as far as capital is concerned, qualitative social and interpersonal relations, even subjectivity itself, are all strictly secondary to the stimulation and manipulation of quantitative flows (of resources, desires, products, work, money) to produce and appropriate a surplus. Yet even as capital axiomatizes social production in this way, it relegates reproduction to an increasingly isolated domestic sphere shorn of its erstwhile productive functions. The power relations of despotism thus don't disappear altogether; rather, they migrate into the heart of the nuclear family, where Father is king: the man's home is his castle, and family members are his subjects. Private obedience is inculcated in the abstract for subsequent transfer into the public sphere onto teachers, coaches, priests, bosses, politicians—but always according to the conditions and directions of the quantitative flows organized by capitalist axiomatization.

For nomadology, by contrast, what has to be accounted for is not the relegation of despotism to the private sphere of the nuclear family by capitalist axiomatization but its resurgence in the public sphere as the very form taken by the capitalist State itself. Far from having simply become subordinate to capital, the State reasserts its power and leads capital in unexpected directions. As we shall see, fascism was supposed to have been a mere transitional stage between the "total war" of Hitler's military war-machine and the even more totalizing economic war-machine of global capitalism; in a somewhat broader context and a different idiom, sovereign power's right to take life by putting its subjects to death was supposed to have given way to biopower's enhancement of life by making its citizens more productive and granting them rights.[6] Instead, under the Bush doctrine of preemption and the so-called War on Terror, a military war-machine returns to reassert the despotic power of the State as a very different way of prosecuting the capitalist conquest of the globe.

Instead of expanding the rights of citizens and enhancing their lives, the Bush regime curtails rights and reduces general prosperity. Given the expectations of the biopolitical State, the return of despotism seems utterly intolerable: the scream of outrage it provokes generates the concept of the Death-State as a means of diagnosing that return. For nomadology, however, a dialectic of sovereign power and biopower, or an alternation between axiomatizing tendencies and despotic countertendencies, does not have sufficient diagnostic force. Just as schizoanalysis insists on diagnosing the neurosis of the Oedipus complex as a specifically capitalist institution from the universal standpoint of a nonneurotic form of psychic organization (which Deleuze and Guattari call "schizophrenia"), nomadology must diagnose the power of the State as a particular form of social organization from the universal standpoint of a nonstate form of social organization. And here the work of Pierre Clastres is indispensable.[7] His analyses of acephalous societies discloses principles of social organization that contrast sharply with, and in some cases get substantially reconfigured in, State forms of social organization. From this standpoint, we will then be able to consider what schizoanalysis and nomadology contribute to our diagnosis of the Death-State.

The Problem Defined: The State

By examining acephalous societies operating without a government, Clastres presents an implicit critique of State power. It is true that the actual societies Clastres examines are in some ways less complex and in all cases considerably smaller than most modern nation-States.[8] But while it is clear that society is not going to get any less complex, it is also clear that the nation-State is not the only, and may no longer be the best, form of or scale for social organization. Globalization in general, and the example of European unification in particular, suggest otherwise. In any case, it is not a question of adopting Clastres's acephalous societies as a model for social organization today but of selecting certain features of those societies for their diagnostic force. And here the details of Clastres's analysis are important.

What Clastres shows is that these societies oscillate between two modes of organization and leadership, depending on the circumstances. Under ordinary circumstances, acephalous societies are led—if that is the right word—by a figure who utterly lacks any authority or power over other members of society. Instead of commanding others to obey, this chief plays two other, very different roles. One is to serve as mediator in the event of conflict within the group. But even here, the chief cannot pass judgment or make binding rulings: instead he can only propose recommendations and must rely on exhortatory eloquence alone; it is up to the parties in dispute to decide whether they will follow his recommendations. When eloquence alone does not resolve the dispute, the chief has recourse to his other main role: that of provider. By means of generous compensation, he mollifies injured parties, redistributes wealth, and thereby restores a measure of harmony to the group.[9] It is significant that these are occasional activities: the chief has no standing power, authority, or function but rather only intervenes when inequities or injuries reach a critical threshold, where they threaten the group's own sense of harmony or cohesion.

The second mode of leadership is equally occasional, but the circumstances that call for it arise from outside rather than inside the group itself: this occasion is war. In times of external conflict, one warrior assumes the role of chieftain and organizes a band of other warriors under his command to protect the group at large from an external threat. In these special circumstances, then, and in these circumstances alone, a figure does arise who enjoys a measure of power over others. But two qualifications to the chieftain's exercise of power are crucial: for one thing, and particularly if the war is offensive rather than defensive, the group as a whole may simply refuse to comply with the chieftain's call to arms. His ability to command, in other words, depends on an initial and punctual consent on the part of those who would support his command function; only once this consent is granted do the chieftain's power to command and obedience to his authority hold sway. Second, and perhaps even more important, he has power only over the band of warriors assembled to prosecute the war. It is true that the group as a whole gives—or refuses—its consent to go to war in the first place. But the chieftain's command only applies fully to the warriors and not to the group itself. So it is that a kind of war-machine takes shape, exceptionally and temporarily, alongside of society itself. And even so, this warrior band's distinctive mode of social organization, characterized by command and obedience, does not completely transform the group's organization in its own image, even temporarily: the group itself remains acephalous even while consenting to the chieftain's command over the warrior band.

We may thus picture acephalous society as a kind of basin of more or less egalitarian, horizontal social relations, punctuated by two less than egalitarian, vertical attractors. Only on occasions when threats to group cohesion or survival reach a certain threshold does an authority figure of one kind or another arise, either within or alongside the group, depending on whether the threat arises from the inside or the outside. The authority of the warrior chieftain seems the more modern of the two: he has the power to command obedience. And yet it fully applies only to the band of warriors operating at the margins or outside edge of the group itself. The authority of the chief, meanwhile, hardly seems to be authority at all: his role is to mediate internal conflict in the attempt to restore or maintain group cohesion through eloquent persuasion and sumptuary generosity. Yet he has no real power over other members of the group, no means other than eloquence and generosity to get them to follow his bidding. Most important, in both cases, authority arises only when a critical threshold of tension has been reached; it arises only with the consent of the group; it subsides as soon as tension abates. A rough egalitarianism, then, is as it were the steady state of acephalous society; departures from this state that induce the emergence of power and authority are in the strictest sense occasional—and temporary.

Now the point of doing a genealogy of modes of social organization is assuredly not to trace a historical evolution from acephalous to State societies. One of the reasons Deleuze and Guattari invoke the ideal-type concept of the *Urstaat* in *Anti-Oedipus* is precisely to *preclude the linear "evolutionism" of such an account*. The State on this view is understood not to have evolved smoothly from acephalous social organization (which exists in part precisely to *prevent* or "ward off" such an evolution) but rather to have appeared abruptly with the violent conquest of one people by another and the imposition of permanent rule by one group over the other.[10] This is meant to suggest (among other things) that being a citizen of the State means ipso facto being a member of an oppressed group—and one of the resounding lessons of the recent history of postcolonialism is surely that it ultimately matters little whether the oppressors, the State rulers, are of a different ethnicity: State oppression is State oppression. In any case, as Derrida has shown in his important essay "The Force of Law," based largely on a reading of Walter Benjamin's essay "Critique of Violence," the founding of the State by any means whatsoever (whether by conquest or not) necessarily entails an initial illegitimate use of force or act of violence.[11] For the laws that could render that initial act legitimate come into existence only after the State has been founded: the founding act itself is necessarily illegitimate (or prelegitimate or alegitimate). Social contract theory thus stands exposed as a convenient fiction, a kind of screen narrative that projects the notions of social contract and consent of the governed retroactively onto the foundation of the State to mask its violence and illegitimacy.

Moreover, even after the founding of the State, consent in representative democracies remains largely fictional. Single-candidate elections are often decried by champions of two-party and parliamentary electoral systems as undemocratic because such elections offer no meaningful choice to the governed, but in an Important sense, the same is true of all elections: in accordance with the logic of choice, "consent of the governed" would only be meaningful in representative democracies if, alongside referendum proposals and the names of candidates for office, something like "no politicians whatsoever" or "some mode of social organization other than State government" were offered as a choice to the electorate or, in a similar vein, if paying taxes to the State were to become completely voluntary. Being able to choose which politician happens to head the State is not the same as being able to choose whether the State exists. But the counterexample of acephalous societies gives the lie to the notion of the consent of the governed in another, more empirical way. For in acephalous societies, as we have seen, the exercise of power and authority is only occasional and really *does* depend on the consent of the members of the group: their leaders are literally powerless without group assent to their actions. Acephalous leadership shows what "consent of the governed" would really amount to and reveals e contrario that State government involves the enforced imposition of permanent rule and the subordination–subjection of State citizens to that rule, whatever the degree of choice as to who rules.

In addition to this stark contrast, a genealogy of modes of social organization shows how elements and aspects of premodern social organization get displaced and reconfigured with the emergence of the modern State. Most important, in absorbing the warrior chieftain's vertical power to command, the State extends that command from the warrior band to the nation as a whole and, at the same time, makes it permanent, instead of occasional and temporary: in addition to or as a result of prosecuting war, the State offers its members protection from external aggression. Instead of the war-machine existing temporarily alongside society, subject to the latter's consent, the State has appropriated the war-machine, made it permanent, and even internalized some of its functions—notably by adding an internal *police* function to the external warrior function typical of acephalous societies. Carl Schmitt will go so far as to claim that it is the ever-present threat of external war that defines State politics in its essence, as we shall see.[12] But for now, the important point is that the State wields power over all its citizens all the time. Organized violence that had been strictly temporary and occasional in acephalous societies and, even more important, directed exclusively outward against other groups[13] becomes permanent in State societies and gets directed inward, at least in part, by the State in its police actions against its own citizens. In an important sense, then, and certainly in contrast with acephalous societies, all States are police states (and vary only in degree).[14]

In a similar way, but to a somewhat lesser extent, the State makes the leader's role of reducing internal tension and adjudicating conflicts permanent as well. Though it is true that actually bringing a case to state court is an occasional act, nevertheless the State does not respond to conflict on an ad hoc basis (as the group leader does) but rather transforms any conflict into an opportunity to apply and enforce the law, and the system of law is indeed permanent. In fact, the intransigence of the law is designed to contribute to social harmony by its very existence, as a permanent reminder of what not to do and of the unalterable consequences of disobeying. Moreover, inasmuch as citizens are absolutely enjoined by the State always to obey its laws, they have none of the latitude members of acephalous societies enjoy regarding their leaders' attempts to resolve conflict: these latter are free to ignore such attempts, whereas citizens are never allowed to ignore the laws of the State or the rulings of its courts. The eloquent pleas of the acephalous group leader have been replaced by the bang of the gavel and the grim proclamation of an irrevocable and inescapable verdict.

The group leader's generosity to the members of acephalous societies, finally, fares very unevenly in its reconfiguration by the State in its various forms of historical development. Under despotism, State subjects are granted at best a vicarious enjoyment of their sovereign's glorious expenditure—even though it is financed by their taxes. In the liberal State, in turn, citizens are granted formal rights, but material prosperity is their private concern. Only with the advent of the Keynesian planning State are citizens granted a measure of prosperity remotely akin to the punctual and strategic generosity of the acephalous leader. It was no doubt this moment of apparent generosity that inspired T. H. Marshall to formulate his famous "three-stage" theory of the historical development of modern citizenship, whereby membership in the State would evolve from merely formal equality of rights and then participation in politics into a mode of fully "social citizenship"—by which he meant that something like a welfare State would progressively integrate all citizens into society on the basis of their sharing some measure of material prosperity.[15] As we shall see, subsequent historical developments may have proven this theory wrong. But for now, it should be clear that, in general, the modern State takes the main functions of acephalous leadership—protection, mediation, and provision—and makes them more or less permanent. Vertical functions and relations that emerge in acephalous groups only occasionally, in times of crisis, become fixed in State institutions on a permanent basis and applied to everyone in society. We need to look more closely, however, at the relations between the modern liberal State and the capitalist economy.

The liberal–capitalist State enjoys not only the permanence and generality characteristic of States in general, as we have seen, but in addition, a mode of existence in a way separate or separated from society itself. Hence the importance of the locution "nation-State"—which I treat here as coterminous with the notion of the liberal–capitalist State. Paradoxically, at just the moment that the economy gains its autonomy from social relations in general, the State loses its autonomy relative to capital, even as it separates out from civil society as a whole.

Reasons for this separation are many. One set of reasons has to do with the emergence of the private sphere in connection with the liberal–capitalist nation-State. Both reproduction and production (accumulation) get privatized in modern nation-States: the former in the institution of the nuclear family, the latter in the institution of the capitalist economy. Another set of reasons has to do with the specific nature of that economy: for capitalist exploitation is not a relation of direct personal subservience subordinating one person to another (slave to master), nor a relation of direct political subjugation subordinating one group to another (the conquered and the conquerors, feudal serfs and lords). Capitalist exploitation is a nominally contractual relation between supposedly "free" labor and privately owned capital. That productive property has become private means that noblesse oblige no longer applies to the new ruling class and that capital has no standing responsibilities to society or to workers, just as free labor means that workers have no standing commitment to any particular job, employer, parcel of land, or society. So inasmuch as free labor owes nothing to capitalists except labor power, and privately owned capital owes nothing to workers except wages, and especially given that this contractual relation is also, to a greater or lesser extent, an antagonistic one, securing the conditions of existence of private capital, free labor, and the contract between them devolves to an instance outside the contract itself—devolves, that is to say, to the State. With its emergence under capitalism, "the economic" as a distinct field sheds both the political and the familial spheres, even while important homologies pertain among all three. We will return to examine the nature of the so-called labor contract in chapter 4, but whatever else must be said about it, the distinctly economic mode of exploitation it institutionalizes represents a stark contrast with the directly personal or political modes of subordination characteristic of slave, imperial, and feudal economies.[16]

The specific mode of existence of the State under capitalism significantly alters some of the basic parameters of social organization. Inasmuch as the capitalist economy institutionalizes a conflictual class relation at the heart of social production, the State's mediation-of-conflict role must not only become permanent, it must more specifically furnish the legal, institutional, and cultural–ideological conditions of existence of free labor, privatized capital, and the contract between them—conditions that cannot be established once and for all but must be constantly re-created to meet the changing circumstances of capital accumulation and class struggle. Indeed, a society based on competition among conflicting private interests and persons will inevitably spawn huge State apparatuses of mediation, both bureaucratic (normative and preventive) and juridical (retributive or compensatory). Meanwhile, the protection function provided by the State expands or shifts to the protection of markets as well as (or even more than) people and territory itself, both in protecting the integrity of the national market from foreign encroachment and (increasingly) in "protecting" access to global markets beyond the territorial sovereignty of the State. The role of provider has expanded considerably as well—but what the liberal–capitalist State provides is largely provided for the sake of private property and capital accumulation. And inasmuch as private capital must maximize its accumulation rates to remain competitive, it will socialize costs to be able to privatize greater profits. It is therefore the State that will provide (in addition to the legal and institutional infrastructure mentioned earlier) the material infrastructure requirements of the market (e.g., for the transportation of goods and materials) and increasingly of production itself (in the form of high-technology transfers from the public sector to the private sector). In a similar vein, because private capital is not itself responsible for the reproduction of labor power (as a slave owner is, by contrast), much of this, too, devolves to the State, which provides all kinds of so-called social services, including education and vocational training. Much of the rest of reproduction devolves, of course, to the privatized nuclear family, with important results we will consider in a moment. Finally, to return to Marshall's notion of social citizenship and the welfare State, but also by way of comparison with the mollifying generosity of the acephalous leader, the State may, from time to time, implement income redistribution, but it does so mainly to prevent or resolve capitalism's recurrent crises of overproduction–underconsumption, if not to stave off social unrest or outright rebellion. These, then, are some of the important ways the modern, liberal–capitalist nation-State reconfigures the basic elements of social organization already present in acephalous society, but now abstracted from social life itself (from what is now called civil society) and made permanent.

We can get some measure of the extremity of this reconfiguration by considering the influential work of Carl Schmitt, particularly his conception of the political. Schmitt elevates the external protection function above all others and makes it the exclusive and absolute defining feature of the political. This view is thus poles apart from the Aristotelian view of humankind as *zoon politikon,* destined by nature to be political animals whose necessarily social existence is political through and through and based on internal friendship and justice rather than external threat. It is also, for that matter, poles apart from a Spinozan or Durkheimian view, according to which political power arises from the imbrication of human beings in social assemblages of any kind or form. For Schmitt, by contrast, the political is determined from the outside in, as it were (as well as top down, as we will see shortly): it is the opposition between friend and enemy and the ever-present possibility of war ensuing from that opposition that alone defines the political; this is the apotheosis of the State's appropriation of the war-machine. It is as if the occasional warrior band operating on the edge of the acephalous group had migrated to and become the very center of social organization, transforming it into a permanent warfare State. This is part of what is meant when Deleuze and Guattari insist that the State appropriates the nomadic war-machine for its own purposes.[17] War and readiness for war have become for Schmitt the very raison d'être of the political.

Any invocation of Schmitt requires serious qualification. For one thing, it must be said that Schmitt's view is an extreme one—and this is one reason that it is so useful: its very extremity reveals key features of the modern nation-State, even if in somewhat exaggerated form; extremity throws into bold relief certain tendencies that are ascendant or even dominant without being exclusive or all-pervasive. But it can also be usefully contrasted with the views of one of his contemporaries, Martin Buber, who considered the relation between State and nation from a very different perspective.[18] Where Schmitt construed State politics as arising from outside, from the opposition between friend and enemy, Buber understood State politics to arise internally, from conflicts within the nation that can't be resolved without recourse to an instance standing to some extent outside and above society, that is, the State. Buber's State is thus defined principally by the role of mediation rather than that of protection. But what is most significant for our purposes is that Buber understood that State power is always in excess of what is needed to resolve social conflict. The very endeavor to resolve internal conflict for Buber generated a State apparatus with a surfeit of power that would eventually turn against the society from which it emerged (or that could be turned outward against societies outside its borders). So where Schmitt viewed the threat of war as a necessary corrective to a mode of social organization (including parliamentary democracy) that had become too lax and therefore needed the mobilization of such a threat to reinvigorate the State's power over society, Buber considered the power of the State over the nation to be inherently excessive, even though it had its origins in legitimate attempts to mediate internal conflict.

For another thing, it must be said that Schmitt's elevation of State over society is hardly new or original. At the moment of consolidation of the modern nation-State, Hegel famously treated the nation as a mere support for the truly important, world-historical work of the State, whose role it was to assure the progress of humankind through history (largely by means of war). Hegel's contemporary Johann Fichte, meanwhile, took an opposing view: the State was to be understood as the expression of the underlying and more fundamental organization of society, and any attempt by the State to impose order or obedience from above would be fruitless (if not counterproductive) in the absence of a people united as a nation by common ties of language, culture, and philosophy.[19]

Finally, as Derrida has argued in an extended deconstruction of the friend–enemy opposition on which Schmitt's conception of the political is based, the distinction between friend and enemy may well be philosophically untenable.[20] If there is ultimately no sure way of drawing that line in the sand between friend and enemy, what happens to a concept of the political based entirely on such a distinction? To some extent, however, it must be said that Derrida's critique of Schmitt falls wide of the mark—for Schmitt himself acknowledges that the friend–enemy distinction is not philosophical, but "existential": it stems from a decision that does not emerge from and is not bound by any rules or laws. And so, like his notion of a sovereignty based on decisions made in a state of exception (to rules, to the law), the concept of the political in Schmitt finally boils down to the—existentially alarming but philosophically rather uninteresting—position that might makes right: the friend–enemy opposition is simply the result of someone in power declaring it to be so, and whoever is in a position to do so makes the declaration by simple and absolute fiat. This is the sense in which political order for Schmitt is imposed top down as well as outside in. But just because the friend–enemy distinction is philosophically untenable, as Derrida argues, does not mean that it is socially ineffective. To the contrary: although it may take some work—dismayingly little work, of the kind often referred to as propaganda—making a distinction between friend and enemy (between us and them, citizens and aliens), and making the distinction stick, is precisely what states and nationalism do. What matters for our purpose is less the formal conditions of possibility (or impossibility, on Derrida's view) of a politics based on the friend–enemy opposition than the real conditions of existence and dynamics of that opposition and the corresponding form of State politics, given the dual privatizations of production and reproduction characteristic of capitalism. And in line with the principles of schizoanalysis, our aim will be to examine the specifically libidinal investments—investments in the family, in the State, in the economy—that compose the contemporary social field.

The Problem Redefined: The Death-State

The starting point for this examination is not, however, the State in general, nor even the liberal–capitalist State in general. New concepts and new diagnoses are called for because problems change and when a situation has become Intolerable. The concept of nomad citizenship not only responds to the problem of the State in general but also diagnoses a specific tendency of the modern State that came into sharpest focus in the United States recently in the wake of the events of September 11, 2001. This tendency—although it coexists with countertendencies, which we will also have to examine—depends so crucially on death and violence as to warrant a specific designation: the Death-State.

It has long been accepted that a defining feature of the modern State is its monopoly on legitimate violence.[21] Members of civilized society refrain from the exercise of violence themselves with the understanding that the State will use force when necessary to mediate internal conflict and to protect them from external threats, thereby safeguarding the interests of the community as a whole. But in his essay "The Force of Law," referred to earlier, Derrida has demonstrated that the founding of states in fact entails two additional types of violence, of very different kinds. The established State's legitimate use of violence (or force) to maintain order and enforce the law in fact depends on an illegitimate, aboriginal use of force or violence to establish order and found the State in the first place. All manner of a posteriori rationalizations of this establishing violence may—indeed, must—be effected, but they merely supplement the initial political violence with further interpretive violence. The forceful imposition of political order is perpetuated, yet obscured, by the forceful imposition of a symbolic order that declares that political order to be legitimate. Ultimately, in the effective establishment of a functioning State, these two moments of violence become indistinguishable: the very legitimacy of the State depends on the retroactive sublimation of the moment of political violence by the moment of interpretive violence. The establishment and ongoing viability of modern States in general thus entail three kinds of violence: the aboriginal, illegitimate–prelegitimate violence of establishment; the legitimating violence of interpretation–decision; and the routine, legitimated violence of enforcement. With the advent of the Death-State, however, additional violence is required for the State to remain viable. More specifically, both the psychic dynamics and the economic dynamics of the Death-State install death and violence at the very heart of the state apparatus, for reasons that schizoanalysis will help us determine.

But schizoanalysis is not the only approach that recognizes the importance of violence to the continuing viability of State rule. Arjun Appadurai, too, has postulated the necessity of violence for the contemporary State's ability to procure what he calls the "full attachment" of its citizens, an attachment that he acknowledges is "more libidinal than procedural."[22] Arguing against the view (which he attributes to Habermas, among others) that "the modern nation-state is able to mobilize, conscript, and deploy its citizens in warfare (or preparation for it) because it already has some prior (and plausible) claim to full attachment," Appadurai suggests, on the contrary, that "the modern nation-state requires various forms of violent mobilization in order to 'produce the people'" as citizens in the first place.[23] For Appadurai, however, the State's ability to produce the kind and degree of affective citizenship that "allows [citizens] to kill and die in its name" remains "an unsolved puzzle."[24] This is precisely where schizoanalysis proves useful: it enables us to understand the psychodynamics of affective citizenship in relation to both family dynamics in the private sphere and economic structures and practices in the public sphere.

One of the signal contributions of schizoanalysis is that it shows that in modern capitalist societies (and in no other), economic and familial determinations tend to be distinct from, yet mirror and thus reinforce, one another: the privatization of production coincides with the privatization of reproduction such that Oedipal relations foster and support capitalist relations, and vice versa. This is more than a mere formal homology— although it can be expressed as such. Adding the figure of the child to a quotation from Marx, Deleuze and Guattari assert at one point in *Anti-Oedipus* that "father, mother, and child . . . become the simulacrum of the images of capital" ("'Mister Capital, Madame Earth,' and their child the Worker").[25] The structures of the nuclear family and the capitalist economy parallel one another: just as capital separates the worker from the means of life (Mother Earth) and defers access to the goods and ensuing gratification until after work, payday, and/or retirement, so the Father separates the child from its means of life (the Mother) and defers access to the opposite sex and ensuing gratification until after puberty and the founding of a new family through marriage. Deleuze and Guattari insist that the nuclear family and Oedipal psychoanalysis are strictly capitalist institutions for this reason (among others): the dynamics of both the nuclear family and standard therapeutic transference effectively program the Oedipal psyche to accept and even relish the structure of capitalist social relations. They even go so far as to say that capitalism "delegates" the social reproduction of subjects to the nuclear family because in their view, capital is a quantitative calculus and not the kind of meaningful system of representation required to foster subjectivity. But this presents a serious problem: the assertion that the capitalist mode of production delegates reproduction to the nuclear family deprives reproduction of its autonomy, implying that the family and psychic life are mere effects of an economic cause.

In this connection, the analysis offered by Norman O. Brown in *Life against Death* is especially important.[26] Like Deleuze and Guattari, Brown focuses on the relationship between psychoanalysis and history ("The Psychoanalytic Meaning of History" is his subtitle), and like them, he is especially interested in the relations between the domestic and public spheres (or between the family and economics) in determining social conduct. But where Deleuze and Guattari tend to favor sociohistorical determination (with capital "delegating" the reproduction of subjects to the nuclear family), Brown insists to the contrary on unilateral psychological determination. In fact, he explicitly sets out to replace what he considers to be inadequate historical (Hegelian, Marxist) explanations for societywide human neuroses with a purely psychological, Freudian explanation—albeit by reading Freud somewhat against the grain and insisting that the repression of death (about which Freud said relatively little) is at least as important as the repression of sexuality (about which he said a great deal).

Now, for Brown to effectively parry the historicizing thrust of schizoanalysis, he would have to specify some determining feature of family life that escapes the historical variability of family forms that Deleuze and Guattari insist on so strenuously and demonstrate so convincingly.[27] And he does so: it is prolonged infantile dependency, which is understood as a biological condition that is invariably true of all family forms (regardless of how extended or privatized they may be) and that has direct and profound repercussions for the human psyche. The human animal, Brown reminds us, is utterly dependent on adults for its very survival for an extended period of time after birth—much longer than most other mammals. This period of dependency of human infants on (let us call them) "caregivers" (rather than mother, father, or even parents—for it makes no difference who) fosters exaggerated expectations for physiological and psychological gratification, intense separation anxiety (since separation from caregivers at this stage means death), and a consequent repression or refusal of death. In effect, the repression of death leaves humans fixated on all the impossible infantile projects they refused to let die in the past, leaving them unable to live in the present and giving motive force to an obsessive orientation toward an imaginary future of total gratification. So the "psychoanalytic meaning of history" is that humans sacrifice "that state of Being which was the goal of [human] Becoming"[28] and compulsively rush headlong into a kind of future no one can ever attain.

Now, from a schizoanalytic perspective, this analysis is suggestive because it coincides with Deleuze and Guattari's analysis of capitalism, which also entails both a crucial measure of dependency (to which we will return in chapter 4) and a "refusal of death"—what they call the subordination of antiproduction (i.e., unproductive social expenditure or consumption) and the corresponding transformation of death into an instinct.[29] Unlike all other social formations that subordinate production to the reproduction of existing power relations, capital does the reverse: it elevates production over social reproduction and systematically sacrifices social expenditure in favor of private accumulation so that the risk of death becomes subordinate to the overproduction and accumulation of means of life. As Bataille never tired of pointing out, consuming goods in the present always entails an element of risk—the risk that those goods might be necessary to sustain life sometime in the future.[30] By neither putting goods to productive use nor saving them for future eventualities, immediate consumption paradoxically aggravates the risk of death, even though it supports life. The curtailment of consumption for the sake of accumulation thus represents a repression of the risk of death. Of course, the repressed always returns—death returns, now as an instinct—but capitalism manages to yoke even the production of means of death to its own self-realization and self-expansion—as when the arms race and weapons production, for example, usurp public spending and contribute massively to capital accumulation. Indeed, from this perspective, bombs are the perfect capitalist commodity and an ideal solution to capital's notorious crises of overproduction, inasmuch as they blow up and immediately call for the production of more bombs to replace them. The death that was refused within the bounds of a State now devoted not to glorious expenditure but merely to furthering capital accumulation gets projected and inflicted outside the bounds of the State through military expenditure in the service of what Eisenhower famously called the military–industrial complex.

These are two very powerful accounts of the state of death in the psychic and social registers, but each assigns causal priority to a different register. So how are we to understand the relation between them? Clearly an obsessive psychological future orientation in search of an impossible state of complete gratification gets captured by—or does it foster?—a society-wide consumerism that contributes directly to, and is indeed required for, the realization of surplus-value and the accumulation of capital, which in turn requires wage suppression so that the drive for gratification is perpetually frustrated. Whatever role our analysis assigns to the mediation of advertising, whether as expression of a psychic compulsion or as mechanism of an economic imperative, the least we can say is that they are mutually reinforcing. And no doubt the Solomonesque solution would be simply to grant psychic compulsion and economic imperative equal determinacy.

The Freudian concept of *nachträglichkeit,* or "deferred action," however, suggests a very different resolution: rather than conceiving of infantile dependency and all its repercussions as determining social conduct and economic dynamics in linear fashion, as Brown's analysis would have it, this concept suggests that it is the refusal of death in social life under capitalism in particular that enables the refusal of death as one infantile complex among many to take center stage in contemporary psychic life.[31] Although infantile dependency is no different in kind in the nuclear family, it is certainly greater in degree, because here one or two parents monopolize caregiving and love, whereas extended families offer many more possibilities for both. There may be an innate psychological tendency in humans to sacrifice the present for an infinitely deferred and impossible future, but it is capitalism that creates the historical conditions for that tendency to flourish and indeed become a predominant dynamic of social life. The separation anxiety over the loss of parental love (which, early in life, means losing access to provisions supplied by parents or caregivers) mirrors and reinforces the separation anxiety over the loss of one's job (which, later in life, means losing access to provisions supplied by the market): part of what is anti-Oedipal about schizoanalysis is the way it reads Freud against Freud this way—or rather Freud against his own Oedipus complex—by suggesting, in line with Brown's analysis, that, under capitalism anyway, separation anxiety is far more important than castration anxiety. This is the first minor theoretical displacement occasioned by schizonomadology: the eclipse of the Father and the phallus and castration in favor of the relationship to the Mother and the loss of access to her.

But this does not mean that market-induced separation anxiety "causes" infantile separation anxiety (for which biology is clearly the cause) nor that capitalism "delegates" the breeding of anxiety-ridden subjects to the family to prepare them for psychic life under market capitalism (which grants capitalism far too much totalizing prescience and agency). It might be better to say simply that the capital–economic and Oedipal–familial instances, which are, in principle, autonomous, turn out in fact to resonate with one another under certain conditions and that they do so today in a mutually reinforcing way, as we will see in the chapters that follow.

Now let us suppose that in addition to these two instances of mutually reinforcing resonance, the economic and the familial, there were a third: let's call it the political, here construed narrowly to refer to affairs of the State. The nation-State plays a key intermediary role as what Deleuze and Guattari call a *model of realization* between the abstract calculus of capital and the concrete reproduction of subjectivity (although it has not always played such a role).[32] And it does so not only through a panoply of intermediary institutions (such as those that Althusser dubbed "Ideological State Apparatuses"—public schools, political parties, and so on) but also as an object of psychic investment in the form of what, more or less following Benedict Anderson, we might call an "Imaginary" (rather than an "imagined") community, to emphasize the psychodynamics involved. Because of the size and complexity of modern societies, Anderson rightly insists, contemporary citizens (unlike their ancient Greek counterparts) have no opportunity to meet face-to-face with their fellow citizens. The nation-State must therefore be imagined by its members: belonging to a nation-State, in other words, unavoidably entails the mobilization of fantasy—and Anderson analyzes some of the means (reading novels, daily newspapers, etc.) by which modern citizens construct and participate in Imaginary representations of the national community.[33] The strength of Anderson's book lies in his examination of how various discourses represent nationhood and thereby solicit citizens' affective investments in their "imagined community"; he is less concerned with the psychodynamics of those investments: this is where schizoanalysis proves invaluable.

Schizoanalysis approaches the question of affective citizenship on the basis of a power principle derived from Spinoza and Nietzsche: libidinal investment in a nation-State depends ultimately on the degree to which belonging to such a State enhances citizens' feelings of power—or to put it another way, loyalty to the State depends on the power rewards it offers to its citizens.[34] Citizen loyalties have often been parsed along an axis of inclusion and exclusion: fellow citizens are included within the bounds of the State, whereas noncitizens are more or less forcibly excluded. As we have seen, the State, on one hand, *provides* for those included among its citizens and, on the other hand, *protects* them from noncitizens who have been excluded, and feelings of power arise from both.[35] More specifically, the modern nation-State has, at least since Fichte, been understood in terms of these two aspects or components: one aspect (which Fichte calls the "nation") involves the feeling of belonging together with fellow citizens in a shared, enclosed space and common culture. Feelings of connection with and responsibility for fellow citizens combine with trust that the Motherland as a community will provide for the well-being of its members. The other aspect (which Fichte calls the "State") involves the sense of order imposed on the nation from above by the State, to bolster and ensure the web of relations composing the community, but also to relate the nation as one people to other nation-States and so that the Fatherland can protect the nation from threats to its well-being coming from outside its borders.[36] Motherland and Fatherland thus represent two poles of the affective investment in nation-States, operating on a continuum marked at the extremes by categories such as inclusion–exclusion, provision–protection, positive–negative, affirmative–defensive, constructive–destructive, and immanent–transcendent—and resonating dramatically with the psychodynamics of the nuclear family and of capital.

We can gauge the depth and breadth of this resonance by briefly examining some of the political rhetoric and juridical theories it generates or echoes in contemporary North American culture. The political rhetoric of the two-party system in the United States, as cognitive scientist George Lakoff has shown, is structured around an opposition between conservatism and liberalism that mobilizes imagery and metaphors based on the figures of the Father and Mother, respectively.[37] Conservative and liberal political positions and the arguments made on their behalf rest squarely, in Lakoff's view, on two worldviews or moral systems built in each case "around a model of an ideal family."[38] The conservative ideal revolves around the "Strict Father," whereas the liberal ideal involves what he calls "Nurturant Parent" or Mother.[39] In brief, the Strict Father ideal, not surprisingly, emphasizes obedience, discipline, respect for authority, and self-reliance, whereas the Nurturant Mother ideal emphasizes love, empathy, care for others, and self-fulfillment.[40] On the basis of these two ideal moral systems or collective fantasies, Lakoff provides a comprehensive account of why conservatives and liberals take the positions they do, or at least make the arguments they make, regarding the principal issues of contemporary

North American politics. Along similar lines, the two collective fantasies also find more elaborated expression in two distinctive theories of justice, which we can call (following Iris Marion Young[41]) the social–connective and the individual–retributive. Whereas the former considers questions of justice systemically rather than individualistically, acknowledges complicity or shared responsibility, and seeks corrective measures in systemic transformation through collective action involving perpetrators, intermediaries, and victims alike, the latter sense of justice seeks to categorically separate victims and perpetrators, to deny significant involvement, and to target discrete individuals or groups for blame to punish and/or exact retribution from them.[42] It may come as no surprise that citizens raised in nuclear families would respond to theories of justice or political rhetoric organized in terms of unconscious investments in the Father(land) or the Mother(land). Equally important for schizoanalysis, however, is the consideration that parental roles and behaviors are themselves modeled unconsciously on the political rhetoric and theories impinging on family life from society at large. Neither the Oedipal structure of childhood nor the agonistic structure of political rhetoric and theory explains the other in any unilateral way; rather the two instances resonate with and reinforce one another.

Given these collective fantasies about the Motherland and the Fatherland, the question then becomes, what conditions would induce investment in one more than the other or even in one to the exclusion of the other? It could be supposed that with the consolidation of a globalizing capitalism, the State would be of declining salience to many of its citizens. But that is only half the story. It is the Motherland that has increasingly "negative salience" for Death-State citizens, as we shall see, while the salience of the Fatherland, on the contrary, continues to increase. Indeed, it will be possible to argue that wounded feelings of abandonment by the Motherland fuel a vindictive rage to punish some foreign Other that is blamed for the betrayal, thereby provoking a compensatory and pathological overinvestment in the Fatherland as rewards from the Motherland diminish.

We can see why this would be the case by examining the State's relations with citizens in three major domains of social life—production, reproduction, and antiproduction—in each of which we see a pattern of decreasing rewards and hence waning loyalties. Starting with the domain of reproduction, it is clear that the nuclear family has suffered severely under neoliberalism so that families require not one but two, three, and sometimes four jobs to support themselves. At the same time, the provision of social services in support of reproduction more broadly conceived—including, most notably, public education but also civil amenities, public health and safety, urban and transportation infrastructures, and so on—has declined radically in quantity and quality. This is no doubt due to capital's successful reduction of its share of reproduction costs and their displacement onto beleaguered citizens, who now shoulder a proportionally larger share of the tax burden than ever before.[43] But in any case, the result is that citizens feel the Motherland is no longer functioning as public Provider, and this feeling translates into diminished citizen loyalty, if not outright resentment and/or a search for alternative and mostly private forms of provisioning elsewhere. This is the context in which feelings of abandonment by the Motherland provoke compensatory investments in compulsive consumerism, among other things. Foreign policy based on expropriating scarce resources around the globe, meanwhile, is perfectly consonant with insistence on the private right to drive a sports utility vehicle; in fact, one function of the Death-State as a "model of realization" for capitalism is precisely to align a psychological compulsion to consume, instilled in subjects since prolonged infancy, with the economic imperative to expand production and consumption in the service of private accumulation—an imperative that, often enough, requires military action abroad to fulfill.

In the sphere of production, the situation is more complicated, even if the resulting pattern is more of the same. In the context of global competition and post-Fordism, income guarantees and, more important, job security itself have been drastically curtailed. That is why what T. H. Marshall has famously called "social citizenship" as the "third stage" in the evolution of modern citizenship—bolstered or guaranteed in the last instance by the welfare state—was either not a stage but a variable within an older stage, or if it was a stage, it is now over, for social citizenship itself is steadily getting stripped away.[44] At the same time, the State is losing economic sovereignty in the face of a number of institutions and agreements, including, most notoriously, the International Monetary Fund and the World Trade Organization but also trade agreements such as the North American Free Trade Agreement (NAFTA) and the General Agreement on Tariffs and Trade (GATT). Especially when it is clear that their government actively supports shipping their jobs overseas, citizens feel neither internally well provided for nor well protected from external competition in the sphere of production—and their affective investment in the State diminishes as a result.

In the sphere of antiproduction, things are more complicated still. Generally speaking, war is a prime mover of citizenship affect, as innumerable polls in recent decades have shown. Indeed, "giving one's life for one's country" may be the ultimate sign of loyalty to the State. And yet the citizen-soldier is virtually nowhere to be found. War is fought instead with a volunteer (or mercenary) army. What was once supposed to be positive affective investment in the Fatherland—the noble fight for freedom in World War II, for instance—has become a more or less purely instrumental exchange relation: volunteers sign up for the Army Reserves (expecting to sacrifice their weekends, not their lives) in exchange for higher educational opportunities they otherwise couldn't afford.

At the same time, however, the Death-State needs war more than ever, and indeed, waging war has become its primary function.[45] For even though wars no longer mobilize positive affective investment (willing sacrifice for a noble cause), they certainly mobilize negative affective investment, that is to say, investment based on trauma and fear. An unending war on some vaguely defined "terror" fits the bill perfectly: citizens are made to feel the need for the State-as-Protector more than ever before, even if the protection it affords is illusory at best. War thus kills at least three birds with one stone: it solves the crisis of overproduction of economic goods by producing endless demand for more weaponry; by commandeering the lion's share of public expenditure, it provokes a compensatory libidinal investment in private consumerism; and it solves the crisis of underproduction of citizenship goods by producing endless demand for mere protection by the Fatherland and a willingness to sacrifice or indeed disparage almost any form of nourishment by the Motherland.

On the basis of what libidinal dynamics could such a State command assent or attract citizen loyalty? The promise of schizoanalysis is to account for Death-State citizenship in terms of a specific libidinal dynamics of affective investment common to the family, capital, and the State in modern societies. We started from the structural homology posited by Deleuze and Guattari between the privatized nuclear family and private capital—"'Mister Capital, Madame Earth' and their child the Worker." But to the considerable extent that the "Imaginary community" of the nation-State mobilizes fantasies of Motherland and Fatherland, we saw that the State, too, operates according to the same structure of affective investment as do the family and capital.[46] We can now take another step. For these three instances share not just the same structure but a common dynamic. In the psychological register, the more conflicted the ego gets due to the repression of needs and desire, the more power the superego wields over the psyche: the superego derives the very force of its power from the repression it exercises. Similarly, in the sociopolitical register, the more conflicted civil society gets due to the clash of private interests, the more power the State wields over society: the State derives the very force of its power from the fear of conflict (internal and external) that it promotes and from the very existence of conflicting private interests that it nonetheless mediates and steadfastly defends.[47] Finally, in the socioeconomic register, the greater the suppression of wages due to competition on the job market, the more surplus-value capital appropriates to wield over social production: capital derives the very force of its power from the labor it divides and conquers to exploit. Furthermore, in all three registers, dependency (rather than brute force) plays a key role in cementing the relation between the subordinated instance and the dominant one. This is perhaps clearest in the case of family dynamics, where Freud and Brown show how crucial infantile dependency on parental care is, both for the physical survival of the infant and for the emotional bonds subjecting it to paternal or familial authority, via the formation of the superego. But dependency, one of the key features of primitive accumulation, is also a crucial aspect of the subordination of labor to capital, as we will see in chapter 4. Finally, dependency is one of the hidden costs of social contract theory: citizens are supposed to gain security and peace of mind by handing over their powers to the State for the mutual safety and protection of all, but in fact, the social contract makes all citizens utterly dependent on the State for the guarantee and enforcement of their rights.[48] In all three registers, convenient fictions serve to mask the wretchedness of generalized dependency: the fiction that the social contract is voluntary and that citizens give consent to be governed by the State; the fiction that the nuclear family is natural or universal and that infants benefit most from the exclusive love of two parents; the fiction that there is a free market in labor and that labor contracts are voluntary. And in each case, dependency produces feelings of inadequacy that, in turn, add compensatory appeal to a figure of transcendent omnipotence—to the omnipotence of the father, the omnipotence of the commander in chief, the omnipotence of capital. We have not just a vicious circle in each case but also a pattern of resonance among the three instances—which turns the vicious circles into an ever-tightening noose.

Of course, to speak of "registers" in this way is partly an artifice of our analysis. And important work has already recognized some of the intersections among them: with the categories of the "performance principle" and "surplus-repression," Herbert Marcuse linked the pressure of economic exploitation in the economic sphere directly to the repression exercised by the superego originating in the family.[49] With the category of "biopower," Foucault forged a link between the dynamics of modern State governance and the capitalist imperative to increase productivity.[50] In a similar vein, the schizoanalytic categories of Motherland and Fatherland underscore the relations between children's investments in the family and citizens' investments in the imagined–Imaginary community of the nation-State. But the relative independence of these registers is also an artifact of modern society, which actually does privatize reproduction in the nuclear family, actually does privatize accumulation under capital, and actually does separate out government from the warp and woof of social relations and lodge it in the State, as we have seen. Yet we need to push the analysis one step farther, inasmuch as we are interested specifically in the psycho- and sociodynamics of the Death-State, not just the modern liberal–capitalist State in general. To this end, the presidential regime of George W. Bush deserves careful scrutiny.

One of the great strengths of schizoanalysis, and its comparative advantage over psychoanalysis, as my first book on Charles Baudelaire demonstrated, is its ability to recover the rich and concrete set of relations that obtain between individuals and their sociohistorical milieus.[51] Baudelaire epitomized the advent of full-fledged modernity in mid-nineteenth-century France, and a schizoanalysis of Baudelaire showed how and why his familial circumstances—his "family romance"—resonated so remarkably with the takeoff of industrial and consumer capitalism and the fitful emergence of a modern State apparatus in France. In a similar way, Bush and his regime epitomize the psychological, political, and economic dynamics of the Death-State. Schizoanalysis enables—and compels—us to diagnose *collective* fantasies or complexes, even as they get expressed in exceptional historical figures such as Baudelaire or (in a very different way) George W. Bush. It would be all too easy—but no less relevant or true for being so easy—to construe Bush's invasion of Iraq as a kind of Oedipal obsession with avenging his father's "defeat" or compromise in the first Iraq war. But the correlations between family romance and State policy, between private-sphere psychology and public-sphere politics, go far deeper than that. To all appearances—whether purely for strategic electoral purposes or not—Bush came across as someone who was intolerant of ambiguity, rigid in worldview, incapable of handling complexity, unwilling to entertain dissent or alternative points of view, and requiring absolute loyalty and uncritical assent from those around him—traits that overlap significantly with the features of so-called born-again fundamentalist Christians.[52] This turns out to be of crucial importance—not only for the electoral support he garnered by courting the Christian vote itself but also for the psychodynamics that explain so much of his broader electoral and presidential appeal.

In brief, born-again fundamentalism has four main features.[53] The first is the feature from which the category gets its name: a literalism that sees Absolute Truth in scripture as the Word of God; this literalism accompanies or derives from an inability or unwillingness to handle ambiguity, nuance, and complexity.[54] It gives rise to a virulent Manichaeism: the world is seen, just as it is in the Strict Father moral system,[55] in simplistic terms of black and white, Good vs. Evil; "you're either with us or you're against us," as Bush famously said. This Manichaeism is central to the second feature of born-again fundamentalism, which is the conversion experience itself: conversion as it were narrativizes the binary opposition constitutive of Manichaeism. The world in general has already been divided into Good and Evil, sin and salvation: conversion, almost always provoked by some kind of trauma (even if only that of "hitting bottom"), then splits the individual personality between past and present, between former sinner and present-day exemplar of salvation. At least it tries to: but of course, the temptations that led to sin cannot be banished so easily; deep-seated desires can be repressed but not eliminated, and the repressed always returns.[56] The born-again split personality therefore stands in constant need of reinforcement, in the attempt to shore up the new sense of self against the old demons of temptation.

This personality type therefore entertains relations with other people of two characteristic kinds—and this is its third feature: on one hand, the born-again fundamentalist will demand unconditional support for his grandiose new self, either by associating regularly with other born-agains who provide and require the same kind of support or by proselytizing in the hope of converting others to the same faith—or both. On the other hand, in relations with those who have not or will not convert, the born-again fundamentalist will treat them with sneering contempt and mete out punishment worthy of the damned—the severity of the punishment matching more or less exactly the degree of sin supposedly relegated by the born again to the past and the degree of temptation actually still suffered in the present. This is the dynamic of "punitive projective identification," by which an element of the personality now considered unacceptable is split off, projected onto others, and punished in them; it is a variant of the dynamic discussed earlier, whereby the superego obtains its power from the very conflicts it seeks to repress, and we will have occasion to return to it later.

The fourth feature of the born-again personality is its apocalypticism. The stubborn fact of the matter is that the world as a whole will not convert to the true faith, despite all the born-agains' proselytizing. And indeed, much of the energy that sustains the born again derives precisely from its undying opposition to an incorrigibly corrupt and inferior world—objective correlative of the abiding temptations and conflicts that continue to haunt its own soul: such opposition is its raison-d'être. To the born-agains' overt chagrin and secret delight, then, the rest of the world refuses to convert. It must therefore be punished and, ultimately, destroyed. So grandiose is fundamentalist self-righteousness that it would prefer to see the world destroyed than allow it to persevere in what it considers evil. If the price to be paid for cleansing the world of sin is its total destruction, then so be it. Clearly this fourth feature is the most extreme of all and may or may not have discernable correlates in the spheres of political rhetoric or culture at large. Moreover, fundamentalism as a whole represents an extreme version of the Strict Father moral and individual–retributive juridical systems diagnosed by George Lakoff and Iris Marion Young. And just as the extremity of Schmitt's views served to highlight important political features of the Death-State, so can the extremity of born-again fundamentalism reveal crucial features of the fantasy investments underlying electoral support for the Bush regime. For although most U.S. voters are not, of course, born-again fundamentalists, Bush's neo-fundamentalist regime nonetheless appealed to an electorate profoundly traumatized by the events of September 11, 2001, and therefore susceptible to a kind of conversion experience intended to restore the moral health of an ailing nation.

Here, although the political conversion experience may be somewhat less clearly defined than that of religious fundamentalism, the trauma that provoked it is more so: it was the World Trade Center and Pentagon attacks, which were immediately and compulsively narrativized in the frame of "things now will never be the same as before." The trauma of this event required the reassurance of a bracing narrative of "before and after" which would, at the same time, signal and promote a decisive change in existential orientation. With the 1960s and the so-called Vietnam syndrome as a distant backdrop, the narrative that developed after 9/11 was that before, we had been too lax, too permissive, too nice, too naive, too sensitive—too "Nurturant"; now and hereafter, we would have to get serious, get tougher, be "Strict" and more "realistic." All complexity—and most of all, our own complicity—were to be eliminated from consideration. Never mind that political structures in the Middle East were imposed by the West during the mid-twentieth century; never mind that a main interest for the region was guaranteeing the continued expropriation of oil reserves; never mind that the Taliban and Saddam Hussein were largely creations of cold war U.S. foreign policy: we were now at war, the enemy was "terror," and the world was suddenly transformed into black and white, friend or foe— "you were either with us or against us." But it is not just complexity that must be denied: so, too, must our vulnerability, our growing interdependence with the rest of the world. Any feelings of weakness or uncertainty must be banished, projected onto others, and punished there in the name of freedom and democracy. The very acquisitive drive that sponsors wars abroad for control of natural resources is denied, split off, and projected onto "terrorists" as their covetous "envy of our way of life." Our actions, conversely, are motivated not by self(ish) interest but by paternalistic concern for others' well-being. Such self-misunderstanding, often referred to as American exceptionalism, is symptomatic of a form of collective narcissism whereby the elaboration of and identification with a delusional, grandiose sense of self (over-) compensates for conflicted feelings of inadequacy and vulnerability that must be projected onto others and thereby denied.[57]

Such a response is not inevitable; it is well-nigh pathological: it reveals a gross overinvestment in the psychodynamics of the Fatherland and a corresponding denial of the Motherland.[58] In contrast to a fantasy of social–connective justice based on the psychodynamics of the Motherland—which would involve acknowledging interdependence and vulnerability, recognizing rights and wrongs on both sides of a porous border, and forging bilateral arrangements to mitigate hostility and repair damages—the fantasy of individual–retributive justice characteristic of the Fatherland draws rigid boundaries between right and wrong, friend and foe (Good and Evil!); assigns unilateral blame to individuals (Bin Laden, Hussein); and seeks vengeance through ruthless punishment executed with a sense of absolute righteousness.[59] But these fantasies are collective and therefore decidedly not purely psychological in nature or in origin: they have sociohistorical determinations, as well. And it is these that we will now consider, from a nomadological perspective.

A Thousand Plateaus adds the notion of the war-machine, as we have said, to the schizoanalytic account of collective fantasy and group dynamics. Relevant here are the fourth and fifth kinds of war-machine mentioned at the end of chapter 1. The third type designates in very general terms the appropriation of the war-machine for State ends, which we examined earlier: here war serves as politics by other means; violence is marshaled to maintain order internally and especially to protect and/or extend territory and markets externally. The fourth and fifth types of war-machine, however, are more historically specific. The fourth war-machine is fascism: according to Deleuze and Guattari, it was fascism that transformed limited war for political ends into total war, whose ends are ambiguous (are they political or economic?[60]), thereby paving the way for the advent of the totalizing war-machine of global capitalism.

Having subordinated the State and its political ends to the aim of capital accumulation on a global scale, the fifth war-machine reverses the means–ends relationship so that now, political means (such as diplomacy) serve economic ends—and the total "hot" war crucial to fascism gives way to a certain kind of peace, the peace of cold war deterrence:

> It was only after World War II that the autonomatization . . . of the war machine had [its] true effect. The war machine . . . no longer had war as its exclusive object but took in charge and as its object peace, politics, the world order, in short the aim. This is where the inversion of Clausewitz's formula comes in: it is politics that becomes the continuation of [economic] war; *it is peace that technologically frees the unlimited material process of total war.* . . . In this sense, there was no longer a need for fascism. The Fascists were only child precursors, and the absolute peace of survival succeeded where total war had failed.[61]

What failed was the Fascists' total hot war in pursuit of the political ends of the Third Reich (and in the face of defeat, the Nazi state turned "suicidal"—to quote the psychological term Deleuze and Guattari borrow from Virilio—or what our schizoanalytic account would instead call apocalyptic[62]). What succeeded, however, was the material process of total war—the more and more complete mobilization or subsumption of all social resources for the war-machine—and its conversion from hot war to the cold war peace of nuclear deterrence and its MAD doctrine of mutually assured destruction. This entails, among other things, a realignment of the relations between the State and the economy, as we suggested earlier in invoking the historical shift identified by Foucault from sovereign power to biopower.[63] But such a shift is not as linear as it may first appear and requires further clarification in this more specific historical context.

Generally or typologically speaking, the difference between sovereignty and biopower involves the subordination of State politics to the economic imperatives of capital accumulation: the despotic State loses its transcendent power of overcoding and becomes immanent to capitalist axiomatization. In the process, and in principle, the authority of the dethroned despot migrates into the heart of the nuclear family, where it gets recoded as the authority of the Father, as we have seen. The apparently dominant tendency, in other words, is for biopower to replace sovereignty; for axiomatization to subordinate overcoding; for the fourth, hot war-machine of fascism to give way to the fifth, cold war-machine of global capitalism: but there are also countertendencies. Generally speaking, we expect global axiomatization to prevail: "the axiomatic [of capitalism] marshals a power [*puissance*] higher than the one it treats . . . [higher] than that of the aggregates serving as its models"—that is, a power higher than that of States serving as models of realization.[64] But as it turns out, despotic authority hasn't completely withdrawn from the public sphere once and for all; the State hasn't become completely immanent to capital—even if the former nevertheless remains subordinate to the latter. The sovereign power of the despot to take life and to demand its sacrifice in war never completely abdicates to the capitalist imperative to produce more life and means of life in the service of private accumulation. "If there is an evolution of the State," Deleuze and Guattari insist, against the grain of any linear periodization, "the second pole, the evolved pole [i.e., the axiomatizing biopower State], must be in resonance with the first [the sovereign despotic State], it must continually recharge it in some way."[65] Even more, there are circumstances in which sovereign power returns to the fore and actually predominates over biopower. This is the context in which nomadology must situate the Bush regime and, by comparison, the Clinton regime that immediately preceded it. Of course, the categorical distinction between sovereign power and biopower, between the despotic State and the axiomatizing State, is an analytic and heuristic one: any and every regime will represent a mixture of both poles or tendencies. But it is also possible that a given regime will favor one tendency rather than the other, and this is why a comparison between what I will call the neo-Conservative Bush regime and the neo-Liberal Clinton regime can prove useful.[66]

The first thing that must be said, however, is that there is a common denominator of tendency and countertendency alike, and it is the continuing development of an economic war-machine, whether for hot or cold war: "the main point," Deleuze and Guattari insist, is that

> the growing importance of constant capital in the axiomatic means that the depreciation of existing capital and the formation of new capital assume a rhythm and scale that necessarily take the route of a war machine.[67]

In this respect, both tendencies are regimes of accumulation based ultimately on capitalist axiomatization. Which type of war-machine prevails under the ubiquitous pressure of accumulation, however—hot or cold, despotic or axiomatizing—will depend on circumstances and choices. At the time Deleuze and Guattari wrote *Capitalism and Schizophrenia,* the global war-machine principally took the form of the cold war nuclear arms race, which translated the military–industrial complex Eisenhower had warned against at the end of World War II into an even more capital-intensive and high-tech enterprise. But those circumstances changed significantly around the turn of the century, first with the end of the cold war (1989) and then with the attacks of 9/11 (2001), and it is important to track these changes to understand the relations between the different kinds of war-machine—and more important, to update them in light of these changed circumstances.[68]

What did it mean for global capitalism that the cold war effectively ended after 1989? What did it mean that the Bush regime in the wake of 9/11 reverted to a preemptive hot war against Iraq (quite unlike the cold war, or even the warm war of recontainment against Saddam Hussein conducted by this father)? One key to understanding the import of these questions is to recall that, as Deleuze and Guattari insist, the fifth war-machine "no longer [has] war as its exclusive object":[69] what really matters instead of war itself is the mobilization of resources on a worldwide scale and the constant formation of new capital.[70] And what the end of the cold war meant was the possibility of converting the State war-machine from military to nonmilitary ends. This is precisely what the Clinton regime had started to do—with considerable success. Now Deleuze and Guattari suggest that with the fifth war-machine, "the world became a smooth space again":[71] that may or may not have been true when they wrote it (and they were speaking from a military perspective, for the most part), but it was certainly not the case by the time Clinton left office. For all the demilitarization of the globe he may have attempted, he simultaneously strengthened and accelerated its systematic axiomatization. That is to say, the striation of global space under Clinton was advanced not by the deployment of GPS or smart bombs but by trade agreements such as NAFTA and GATT, which provided globalizing capital with firm and legally enforceable strangleholds on markets in countries throughout the world. Not only was he able to balance the federal budget and address the trade deficit, but by his second term, the domestic and foreign trade policies he championed had generated a substantial surplus. In terms of affective citizenship, the Clinton regime was restoring the Motherland to something approaching a more equal status with the Fatherland; development of productive force regained some ground relative to the exercise of power through military domination; providing for the citizenry came to seem just as feasible and important as protecting them. Indeed, for a brief moment, the question on the agenda was how to spend the "peace dividend." Under Clinton's neo-Liberal regime, then, the State operated principally in the service of capitalist axiomatization of the globe, with few political or military ends of its own.

All this changed dramatically under the Bush regime—due in part to the calamity of 9/11 but also to the way the Bush administration and much of the mass media managed it so as to bolster the sovereign power of the State. The contrast between the Clinton regime's embrace of global trade and free markets and the Bush regime's insistence on military supremacy and armed conquest could not have been sharper. In this context, the concerted right-wing attack on the Clinton legacy involved far more than the Lewinski affair for which he was impeached (unsuccessfully), the "return to the 1960s" he represented, or the supposedly pro-gay "don't ask, don't tell" policy he proposed to the military—far more than any or all of these culturalist failings for which the fundamentalist Christians reviled him. For their neo-Conservative allies in the Bush administration had other grievances: the Clinton administration was out to conquer the world and impose U.S. rule not by force of arms but by the force of trade (albeit on terms most favorable to North American and northern capital, of course)—that is, to axiomatize it economically rather than subjugate it militarily. This could only lead, in neoconservative eyes, to a weak-kneed spirit of multilateral cooperation and hence a deficit of military vigilance and assertiveness abroad, combined—in the words of a Trilateral Commission report's reflections on the prosperous 1950s and 1960s—with an unmanageable "excess of democracy" at home.[72] The Clinton administration, in other words, represented—and had begun to institute—a dramatically different regime of capital accumulation: one that threatened to the core the neo-Conservative right's favored, military–industrial accumulation regime—what we would today (updating Eisenhower's original concept) have to call the "high-tech-engineering–military–cybernetic–industrial–fossil-fuel complex."[73] In contrast with the Clinton regime, the Bush regime of capital accumulation reasserted the prerogatives of big engineering, big energy, big oil, and defense and security industries over the rest of the economy, using the so-called War on Terror both at home and abroad to secure an enhanced rate of profit for certain sectors of capital, to be sure, but also to significantly expand the powers of the State.

These, then, are the sociodynamics of the Death-State. Bush "recharges" the first, despotic pole of the State, mobilizing Schmittian friend/enemy politics to terrorize citizens into agreement to wage war for the sake of the Fatherland at the expense of the Motherland, and combines this with a decisive boost to profit rates in the high-tech-engineering, military, and fossil fuel sectors of capital that he and the vice president so clearly represented, through the prosecution of an interminable hot war. Given the ongoing development of the capitalist war-machine, the power regime of the Death-State might be more appropriately categorized as neo-despotic rather than despotic. For death and terror under true despotism are largely incidental, or at least clearly subordinate to transcendent political ends:

conquest or defense of territory and the establishment or maintenance of taxation. Under neo-despotism, by contrast, military and police actions are inherently or immanently related both to the accumulation of capital and to the preservation or extension of State power.

This return of State despotism is difficult to account for in the terms of *Anti-Oedipus*: despotism was supposed to have disappeared from social production as State politics became increasingly immanent and subordinate to economic axiomatization; it was supposed to have endured only in the private sphere of the nuclear family, in the form of the Oedipus complex. Although the first volume of *Capitalism and Schizophrenia* may have actually deployed despotism (along with savagery) only for the sake of a genealogy of the Oedipus complex, it was all too easy to read it as a linear account of the State becoming immanent to capital. The second volume emphatically rules out such a misreading: *A Thousand Plateaus* is clearly nonlinear, in style and organization as well as substance. Fascism may have served historically as a transition from the hot war-machine of Nazi despotism to the cold war-machine of deterrence and global axiomatization—but not once and for all. The axiomatizing, biopower State must always resonate with the "older," sovereign form, which continually or periodically "recharges" it. The total hot war of military domination and the total cold war of capitalist axiomatization are thus not to be understood in linear terms as two historical stages but in nonlinear terms as two basins of attraction, between which actual historical developments may oscillate—with no guarantee that one basin will ever ultimately win out over the other. The military hot war of neo-despotism, in other words, has not been relegated to the legendary "dust-bin of [linear] history": to the contrary, it can recur, as the Bush regime has demonstrated—and there is no saying that it may not ultimately prevail.[74]

In this light, we can provide more complete answers to questions raised earlier concerning the kind of appeal the Death-State has for its citizens, the kinds of loyalty it evokes (and does not invoke), and the kinds of fantasy investments and psychodynamics it mobilizes. Death-State citizenship comprises three resonating structures of dependency: that of infants on parents in the nuclear family, that of labor on capital in the market economy, and that of citizens on the State. Feelings of insecurity and inadequacy deriving from dependence in turn make dependence all the stronger, inasmuch as Death-State citizenship offers to transmute those feelings (denied and projected onto others) into triumphant identification with a grandiose, vindictive, and punitive authority figure (or Strict Father) possessing or projecting an aura of absolute certainty and supreme confidence. As Schmitt's work shows, to make the Death-State conversion absolute requires the declaration of war, the identification of an enemy, investment in the Fatherland at the expense of the Motherland. And this is precisely what the Bush regime was able to do. Economic investments responding to the renewed and apparently limitless demand for capital-intensive, high-tech munitions, along with psychic investments in authority figures responding to the demand for greater measures of protection and political investments in the renewal of sovereign State power, were all mobilized simultaneously through the prosecution of the never-ending War on Terror.

The Death-State thus entails a fourth kind or degree of violence—a violence beyond the legitimated monopoly on violence by which Weber defined the state; a violence beyond the prelegitimate violence of foundation and the legitimating violence of interpretation or a posteriori rationalization identified by Derrida. The Death-State entails the violence of permanent war, conducted, as we have seen, to produce both surplus-value for an important sector of capital and surplus power for the neo-despotic State—along with abject submission in its citizens. Here again, Schmitt's abysmal standpoint is illuminating. For the State at war commands loyalty not just by demanding that its citizens consent to kill others; it also does so by demanding that they consent to sacrifice—their well-being and, ultimately, their lives—for the sake and at the behest of the State. The Death-State, in other words, specifically aggravates the very vulnerability it transforms into irrevocable loyalty to itself and to the cause of war. The strategic effectiveness of repeated calls to "support the troops" was clear evidence, based on the staggering power of cognitive dissonance, that people become incapable of questioning a cause to which citizens' lives are sacrificed—because of the very fact of that sacrifice; and it is testimony to the strength of their abject identification with the Death-State. State power thus derives not just from being in the position to decide and declare who is friend and who is enemy but from being in the position to demand the ultimate sacrifice: to give one's life for one's country. Because of this demand, the Death-State enjoys a monopoly not only on violence but also on citizenship, on people's sense of belonging and the degree and kind of their investment in social groups.[75]

The concept of nomad citizenship is designed in this context to break the Death-State monopoly on people's investment in social organization, on their sense of belonging, responsibility, and engagement with others. Schizoanalysis and critical nomadology have diagnosed the ills of Death-State citizenship; it will be up to affirmative nomadology to articulate the problem differently and to highlight other possible solutions. It is significant in this context that, in his commentary on Benjamin's discussion of the use and abuse of force in "Critique of Violence," Derrida overlooks the single most dramatic instance of nonviolent social rebellion mentioned by Benjamin: the general strike. Most forms of rebellion, Benjamin argues, repeat the alegitimate violence accompanying the founding of any new social order in their attempt to overthrow the old. Most strikes, meanwhile, are also violent, according to Benjamin, inasmuch as they seek to extort benefits from and within the existing social order. The general strike is exceptional for Benjamin: it is not violent because it is not an act; it is a nonact, a refusal to act (and a refusal to extort), a withdrawal of labor; it is a concerted disengagement from, rather than a violent counterengagement against, the old social order. This is a crucial insight and presents the general strike as an ideal of nonviolent revolutionary (non-) action.[76] However, for the general strike to point to some kind of strategy rather than remain just an eternal ideal or a short-lived symbolic gesture, there would have to be some way to *sustain* such a strike. This is one index of the importance of identifying and exploring viable and actually existing alternatives to the capitalist domination of the market economy, as we shall see in chapter 4. In the next chapter, in a similar vein, it will be a matter not of theorizing or justifying forms of struggle against the State but of identifying and exploring viable and actually existing alternatives to Death-State citizenship.

CHAPTER THREE

Nomad Citizenship

Affirmative nomadology seeks to identify modes of social organization and interaction that represent experimental alternatives to Death-State citizenship. Improvisational jazz has served so far as our prime example of nomad social organization and dynamics: coherence is generated internally and immanently, from the bottom up, instead of being imposed in top-down fashion from on high. But there are other actually existing experiments in nomad social organization. In this chapter, we will examine nomadism in enterprise management, in neighborhood organization, and in Internet development.

Enterprise Management and Self-Organizing Groups

The opposition of jazz bands to classical orchestras enabled us to contrast two forms of organization of the social field, one featuring top-down, transcendent command and the other bottom-up, immanent self-organization. But such an opposition is by no means absolute; it has mainly heuristic value. There is a noteworthy exception that belies a simplistic opposition between jazz and classical music: it is the Orpheus Chamber Orchestra, which is often referred to as "the world's only conductorless orchestra." (Orpheus is one of the two orchestras sponsored by and housed at Carnegie Hall; its worldwide performances and recordings regularly receive prizes.) Ever since its founding in 1972, Orpheus has prided itself on being "the only major orchestra in the world to consistently rehearse, perform, and record without a conductor."[1] How can a world-class orchestra perform without a conductor? Although Orpheus still reproduces precomposed music from a score, nearly all its other procedures are quite unlike those of a standard classical orchestra. For one thing, the function of conducting has been deducted from the figure of the conductor, which has disappeared: instead of being assigned exclusively and permanently to one person—*the* conductor—the conducting function circulates among various members of the orchestra. Whoever is collectively considered to have the best knowledge of and/or feel for a certain piece of music is chosen to conduct it; when the piece of music changes, so does the conductor. The role of section leader also circulates among the members of those orchestra sections large enough to have a leader (violins, winds, etc.). More important for our purposes here, the principles of immanent self-organization have in the last few years been extended from the artistic to the business side of the orchestra: the Orpheus Chamber Orchestra now operates with neither a CEO, an executive director, nor a conductor.[2] And similar principles apply to the function of artistic director, repertory manager, and so on: the twenty-seven members of the orchestra decide as a group who will temporarily fulfill various business functions for specific musical choices or periods of time. The figures of CEO, CFO, marketing director, and so on, have been eliminated, and their functions circulate on a regular basis among the members of the group, depending on collective assessment of relative talent and skills in various areas and of the quality of members' actual performance in the different roles. Despite the type of music it performs, Orpheus has managed to recast the entire "organization of the social field" of a classical symphony orchestra along the lines of improvisational jazz.

The emergence in the 1970s of Orpheus as a highly successful experiment in self-organization coincides in the field of management science with a wave of proposals for the reform of hierarchical bureaucratic organization in accordance with notions of employee involvement, quality of work-life, and workplace democracy.[3] In fact, Harvey Seifter, the former executive director of Orpheus who stepped down in 2002, has offered seminars and served as management consultant for a number of successful businesses (including J. P. Morgan Chase, Ritz-Carlton, Intel, and Stonyfield Farms) that adopted or adapted Orpheus practices and principles of organization to their own enterprises.[4] The rise of the information economy and of Japan as a serious economic competitor in the 1990s ushered in another wave of management reform theory, led by Peter Drucker at Harvard, under rubrics such as networking, team working, delayering, and flat management. Yet it is now widely acknowledged that the key ideas for these reform movements (as well as for the participative management movement of the 1950s and 1960s) lie in the management theory of Mary Parker Follett, a Progressive-era social reformer turned management consultant whose most important writings appeared in the 1920s.[5]

Looking back from our present-day "information society," it is easy to see that much of Follett's importance and influence stems from her very early recognition that "fact-control" would become far more crucial than "man-control," that the management of information would become at least as important as the management of people.[6] The importance of information management is in turn related to what Follett called the principle of *depersonalization*. One instance of this principle we have already seen: important functions are no longer the permanent prerogative of an individual figure (such as a conductor or CEO) but instead circulate among members of the group. Even more important, authority in a given situation, according to Follett, does not reside in an individual or a position but in the situation itself: "One *person* should not give orders to another *person*," she insisted, "but both should agree to take their orders from the situation." The task of the management consultant, therefore, "is not how to get people to obey orders, but how to devise methods by which we can best *discover* the order integral to a particular situation."[7] In a prescient formulation of what we now call bottom-up or emergent self-organization, she maintained that "legitimate authority flows from co-ordination, not co-ordination from authority."[8]

Equally as important as her insistence on the principle of depersonalization was Follett's critique of what she called *particularist* individualism: the notion that individuals were discrete atoms and that good management amounted to knowing how to combine them in the most efficient way. Her unit of analysis was instead the group, and the individual was always understood only as a member of a group—indeed, of a multiplicity of groups: "the individual is not a unit but a centre of forces (both centripetal and centrifugal), and consequently [the group] is not a collection of units but a complex of radiating and converging, crossing and recrossing energies."[9] But Follett was, at the same time, very careful to define what kind of group was involved and the nature of the relation between the group and the individual.

The group was to be distinguished most of all from a herd or crowd, from an undifferentiated mass. For what distinguished true group dynamics from both mechanical and organic totalities was what she called the *integration* or *interpenetration of difference*. "Democracy," she insisted, "rests on the well-grounded assumption that society is neither a collection of units nor an organism but a network of human relations. . . . The essence of society is difference, related difference."[10] *The power of human groups arises from the articulation of differences,* not from the simple aggregation of units, and the articulation of differences cannot occur via the simple addition of individual votes in a ballot box or of individual consumer preferences at the cash register. The power of human groups requires, instead, a group process that, through discussion and interaction, generates

what Follett calls a "common thought" that—like a jazz improvisation—
"harmonizes difference through interpenetration."[11] The active, genera-
tive nature of group process is key, for "the essential feature of common
thought is not that it is held in common, but that it has been produced in
common."[12] Common thought is the outcome of a process whereby differences are not suppressed or superseded but integrated into a working
whole, and the strength of this whole lies precisely in the preservation and
interrelation of difference:

> [the group] needs my difference, not as an absolute, but just so
> much difference as will relate me. Differences develop within the
> social process and are united through the social process. . . . It is
> not my uniqueness which makes me of value to the whole but my
> power of relating.[13]

The group articulates or integrates difference from the bottom up, whereas
the crowd has order imposed on it top down. Crowds, moreover, operate on the principles of imitation or likeness and obedience rather than
difference and articulation.[14] Members of an undifferentiated crowd are
simply all alike; but even members of a differentiated crowd do not contribute their differences to a group process, but merely imitate roles that
have been assigned to them from on high (like football players obediently
executing set plays designed by the coach and called by the quarterback).
    What emerges from group dynamics is a kind of horizontal rather than
vertical authority, an authority that Follett insists

> does not come from separating people, from dividing them into
> two classes, those who command and those who obey . . . [but]
> from the intermingling of all, of my work fitting into your work
> and yours into mine, and from the intermingling of forces a power
> being created which will control those forces.[15]

> The skillful leader . . . controls his group not by dominating but
> by expressing it. . . . The [true] . . . leader is he who can liberate
> the greatest amount of energy in his [group].[16]

Follett thus formulates a crucial distinction between power-with and
power-over.[17] Power-with develops out of the articulation of differences,
each of which contributes positively to an emergent whole that is greater
than the merely arithmetic sum of its parts: horizontal authority expresses
and thereby simultaneously enhances the power of the group. The vertical

authority of power-over, by contrast, operates by constraint and limitation and thereby diminishes individuals' contribution to the group: power-over is the power to say no, to limit others to the imitation or reiteration of predetermined roles; it is, in short, the power to command obedience.[18]

It may be worth contrasting Follett's distinction with the more familiar distinction between positive and negative liberty, between freedom-to and freedom-from. Negative liberty is simply *freedom from* constraint, whereas positive liberty is the *freedom to* actually do something. Negative liberty and power-over are diametrically opposed: negative liberty is precisely freedom from control exercised by someone who has power over you. But positive liberty and power-with are not the same. For the "freedom-to" do something entailed by positive liberty characterizes both groups and crowds: a football team or an army battalion certainly has the freedom and the ability to do something, despite being organized vertically rather than articulated horizontally.[19] Like her definition of immanent authority, the distinction Follett proposes between power-with and power-over involves the difference between a force immanent to group process and the imposition of transcendent control from outside or above:

> the best philosophical as well as the best psychological principle
> by which to test the legitimacy of "power" . . . [is to] ask whether
> it is integral to the process or outside the process, that is . . .
> whether it grows out of the actual circumstances, whether it is
> inherent in the situation.[20]

The concept of power-with thus designates both less and more than the mere ability to accomplish something: it highlights the specific quality of the "organization of the social field" entailed by the *form of activity* doing the accomplishing.

Follett was a contemporary of the other, more famous, turn-of-the-century North American management theorist Frederick Winslow Taylor, and the stark contrast between their views is revealing. Following in Sir Francis Bacon's footsteps, Taylor advocated replacing the rule-of-thumb procedures developed informally by workers themselves with formal rules developed independently of them by "scientific" managers.[21] Where Follett endorsed a form of authority arising immanently from an internally differentiated but nonhierarchical group, Taylor insisted on a sharp, hierarchical distinction between the managers, who would analyze the work process to formulate rules of procedure, and the workers, who would merely carry them out. Far from being a common thought produced and held in common, management's procedural rules were based on minute dissection of every single gesture and movement of the work process, followed by the promulgation of formal rules imposed on it from outside and above the process itself, designed to maximize worker efficiency. Whatever power-with may have existed among the workers is banished by the exercise of absolute managerial power-over the work process and the workers engaged in it:

> the workman who is best suited to handling pig iron is unable to understand the real science of doing this class of work. He is so stupid that . . . he must consequently be trained by a man more intelligent than himself into the habit of working in accordance with the laws of this science.[22]

> It is only through *enforced* standardization of methods, *enforced* adoption of the best implements and working conditions, and *enforced* cooperation that . . . faster work can be assured. And the duty of enforcing the adoption of standards and of enforcing this cooperation rests with the *management* alone.[23]

An absolute and categorical demarcation between conception and execution, command and obedience, was thus central to Taylor's view of management and the "organization of the social field" it entailed.

Although Taylor and Follett were contemporaries, it must be said that Taylor's view was the more influential of the two for much of the twentieth century. This may be because Taylorization better suited a manufacturing economy, up to and including the mass production and mass marketing of commodities characteristic of Fordism, while Follett's management theory is better suited to the growing importance of what we now know as "immaterial labor" in the post-Fordist information economy. A very different, sociological rather than economic explanation is offered by Luc Boltanski and Eve Chiapello in their study *The New Spirit of Capitalism,* which shows that ideas of delayering, flat management and network enterprise represented the nouvelle vague in management theory in France as well as the United States and Japan at the end of the twentieth century.[24] But in their view, this new spirit represents capital's response to the crisis and criticisms of the May 1968 movement rather than gains in economic efficiency. Both explanations may be true. But Boltanski and Chiapello go so far as to say that the managerial transformation they describe represents a defeat of the spirit of 1968 and of the theories (like that of Deleuze and Guattari) inspired by it. And this is partly true but ultimately false. It is true that neoliberalism has indeed absorbed much of the critique of alienated work and rigid workplace hierarchies by making work activity more flexible, innovative, and collaborative—largely as a way to improve productivity but also with the result of making employment itself more precarious. But the transformation only goes so far: what Boltanksi and Chiapello call "project-centered" work may indeed be far more creative and collaborative than earlier modes of work, but the essential fact is that the project itself is still assigned by management, and the benefits of the work still accrue disproportionately to management and capital. This is the symbolic significance of the evolution of the Orpheus Chamber Orchestra: after having made the work process itself collaborative and self-organizing, they made the business itself a collaborative and self-organizing enterprise. It would thus be more appropriate to say that the impact of 1968 has been a qualified success—inasmuch as the quality of work has improved for some people in some sectors of the economy—but only a partial success in that most work ultimately remains alienated and exploited under the control of management and capital.

Follett's perspective suffers from similar limitations: though she usefully highlights the gains to be had from the articulation of difference in work groups that self-organize immanently, that is, without the limitations of power-over, her perspective presupposes a fundamental congruence of interests in such groups so that "difference [can be] harmonize[d] through interpenetration." But what if there are profoundly different or even antagonistic interests informing those points of view?—interests as different or opposed as those of management and workers, labor and capital, with aims as different or opposed as the quality of work and the maximization of profit? Follett is well aware of this objection, but her response does not get us very far. All she can propose is "making capital and labor into one group," a change that will enable us to

> distinguish between true and apparent interests, or . . . [between] long-run and immediate interests; then we shall give up on the notion of "antagonisms," which belong to a static world, and see only differences—that is, that which is capable of integration.[25]

Although her distinction between a static world of antagonisms and a world of differences may prefigure much postmodernist theory, the belief that capital and labor could simply agree to form a group and abandon their antagonism in favor of "true," "long-term" common interests marks a weak point in her theory. And certainly, despite the pertinence and undeniable influence of her theories of group self-organization, their widespread business application in recent years has done little to mitigate the antagonism of capital and labor in most enterprises or throughout society as a whole.

Such limitations do not entirely invalidate Follett's perspective, for they are shared by most management theory and indeed by most social theory, according to the overview Hardt and Negri present in *Labor of Dionysus*.[26] Taking the Italian constitution of 1848 as an exemplary starting point, they argue that postwar liberal–capitalist States have tried to acknowledge and incorporate the immanently self-organizing capacity of much social activity but have ultimately failed and had recourse to transcendent authority, instead:

> In the first (utopian) schema of the model, the unification of the
> multiplicity was configured as a simple result of the completion
> of the process [of self-organization]; now, instead, the unification
> is imposed in the form of authority. While the first unification
> wanted to be immanent to the process, this second one seems to
> transcend it. . . . The democratic character of the management
> of social capital is subordinated to the conditions of the growth
> of profit. . . . The model, in short, although it was entrusted to
> an immanent justification, collapsed. Only the transcendence of
> power can serve to give it real sustenance.[27]

This theoretical collapse mirrors one of the paradoxes of neoliberalism. It endeavors to release individuals' innovative work activity and creative energy from the constraints of authoritative yet stagnant institutions, conventions, and contracts yet still does so to better capture the surplus generated by any and all such activity. In the immediate context, authority may derive immanently from within the self-organizing work group itself, as Follett proposes, but in the larger context, all local authority remains subordinate to the command of management and capital. This is a problem we will want to pose anew in the next chapter.

For now, it is sufficient to acknowledge how prescient Follett's management theory was and how influential it has become. But it is also important to recognize that her ideas about self-organizing groups did not originate in the business world and were not limited to that arena. Indeed, she came to management theory rather late in life, after an extended period as a community activist and theorist in the years preceding the First World War. Ironically, the Follettian principles that have become so fashionable in post–World War II management science in fact arose out of her experience in the neighborhood organization and urban community center movements of the Progressive era.

Neighborhood Organization and Urban Complexity

After writing a brilliant but rather conventional political science study of the House of Representatives, Follett spent the first decade of the twentieth century, like so many highly educated women of her era, engaged in social activism on behalf of the urban poor. In the quarter-century following the Civil War, migration from the South, immigration from Europe, rapid industrialization, and innovations in transportation had completely transformed the American city, and it had become clear to many that representative democracy, bent largely to the bidding of big business, was unsuited to addressing the attendant problems. But many activists, Follett included, treated these problematic developments as an opportunity to revitalize American democracy from below. New to the post–Civil War industrial city was a growing spatial separation of work from the home, and this gave rise to a new configuration of city space, which now combined a set of predominantly industrial or commercial zones with a patchwork of specifically residential neighborhoods. Whether through settlement houses, community centers, or neighborhood organizations, the new urban residential space became a locus of intense grassroots political activism. "We can never reform American politics from above, . . . by charters and schemes of government," Follett warned:

> Political progress must be by local communities. Our municipal
> life will be just as strong as the strength of its parts. We shall
> never know how to be one of a nation until we are one of a
> neighborhood. . . . We who believe in neighborhood organization
> believe that the neighborhood group is a more significant unit to
> identify ourselves with than any we have hitherto known. . . . The
> organization of men in small, local groups must be the next form
> which democracy takes.[28]

Follet's experience in Progressive neighborhood activism would have a decisive influence on her political theory and eventually contribute to her management theory as well.

For Follett, the neighborhood had some of the advantages Deleuze and Guattari see as characteristic of the plane of immanence of the Greek agora. The neighborhood is composed, not exactly of friends and rivals in a common philosophical enterprise, but of neighbors who are all more or less on the same footing, who share an interest in their common residential space, and who have no obvious or designated authority figure standing above or among them (elected city officials being too remote to serve in this capacity). Whatever authority there is in the neighborhood emerges horizontally. Unlike Deleuze's Greek citizens, however, who are all alike, that is to say, undifferentiated as well as equal, the citizens of neighborhoods are equal (as neighbors) yet diverse. This diversity is what distinguishes the neighborhood group from other groups and elevates it above them:

> In a more or less mixed neighborhood, people of different
> nationalities, or different classes [or occupations] come together
> easily and naturally on the ground of many common interests: the
> school, the recreational opportunities, . . . hygiene, housing, etc.[29]

> On the other hand consider how different it is when we *choose*
> the constituents of our group—then we choose those who are
> the same as ourselves in some particular. The satisfaction and
> contentment that comes with sameness indicates a meager
> personality. . . . In a neighborhood group you have the stimulus
> and the bracing effect of many different experiences and ideals. . . .
> Life [is] enlarged and enriched by the friction of ideas and ideals
> which comes from the meeting of people of different opportunities
> and different tastes and different standards.[30]

Moreover, diversity enables neighborhood authority to operate not just horizontally but according to the principle of depersonalization we saw illustrated earlier, in the conductorless Orpheus Chamber Orchestra:

> In neighborhood groups where we have different alignments on
> different questions, there will be a tendency for those to lead at
> any particular moment who are most competent to lead in the
> particular matter in hand. Suppose the subject is sanitation. The
> man who is most interested, who has the clearest view of the need
> and who is its most insistent champion, will naturally step forth
> as the leader in that. The man who knows most about educational
> matters will lead in those. . . . Thus the different leaders of a
> democracy appear.[31]

The organization of small, local groups seemed the perfect proving ground for revitalizing American democracy from the bottom up.

As cogent as the theory that emerged from Follett's engagement with neighborhood organization is, the community-organizing experiment itself was by no means a complete success. For one thing, economic stratification steadily drained the lower-class neighborhoods that were the focus of community organizing of internal resources (such as job skills and professional expertise), while members of upper-class neighborhoods did quite nicely on their own, without any need for community support. More crucially, World War I intervened: the burgeoning national neighborhood organization movement was quite literally taken over by the Defense Department to propagandize for the war effort. The experiment in immanent, grassroots democracy succumbed to the imperatives of war mobilization from on high.[32] By the 1920s, Follett had shifted her focus to business, effectively transferring the understanding of group dynamics she gained in neighborhoods to the fields of management and political theory.

Yet the Progressive-era neighborhood organization movement was by no means a total failure, either—even leaving aside the important contributions to management and political theory it inspired from Follett herself. For one thing, the neighborhood and community organization movement eventually recovered from its subordination to the First World War effort and continues to this day. Saul Alinsky is no doubt the best-known proponent and practitioner of neighborhood organization as a political weapon for the urban dispossessed, although it is not clear the extent to which his and his followers' neighborhood groups are self-organizing and the extent to which they are organized in top-down fashion by more or less professional community organizers (community organizing having become a branch of the social work profession after World War I). Alinksy started organizing in the infamous "Back of the Yards" area of Chicago (featured in Upton Sinclair's *The Jungle*) in the late 1930s and had developed a nationwide strategy for and network of neighborhood organizations by the time he died in 1972. And neighborhood organization has been and continues to be pursued by a variety of groups, including the American Communist Party, labor unions, the Black Panther Party, and others less well known and too numerous to mention. In the waning decades of the twentieth century, there may have been as many as ten thousand neighborhood organizations in New York City alone and six times that many in the country as a whole.[33]

Whatever the practical successes and failures of the neighborhood organization movement on the ground, Follett's perspective harbors a more serious, theoretical problem: like anarchists and communitarians in this respect, she focuses for the most part on fairly small-scale, territorially concentrated, face-to-face groups (first the neighborhood organization, later the business enterprise). The problem with an exclusive focus on face-to-face groups, as Iris Marion Young has shown, is that it can construe any kind of mediation as alienation, and privilege instead immediacy and transparency; it tends, in short, to deny some kinds of difference.[34] Such a focus is not only theoretically untenable (Young argues that it falls afoul of the Derridean critique of unified subjects present to one another[35]), it is also totally impractical: urbanization and hence intensifying social mediation and complexification are long-standing and worldwide trends that must be worked with, not wished away in a nostalgic attempt to restore something like small-town, gemeinschaft social life. Drawing directly on the work of Jane Jacobs—arguably the second great twentieth-century American theorist of urban neighborhoods, after Mary Parker Follett herself—Young proposes city life as an alternative to the neighborhood group, "an ideal of city life as a vision of social relations affirming group difference," and as a venue for "different groups that dwell together . . . without forming a community"[36]—or while forming at most what van Gunsteren would call a "community of fate."[37] If the essence of society is not just difference but "related difference," as Follett insists, it is city life as a whole that concentrates and composes related differences, even more than the neighborhood group alone.[38]

We saw that for Follett, the neighborhood group already possessed this advantage compared to the Greek *polis*: whereas Greek citizens qua citizens were all alike (land- and slave-owning males), neighborhood citizens were different—occupationally, at least—and those differences contributed directly to the strength of the group. Occupational differences aside, however, neighborhoods were largely (and have become increasingly) homogeneous in class and racial terms. In this respect, the neighborhood community always risked folding back in on itself, privileging sameness over difference and systematically (often violently and/or illegally) excluding others.[39] City life itself, which Young characterizes as the "being together of strangers," can serve as an antidote to the dangers of exclusionary neighborhood communitarianism. This is because, while the city contains affinity groups of many kinds (families, voluntary associations, recreational clubs, neighborhood organizations, occupational groups, and so on), urban dwellers must, in the course of daily life, venture outside the bounds of these groups, traversing a variety of public spaces where they meet and interact with total strangers. The very density, anonymity, and complexity of city life counterbalances the centripetal force of community self-organization and self-identification, compelling or encouraging urban dwellers to frequent "public spaces [where] people encounter other people, meanings, expressions, issues, which they may not understand or with which they do not identify."[40] City living not only fosters the development of multiple, different affinity groups but also brings members of those groups into regular contact with others: the complexity of the city thus fosters not just self-contained difference but related difference.

In *The Death and Life of Great American Cities*, Jacobs provides a pioneering account of the city as matrix of immanently related difference. Her work opposed not only the practices and programs of urban renewal rampant in post–World War II America but also the modernist view of city planning promulgated by Le Corbusier and others starting early in the century.[41] The modernist city planner sought to simplify and rationalize the city: his ideal was a gridlike plan whereby various urban functions—commercial, recreational, industrial, residential, and so on—would be carefully segregated from one other and the "formal layout" of city structure purified accordingly.[42] To Jacobs, such single-use functionalism and geometrical moralism were anathema: she favored, instead, the rich complexity of multiuse urbanism as it emerged over time, without the need for top-down planning.[43] And where Follett emphasized the self-sufficiency of the neighborhood, Jacobs emphasized its necessary imbrication in the larger structures and dynamics of the surrounding city.

Jacobs is interested in what makes neighborhoods in some older, unplanned cities so livable—both safe and enjoyable—for their inhabitants. The key factor is diversity: vibrant neighborhoods thrive on a diverse mix of activities (residential, commercial, recreational, etc.) as well as a diverse mix of people and of reasons for being in the neighborhood. The people responsible for the vitality of Jacobs's neighborhoods are not just the residents themselves but also nonresidents who come to the neighborhood to work, eat, drink, shop; even those who may just be passing through the neighborhood contribute to the interpersonal fabric that keeps the neighborhood secure and makes it interesting. It is just such a rich mix of inhabitants and users keeping watch on the neighborhood that keeps it safe and conversely makes it an interesting place to be and to observe. Empty streets are dangerous streets, according to Jacobs, and so keeping neighborhood streets full of a variety of users at most times of day and night is key to keeping the neighborhood safe and attractive. People watching and people-watching form a virtuous circle, as seeing and being seen reinforce one another and enhance the vitality of the neighborhood.[44]

Jacobs thus introduces a third figure to the cityscape, a type located somewhere between the close neighbor, about whom one knows nearly everything, and the total stranger, about whom one knows nothing all: the "public acquaintance."[45] *Public acquaintances* are people I see in the neighborhood with some regularity and who are therefore known to me, as I am

to them, but whom I don't know very well at all: they may include the office
worker who comes to the neighborhood deli on weekdays for lunch; the
college student on her way to and from classes; the joggers who stop by the
neighborhood park with their dog on the way back across town. Familiar
acquaintances combine with neighborhood residents in composing a web
of interpersonal connections that makes it possible not only to tolerate the
presence of strangers and passers-by without undue concern but to enjoy
and appreciate their novelty and their differences. It is the haphazard mix
of residents, regular users, mere passers-by, neighbors, strangers, and acquaintances that, for Jacobs, both enlivens and secures the neighborhood.

In one important respect, the Jane Jacobs neighborhood is quite unlike the neighborhood watch groups her work partly inspired and quite
unlike the Progressive-era neighborhood organization championed by
Mary Parker Follett and others—not to mention the radiant city of Le
Corbusier—because the Jacobs neighborhood is completely unplanned
(*unconscious* is the word she often uses). The continual crisscrossing of
paths, the consistent overlapping of lines-of-sight, the comings and go-
ings and the staying in place, the seeing and being seen, the buildup of
a thick texture of social relations and related difference—all this occurs
totally without design. And yet it is more effective at making cities livable
than a strong police presence and top-down surveillance. "No amount of
police can enforce civilization," Jacobs insists, "where the normal, casual
enforcement of it has broken down."[46] It is thus the very complexity of
city life that makes the city livable, safe, and enjoyable.[47] She compares
the complexity of city life to an "intricate ballet":

> Under the seeming disorder of the old city, wherever the old city
> is working successfully, is a marvelous order for maintaining the
> safety of the streets and the freedom of the city. It is a complex
> order. Its essence is intricacy of sidewalk use, bringing with it
> a constant succession of eyes. This order is all composed of
> movement and change, and although it is life, not art, we may
> fancifully call it the art form of the city and liken it to the dance—
> not to a simple-minded precision dance with everyone kicking
> up at the same time, twirling in unison and bowing off en masse,
> but to an intricate ballet in which the individual dancers and
> ensembles all have distinctive parts which miraculously reinforce
> each other and compose an orderly whole.[48]

But ballet it not quite the right comparison. From all the recurring movement and change, order can emerge, to be sure, and often does—but this

order is totally unchoreographed, unscripted, unscored, and unplanned. In other words, the "complex order" of city life is self-organizing, and hence it is much less like ballet and more like improvisational jazz.

Such order can emerge but cannot be guaranteed to do so. The Jacobs ideal neighborhood can fail, as Marshall Berman (among others) has pointed out.[49] By definition, emergent complex order is difficult (if not impossible) to program from on high—although conditions for its emergence may be specified (as Jane Jacobs does) and efforts subsequently made to sustain or foster them. As we saw with Follett's neighborhoods, a minimum floor of resources (skills, income, services) internal to the neighborhood is probably necessary to make the benefits of urban complexity described by Jacobs self-sustaining; such resources were already on the wane in many American urban neighborhoods even as she wrote. But in addition, for Jacobs, the neighborhood itself had to be well situated in relation to a larger urban space that would provide a supportive context (of pedestrian flows, adjacent destinations, etc.) for the neighborhood. Jacobs was writing more or less explicitly against the utopian programs of urban renewal that posed one kind of challenge to her ideal of complex urban order; Berman cites another: suburbanization. In the decades following World War II, not only were older neighborhoods being wiped clean for urban renewal but jobs and those lucky enough to have them were being moved out of inner cities to suburban spaces, leaving the inner city to wither and die. For Berman, this more or less gradual process was made catastrophic in New York by the expressway system masterminded by Robert Moses, which ravaged the fabric of the five boroughs to make Manhattan accessible to suburbanites commuting by car. Jacobs's ideal of urban complexity was not likely to survive the growing disparities of wealth that beset most large American cities through suburban exodus after the war and that have continued to worsen ever since.

This contrast between Mary Parker Follett's more or less self-contained neighborhood organizations and a more expansive account of urban complexity in Jane Jacobs is not entirely fair: Follett's vision was not, in fact, limited to face-to-face neighborhood groups or business enterprises—even though that may have been the focus of most of her best work. Without the careful observation and attention to detail that characterizes Jacobs's work, Follett nonetheless does extend her insights regarding related difference to society at large, which she conceives of simply as a larger group composed of multiple smaller groups:

> Progress from one point of view is a continuous widening
> of the area of association . . . [from neighborhoods to] labor

organizations, cooperative societies, consumers' leagues,
associations of employers and employed, municipal movements,
. . . the Men's City Club, the Women's City Club . . . professional
societies.[50]

And the same principle of immanent articulation and integration of differences would govern the formation of larger out of smaller groups as
governs the formation of a group out of individual differences to begin
with: "the same force that forms a group may form a group of groups."[51]

This process of forming a group of groups is not merely additive:
"society . . . does not consist merely of the union of . . . various groups.
There is a more subtle process going on—the interlocking of groups."[52]
Perhaps more important—and this is one way Follett characterizes the
"interlocking of groups"—the multiplicity of groups composing society
is a correlative of the multiplicity of individuals themselves. We have already seen that for Follett, "the individual is not a unit but a centre of
forces (both centripetal and centrifugal)";[53] these forces correspond to the
various groups to which an individual belongs:

> In some groups I may be an employer, in others an employee. I
> can be a workman and a stockholder. I may belong at the same
> time to the college club and the business women's club. . . . I may
> have to say the collective I or we *first* of my basketball team, *next*
> of my trade-union, *then* of my church club or citizens' league or
> neighborhood association, and the lines cross and recross many
> times. It is just these cross lines that are of inestimable value in the
> development of society.[54]

In stressing the nonlinear rather than merely additive nature of the self-
organizing whole formed by these crisscrossing lines of force, Follett distinguishes her view from two other views current at the time she was
writing: occupational representation and organicism.

Occupational representation can in fact appear as a version of organicism,[55] but it played a special role in the neighborhood organization movement of which Follett was a part. Members of neighborhood
groups not only shared a common interest in the neighborhood, they
also brought diverse skills and professional expertise to contribute to
the neighborhood. A major function of neighborhood councils was to
match the needs of the neighborhood group with goods and services provided by the various occupational and professional groups. Along with

neighborhood representatives, the occupational representatives played a major role in the neighborhood organization vision. Now Follett had no objection to this aspect of neighborhood organization, as far as it went. But she insisted that "man has many functions or rather . . . *is* the interplay of many functions."[56] And hence to limit anyone's social representation to their occupation—or even to their occupation combined with their residential representation—would be to impoverish the individual as well as society as a whole: "our place in the whole can never be bounded by any one function. . . . If you shut a man up in his occupation, you refuse him the opportunity of full growth."[57] "My citizenship," Follett concludes, "is something bigger than my membership in a vocational group."[58] And a similar critique applies to the restrictive functionalism typical of organic social theory in general:

> while the cell of the organism has only one function, the individual may have manifold and multiform functions: he enters with one function into a certain group of people this morning, and with another function into another group this afternoon. . . . This self-detaching, self-attaching freedom of the individual saves us from the danger to democracy which lurks in the organic theory.[59]

Just as the individual enters and leaves a variety of groups that express his "manifold being," so, too, should society be composed of myriad groups: "you must have as many different kinds of groups as there are powers in man."[60] Given her emphasis on the reciprocal multiplicity of the individual and of society, and on the multiplicity of groups composing both, Follett is led to conclude that "multiple citizenship in its spontaneous unifying is the foundation of the new state."[61]

But for such multiple citizenship to form a State, the groups composing it cannot merely remain parallel: they must interlock or "compound" with one another to form larger and larger groups. "Every man and woman to-day," she insists, "must create his small group first, and then, through its compounding with other groups, it will ascend from stage to stage until the federal state appears."[62] Follett takes care to distinguish this immanent, federal State from the State as it appears in what she calls a "misunderstood Hegelianism,"[63] which results in "nationalization" instead of federation. As it turns out, Hegel himself is among those who have misunderstood the proper dynamic of the State[64] by conceiving of it as a transcendent absolute, "something 'above and beyond' men,"[65] instead of seeing it as an expression of compounded group life. For "the true state

does not 'demand' my allegiance," according to Follett. "It is the spontaneously [sic] uniting, the instinctive self-unifying of our multiple interests."⁶⁶

Here, however, we reach the ultimate limit of Follett's perspective. Her
notion of "multiple citizenship" becomes a key component in the concept
of nomad citizenship, but the idea of it "spontaneously . . . unifying" to
become the foundation of a new State is open to question. Though it is
true that she invokes "spontaneous uniting" and "instinctive self-unifying"
mainly to distinguish the immanent process of compounding groups into
a federation from their nationalization by a transcendent, absolute power,
she does not, however, present any mechanisms or vehicles by means of
which such federation might occur. As invaluable as her analysis of face-
to-face group dynamics is, we will need to look elsewhere for comparable
visions of immanently self-organizing group dynamics on a larger scale; we
turn to this task later in this chapter and in chapter 4. But before moving
beyond the small-scale group dynamics of the business enterprise and the
neighborhood organization, it is worth highlighting the view of federated
State sovereignty propounded by Mary Parker Follett for the contrast it
provides with the views of Carl Schmitt examined in the previous chapter. How does the sovereignty of Follett's Motherland compare with the
sovereignty of Schmitt's Fatherland?⁶⁷

Follett's conception of State power and her definition of State sovereignty
are perfectly consistent with what she had seen in the dynamics of neighborhood and other local group associations:

> The sovereign is not the crowd, it is not millions of unrelated
> atoms, but men joining together to form a real whole.⁶⁸

> A group is sovereign over itself as far as it is capable of creating
> one out of several or many. A state is sovereign only as it has the
> power of creating one in which all are [sovereign]. Sovereignty is
> the power engendered by a complete interdependence becoming
> conscious of itself . . . it is the imperative of a true collective will.⁶⁹

In the compounding of smaller groups into larger ones, a "collective sovereignty is evolved from a distributed sovereignty,"⁷⁰ Follett explains, and
this collective sovereignty does not constrain but rather expresses the mutual benefits of articulated difference:

> The state must be no external authority which restrains and
> regulates me, but it must be myself acting as the state in every

smallest detail of life. Expression, not restraint, is always the
motive of the ideal state.[71]

In Follett's view, the process of articulating the differences among smaller
groups into larger ones and the forging of a large-scale collective sovereignty from the distributed sovereignty of face-to-face groups would
eventually move beyond even the State and compound States into a single
world-State or league. (She was a strong supporter of the contemporary
idea of a League of Nations.)

What prevailed in place of Follett's conception of collective sovereignty
was precisely that "misunderstood" Hegelian view that saw the role of the
State not as articulating and enriching the lives and interests of its citizens but rather as transcending all such private interests and subordinating them to the advancement of the "objective spirit" of a nation through
warfare.[72] Where for Follett, the unification of the State—up to and including a world-State—is to be determined immanently and *internally*,
by the growing strength of groups whose differences are articulated to
their mutual benefit, for Schmitt, the unity of the State is to be determined
purely *externally*, by the relation of enmity between friend and enemy. As
we saw in the preceding chapter, he insists that

> [any] political entity presupposes the real existence of an enemy
> and therefore coexistence with another political entity. As long as
> a state exists, there will thus always be in the world more than
> one state. A world state which embraces the entire globe and all of
> humanity cannot exist.[73]

Schmitt recognizes, of course, that any social body will contain a number
of heterogeneous allegiances in addition to allegiance to the sovereign
State: someone can be "a member of a religious institution, nation, labor
union, family, sports club, and many other associations."[74] Characteristic
of what we can call these "horizontal" affiliations is that they "impose
on him a cluster of obligations in such a way that no one of these associations can be said to be decisive and sovereign."[75] But there is, according to Schmitt, one "vertical" allegiance that transcends all others and
stands out from them as the *master-allegiance*—and this is, of course,
allegiance to the State. And the reason the State commands supreme allegiance from its citizens is that it has a near-monopoly over matters of
life and death and an absolute monopoly on declarations of war between
friend and enemy:

> The ever-present possibility of a friend-and-enemy grouping
> suffices to forge a decisive entity which transcends the mere
> societal-associational groupings. The political entity is something
> specifically different, and vis-à-vis other associations, decisive.[76]

Over against liberal and pluralist—or Follett's federal—conceptions of the State, according to which it appears "at times . . . as one association among other associations, at times as the product of a federalism of social associations or an umbrella association of a conglomeration of associations,"[77] Schmitt's State distinguishes itself absolutely from all other forms of social allegiance because it can declare war and thereby legitimate killing in its name and demand the sacrifice of citizens' lives for its own sake: "by virtue of this power over the physical life of men, the political community transcends all other associations or societies."[78] Political or State citizenship, for Schmitt, thus turns entirely on the distinction between friend and foe, and it is the role of the State—and only the State—to decide for a social body who its enemies are and thereby mobilize it for war. In this Important respect—or according to this definition of politics, at least—*every* State is to some degree a Death-State.

Now if Schmitt's transcendent view of State sovereignty and the corresponding State monopoly on citizenship have prevailed over Follett's immanent conception, this is not because that view is more cogent (it is not) but because it reflects and reinforces one of the actual proclivities of the modern Death-State, which, as we saw in the preceding chapter, has been and continues to be to wage war. It is in this context that the concept of nomad citizenship is so useful, inasmuch as it presents a mode of multiple citizenship and distributed sovereignty not limited to politics and the State. As Appadurai insists, there are "strong alternative forms for the organization of [social belonging] . . . forms that either contest the nation-state actively or constitute peaceful alternatives for large-scale political loyalties."[79] In light of such alternatives, nomad citizenship proposes a mode of social allegiance that would ideally eclipse political citizenship as it is conventionally understood and supplement it with other modes of citizenship on a variety of scales.

To the State monopoly on citizenship based on declaring war and promoting or demanding self-sacrifice and slaughter, then, nomad citizenship offers a fundamental and vital alternative. Its main thrust is to redefine citizenship so that it includes and legitimates a wide range of group allegiances of the kind Follett emphasized—and especially to deprive the State of its claim to any transcendent master-allegiance. It may indeed, as Appadurai suggests, be "time to rethink monopatriotism, patriotism directed exclusively to the hyphen between nation and state," so as to "allow the material problems we face—the deficit, the environment [etc.] . . .—to define those social groups and ideas for which we would be willing to live—and to die."[80] If so, it would be Important for the form of these multiple group allegiances to be, in the sense that Deleuze and Guattari, along with Follett, describe, immanent: their power—their power-with—would arise from participatory democracy and the self-coordinating articulation of differences to the mutual benefit of all concerned; they would serve and foster the enrichment of life internally or locally rather than thrive on and foster external threats to it, as the transcendent allegiance of State citizenship does. Developing multiple allegiances to social groups "beneath" the level of the State would extend the benefits and responsibilities of citizenship throughout social life, would in effect dissolve the boundaries separating the State and electoral politics from civil society, and would ideally encourage the growth of smaller-scale participatory democracy in numerous venues to supplement (if not supplant) the large-scale representative system we have now. The question is, what venues might sustain nomad citizenship and distributed sovereignty, beyond face-to-face groups such as work teams, business enterprises, and neighborhood organizations? We turn first to the Internet before considering in chapter 4 the role of markets in supporting widely distributed nomad citizenship.

Internet Developments

It is often said that the Internet is rhizomatic, that is, organized horizontally without any hierarchy. This is only partly true. Whereas much of the physical structure and the routing patterns of the Internet are indeed rhizomatic, in the sense that there is no center and no hub-and-spokes or trunk-and-branch pattern to traffic on the Internet, the current domain-naming conventions, and hence the logical structure of the Internet, are indeed hierarchical and conform very clearly to a trunk-and-branch model.[81] In any case, and regardless of the proportion of its rhizomatic and hierarchical features, what counts here is rather the manner in which the Internet "contributes to the organization of the social field." The Internet not only turns out to be an especially propitious medium for nomadic social relations beyond face-to-face groups, it also turns out to be the locus of a pitched battle between an older mode of organization and ownership and a newer mode whose property relations are incompatible with the old.

There may be no better-known Internet development corresponding to Follett's dictum that "the essential feature of common thought is not that it is held in common, but that it has been produced in common"[82] than the online encyclopedia Wikipedia. Founded in 2001, Wikipedia is a compendium of information coauthored by some fifty thousand contributor–participants (so far). *Wiki* (from a Hawaiian-language term meaning "rapid") refers to a software platform that enables visitors to the Wikipedia Web site to contribute information and/or correct existing information almost instantaneously. The software platform also logs all changes to any article, making them visible to anyone who wishes to consult them, and enables the instant restoration of an earlier version of the article if any changes made prove deleterious. Without any command hierarchy, without an editor in chief or a stable of contributing experts, the Wikipedia project has mobilized thousands of people utterly unknown to one another to collaborate in writing and editing a cooperatively produced encyclopedia for the twenty-first century. The result is an oft-cited and constantly growing reference tool containing (at last count) over three million articles in English, over a million each in German and French, and over a half million each in Japanese, Dutch, Spanish, Polish, Portuguese, and Italian.

This is not to say that the Wikipedia experiment has been an unmitigated success. There may be good reason to worry about the accuracy of an encyclopedia to which absolutely anyone may, in principle, contribute, regardless of his level of expertise or indeed his ulterior motives. Unlike other experiments in nomadic Internet development, Wikipedia has almost no filters or barriers to participation whatsoever, relying instead on voluntary cooperation with social norms (such as maintaining a neutral point of view), which are spelled out on the Wikipedia Web site.[83] For the most part, these self-enforcing social norms seem to work. In a 2005 study by the prestigious science journal *Nature* that compared entries in Wikipedia and in *Encyclopedia Britannica,* the two works were found to have the exact same number of major errors, while Wikipedia had only slightly more minor errors.[84] Only science entries were considered because factual errors would presumably be easier to detect in hard science subject matter. But that a self-organizing, collectively authored and edited online encyclopedia could practically match the accuracy of the most respected expert-produced encyclopedia in the world says a great deal about the potential of the peer-production process.

So does the Wikipedia response to criticism from Robert McHenry, a former editor in chief of *Encyclopedia Britannica* who called his rival a "faith-based encyclopedia."[85] McHenry noted (among other things) that the Wikipedia article on Alexander Hamilton did not mention the uncertainty regarding Hamilton's date of birth, which (as the *Britannica* article makes clear) was either 1755 or 1757. The Wikipedia article chose one date and did not acknowledge the uncertainty. But in this respect, it was just as "accurate" or "inaccurate" as every other online encyclopedia, except the *Britannica*: most online encyclopedias—whether peer or expert produced—agreed that the two-year discrepancy between possible birth dates was too trivial to include in an encyclopedia entry. But McHenry went further: he also noticed (since the wiki platform logs make accessible all versions of each article) that the Wikipedia article had originally given one date of birth but had, in a subsequent revision, switched to the other; this created inconsistencies later in the article regarding the age at which Hamilton did this or that, inconsistencies that the peer-editing process had not noticed or corrected. It may be telling that McHenry did not participate in the peer-production process and correct the Wikipedia article himself. It is certainly richly ironic that within a week of the publication of his critique, the Wikipedia article had been revised to acknowledge the birth date uncertainty and eliminate the inconsistencies: living up to the wiki name, the peer-produced encyclopedia had corrected itself almost immediately and was now one of only two online encyclopedias providing details about Hamilton's uncertain birth date.

In more controversial matters—the *Nature* study mentions climate change, but the entries on abortion and on Carl Schmitt also fit this category—acceptable levels of correctness and neutrality are far harder to agree on, and there have, in some cases, been "reversion wars," in which certain participants repeatedly remove other participants' corrections by restoring an article to the version they themselves authored. The editors have, on occasion, felt it necessary to intervene (by blocking or limiting certain participants' ability to alter content), thereby superimposing external or transcendent control over the otherwise immanent peer-production process. Yet it may be better for an encyclopedia to reveal healthy debate about controversial topics than to purvey expert opinion as gospel truth. Should a single editor or editorial committee decide once and for all whether to mention Schmitt's ties to the Nazi Party? Or should the debate about how important this fact is to our understanding of Schmitt be part of what an encyclopedia reveals to its readers? Although this may not have been what Follett meant when she maintained that "the essential feature of common thought is not that it is held in common, but that it has been produced in common,"[86] the peer-production process of Wikipedia makes the socially constructed and socially contested character of knowledge regarding controversial topics evident to its readers. And so, as a contribution to the social field of a more participatory democratic culture, Wikipedia may be better than the expert-produced *Britannica*, even if their degree of accuracy turns out to be more or less the same.

However one judges the success or failure of the Wikipedia project, it serves here as an illustration of the cooperative peer production of knowledge, a strong version of so-called distributed cognition whereby the people involved have no face-to-face contact whatsoever. In two important respects, it resembles the classical Greek agora that for Deleuze and Guattari gave rise to the practice of philosophy—even though Greek citizens, of course, did meet face-to-face. For one thing, like Greek citizens, practically all the participants in the Wikipedia project are equal—not exactly friends and rivals, perhaps, but nonetheless all on the same level as participants. And second, there is no ultimate authority figure or expert standing outside and above the process that would decide whose entry is correct or whose version will stand.[87] This lack of ultimate authority and the ensuing potential for damage from disruptive participation have troubled the creators and managers of other information portals on the Internet, some of whom have tried to balance free and open participation with controls on disruptive behavior without resorting to transcendent editorial command over the peer-production process.

Attempts like Wikipedia to combine distributed intelligence and distributed sovereignty abound on the Internet. Slashdot and Kuro5hin are both cooperative online information portals (and therefore somewhat different from full-fledged encyclopedias): they are designed to make breaking information—either pulled from elsewhere on the Web or written specifically for the sites—available to their members. Anyone can join Slashdot or Kuro5hin, although both are intended for people specifically interested and involved in Internet technology. (Slashdot presents itself as "News for Nerds. Stuff that Matters"; Kuro5hin's declared focus is "technology and culture, from the trenches.") The two sites attempt to promote both open-access and high-quality debate without resorting to top-down control of either content or participation. Slashdot does exercise a modicum of top-down control regarding content: its editors decide which of the hundreds of items sent to them by members each day will be posted to the homepage or one of the special-topic sections of the Web site. But the debate portion of the site is self-moderated in bottom-up fashion. Anyone (member or not) can post comments in response to an article, and moderators then rate the quality of the comments. Readers can set their comment threshold to read only the best ones, or only the comments not found objectionable by moderators, or all the comments. Almost anyone can serve as moderator, although there are criteria set to ensure their quality: moderators must be regular and fairly long-standing members of Slashdot (to discourage people signing up new accounts simply to disparage another member), and the comments they themselves have posted must have positive "karma"— they must have received an average rating of good or better from other moderators (this is to discourage people with little expertise or bad attitudes from moderating others' comments). Moderators are selected by machine at random from the eligible pool of members and are awarded a certain number of points with which to rate comments; if they are not used within three days, they expire. This is meant to ensure that the moderation function is distributed as widely as possible among members in good standing; being selected to moderate comments is likened to being called for jury duty and is considered both a privilege and a responsibility. (The sole exception to the random distribution of moderating power is that editors are given unlimited moderating points, to use in extreme situations when repeated malicious commenting threatens the readability of the site: editor moderation represents only 3 percent of the total and is statistically on par with or slightly fairer than member-at-large moderation. This latter fact is known because Slashdot has recently added a second tier of moderation, by which a randomly machine-selected group of members rate moderators' ratings for fairness.)

Kuro5hin takes the idea of a self-moderating distributed-sovereignty information site one step further: here what articles get posted to begin with is determined by a vote of the members. Submitted articles first appear in a voting queue, where each member can vote either to post the article to the front page, to post it to a topical section page, not to post it anywhere, or to express no opinion about the article (which is discouraged). As soon as an article appears, members are encouraged to respond to and comment on it, and the comments then get rated; once again, the point is not just to publish information on important issues but to encourage broad discussion of those issues, while at the same time maintaining the highest possible quality of discussion. The comment-rating system allows members to set their site preferences to see only the best comments or to see the comments not found objectionable by other readers; it is also possible to set one's reading preferences to see all the comments posted, regardless of rating. (Six different members must rate a comment before it gets machine tagged as either good, average, bad, or so bad as to be hidden; only one rating per comment is accepted from a given ISP address to discourage the use of multiple accounts to unfairly influence the rating process.) More recently, a Web site for free software developers called Advogato has undertaken the development of a "trust metric" that would assure a near-perfect self-moderating process by eliminating the possibility of any one participant or group of participants unfairly distorting peer input and ratings; it remains to be seen how successful the attempt will be and how widely it will be adopted. The posting, comment, and moderation systems used by Slashdot and Kuro5hin and proposed by Advogato may seem complicated, but the aim is to offer both open-access and high-quality debate and to do so with little or no top-down interference from the editors: the sites are designed to offer a self-moderating platform for the dissemination and discussion of important information for specific subgroups of the Internet community.

Slashdot and Kuro5hin are by no means the only sites attempting to combine distributed intelligence and distributed sovereignty by capitalizing on the ability of Internet-linked computers to collect and make use of vast amounts of information for the benefit of users. Amazon.com, for instance, offers purchase recommendations based on the automatically calculated relationship between the specific set of products one buyer has purchased and all the products purchased by other consumers who purchased any of that set of products; it also posts readers' reviews of the books it has for sale and enables readers to rate those reviews (as helpful or unhelpful). Ebay, in a similar vein, offers a rudimentary trust metric that allows buyers to rate sellers and sellers to rate buyers after every transaction; the site then compiles and publishes the ratings of each Ebay member for all other members to see. The aim is to compensate in a way for the anonymity of the Internet marketplace so that people who never meet one another face-to-face can nonetheless trade with some measure of confidence in one another. Shame and reputation play an important role in this system: buyers and sellers with good reputations get more business; those with bad reputations are shamed into compliance with Ebay norms or end up being shunned altogether. But it is important to note that this compensatory rating system does not actually make buyers and sellers known to one another; shame and standing do not operate quite the way they do in small-community, face-to-face relationships: all that Ebay members know about one another is how they behave as Ebay traders, nothing more. This form of shame-based enforcement of social norms does not require or entail total transparency but merely a kind of minimal market transparency whereby the rating system enables Ebay members to conduct business with a measure of trust in one another, while nevertheless remaining fundamentally anonymous. In fact, the Ebay rating system provides more readily available information for anonymous Internet-mediated shopping than most face-to-face shopping does (for how can one gauge trustworthiness at a garage sale, or even in a shopping mall?). This is not to say that the Ebay system is perfect; it has its share of complaints, broken contracts, and lawsuits. But it offers nonetheless another illustration of the potential of Internet-based, peer-produced information flows to construct and maintain cooperative social relations on a larger-than-face-to-face scale.

By far the most Remarkable and Important experiment in Internet-based peer production is the free open-source software (FOSS) movement.[88] In this case, it is fair to say that the experiment has been an unqualified and overwhelming success. Nearly three-quarters of all Web servers use FOSS (the Apache Web server program), as do major Internet sites such as Amazon, Google, and CNN.com (which all run on the open-source GNU–Linux operating system). All the major alternatives to Microsoft's Internet Explorer Web browser (including Netscape, Mozilla, and Firefox) are FOSS programs. In the first three years of the twenty-first century, computing giant IBM saw its GNU–Linux-related revenues rise from almost nothing to more than double the revenues generated by its own patented software applications; it now invests billions of dollars in FOSS development and donates patents to the Free Software Foundation. Equally remarkable as this level of success (especially since the GNU–Linux operating system competes head-to-head with monopolistic Microsoft's Windows operating system) is that FOSS is not only available for free, it is produced for free. In this respect, it resembles other experiments in Internet-mediated peer production such as the NASA Clickworkers Project and Project Gutenberg's Distributed Proofreaders (DPs).

In late 2000, NASA scientists decided to try to make some use of the roughly 80 percent of scientific data from space missions that never get properly analyzed by drawing on the distributed network of potential human processing power available through the Internet. Anyone who visited the Mars Clickworkers Web site was presented with Mars orbiter photographs and asked to identify and/or classify craters. Some eighty-five thousand people visited the site in the six-month experimental period, submitting a total of over two million entries—enough for the subsequently machine-averaged clickworker responses to easily match the accuracy of geologists with years of training. On the basis of this astonishing success, NASA has renewed and extended the project, with clickworkers now mapping craters and other surface features on asteroids as well as Mars.[89] DP has had similar success with similar methods: started in 2000 to assist Project Gutenberg's aim of "preserving history one page at a time" by creating an immense online library of all works not subject to copyright restrictions, DP mobilizes some fourteen hundred volunteer proofreaders per week (on average) to check and recheck scanned pages of books against digital photographs of the original text. While most proofreaders check just a few pages, some have done literally tens of thousands.[90] The result is a total of over nine thousand proofread digitized volumes submitted to Project Gutenberg for online preservation in the past six years.

Like NASA, with its volunteer clickworkers, and Project Gutenberg, with its DPs, FOSS mobilizes thousands of Internet-mediated participants—participants who, in this case, create, debug, and improve open-source software programs, including, but not limited to, the well-known and widely used GNU–Linux operating system. One major difference is that most contributors to FOSS have a considerable degree of expertise in computer programming. But such expertise is not an absolute requirement to participate: in principle, anyone could notice and report a problem with a FOSS program, thereby mobilizing any number of peer programmers to debug the program and solve the problem; moreover, someone without any expertise at all could propose the addition of some desirable feature to an existing program, or indeed the creation of an entirely new program, to which expert programmers would then respond (either by writing code for the new feature or program or declaring it impossible). Although Richard Stallman started programming elements of what would become the GNU–Linux system in the mid-1980s, his most important contribution was to devise and institute the system of cooperative peer production that would become the hallmark of the FOSS movement. (He was awarded a MacArthur Fellowship in 1990.) GNU–Linux would be free, open-source software, which meant that anyone could not only use the program for free but also freely access the source code to modify the program for their own purposes and/or improve it—with one crucial stipulation: the modified program would itself have to remain free and open source so that future collaborators could, in turn, make modifications and improvements of their own.[91] By the end of the decade, an undergraduate computer science student named Linus Torvald had started the process of programming an operating system kernel (derived from a teaching software program called MINIX) that would run GNU programs on any 386 processor (then the staple of the PC industry); he would gradually assume the task of coordinating contributions to GNU–Linux coming from programmers around the world. By the end of the century, the full-fledged GNU–Linux version 2.2 operating system could run on a variety of machine architectures in addition to 386 processors; it and Windows NT were the only two operating systems in the world gaining market share.[92] A new Internet-mediated, commons-based process of peer production had come into its own: GNU–Linux and other FOSS programs would continue to evolve through the attention of hundreds of users who noticed problems or foresaw possible innovations, and then through the distributed programming intelligence of hundreds and then thousands of programmers who solved those problems and continue to improve and expand the system's capabilities to this day.

This new system of peer production is Important for several reasons. For one thing, it is far more efficient and powerful (in the realm of Internet development, at least) than the older capitalist mode of production based on private ownership and industrial production models.[93] Sourceforge.net, perhaps the major Internet clearinghouse for FOSS development (but not the only one[94]), has well over one hundred thousand software development projects under way, and they draw on the expertise of nearly a million and a half registered users—many times more than even monopolistic giants like Microsoft or Oracle could ever afford. Moreover, software updates are published with much greater frequency and flexibility on the peer-production model, so changes small or large get incorporated and distributed more quickly, and the rhythm of the evolutionary process itself is that much more rapid. A second Important feature of the peer-production system is that its products are, in a critical sense, not economic goods at all; they are what economists sometimes call *nonrival goods*: sharing information is not like sharing food, inasmuch as my imparting some information to you does not diminish the amount of information I still hold, whereas my sharing food with you means that I have less nourishment than I otherwise would. Indeed, there is an important sense in which sharing information and ideas can increase the amount of information for both parties, as the FOSS movement clearly shows (and as Mary Parker Follett never tired of insisting). The third distinctive feature of the new system of production follows directly from the second: FOSS peer production is commons based, meaning that FOSS products cannot be privately owned; anyone can use then, and anyone can improve them. The General Public License (also known colloquially as copyleft), which was developed for the Free Software Foundation by Richard Stallman and Eben Moglen, assures that FOSS cannot become private property and remains instead a Common Good from which anyone may benefit and to which anyone may contribute (if she is able). This Internet-mediated intellectual commons is a key feature of the peer-production system, and we will return to it later.

The final Important feature of the new system is that peer production is based neither on incentives coming from the market nor on orders coming from a boss or managing supervisor. A now-classic analysis of capitalist production spearheaded by Ronald Coase in the 1930s and developed subsequently by Oliver Williamson and others examined the relative transaction costs to a business firm of buying goods and services on the open market compared to hiring people to produce those same goods and services within the firm.[95] Where transaction costs of buying on the open market are high, production is integrated into the firm and triggered by managerial command; where they are low, production is outsourced and triggered by market pricing mechanisms. Commons-based peer production breaks completely free of this paradigm: participating programmers are not paid for their contributions, nor are they told what to do by some supervising manager. Instead, they engage and contribute on their own free initiative.

It is worth being clear in this regard about the role of Linus Torvald in the peer-production process, for he is nothing like an orchestra conductor: programmers are not obeying his commands to write or patch a certain piece of software; this is taken care of immanently and voluntarily through the mediation of Web sites like SourceForge and Savannah. Problems and possibilities are posted more or less anonymously, and whoever is willing and able to take up the challenge responds and submits solutions, which are freely available to everyone. All Torvald does is subsequently decide whether a given solution is worth incorporating into the next standard release of the GNU–Linux package. Any items he decides against including in a general release remain available to all and can be incorporated into future releases by others. Yochai Benkler puts it this way:

> Torvalds's authority is persuasive, not legal or technical, and certainly not determinative. He can do nothing except persuade others to prevent them from developing anything they want and adding it to their kernel, nor from distributing that alternative version of the kernel. He can do nothing to prevent the entire community of users, or some subsection of it, from rejecting his judgment about what ought to be included in the kernel. Anyone is legally free to do as they please.[96]

Torvald thus fulfills a leadership role resembling those described by Clastres and Follett: his authority depends entirely on persuasion rather than command, and at his best, he succeeds in expressing the common thought of the FOSS community as to what the general release program should contain; if at some point, he did not, the community could easily sidestep him and correct his misjudgment. Indeed, the FOSS movement fulfills most of Follett's criteria for self-organizing business groups, with the important difference that FOSS participants form a so-called virtual community and, as a rule, never meet one another face-to-face.

Given its Remarkable success in the realm of knowledge and information, Internet-mediated commons-based peer production is an Important alternative to the now-dominant but clearly threatened capitalist mode of organizing knowledge production, appropriation, exploitation, and dissemination, and it represents an Important instance, alongside neighborhood organizations and flat-hierarchy business management, of a nomadic organization of the social field. The virtual potential of networked personal computing is undeniable: how—or indeed if—it ultimately gets actualized is a different kind of question altogether.

The new system of peer production is in fact under attack by proponents of the already established industrial–private property model. Private ownership of intellectual and cultural property rights was once defended on the grounds that the high capital cost of producing such knowledge (investment in expensive equipment, training of professional workers, etc.) deserved a substantial return on investment. Yet trends in microelectronics and information processing (including the ready availability of inexpensive digital video and camera equipment as well as personal computers and of software programs to seamlessly interlink all three) along with the development of legal instruments (such as copyleft) and virtual communities such as DP and SourceForge have, for the most part, made the return-on-capital-investment defense of private intellectual property rights an anachronism—especially when the FOSS movement actually gives away software programs that are far superior to those sold by Microsoft at a considerable markup.[97] The capitalist economy is nevertheless fighting back, actively pursuing what has been called a "second enclosure" in attempts to extend the duration of copyrights, enlarge the domain of what is patentable (e.g., to include the genetic code[98]), limit the reproducibility of digital material and restrict the sharing of digitized information, and even convert Internet traffic into a privately appropriable revenue stream.[99] The reference to enclosure acts underscores the similarity between this attempt to appropriate the commons and the successful attempt at so-called primitive accumulation that contributed so much to the emergence of capitalism in England, as we will see in chapter 4. What the example of software peer production already makes clear, however, is that capitalism tends to give rise to social innovations that it then has substantial difficulty bringing back under its control for the sake of private accumulation.

Conclusions

By now, considerable resonance will have emerged among the prospects for and obstacles to nomad social formations in self-organizing business enterprises, urban neighborhood dynamics, and Internet developments. Mary Parker Follett saw the potential for groups within business enterprises to collectively develop, recognize, and respect a kind of authority emerging from the immanent articulation of different points of view on a given situation. But the starkly divergent interests of capital and labor, management and workers, makes such an articulation practically impossible; only with the elimination of absentee ownership and its power-over the workforce, as we will see in chapter 4, can the convergence and integration of related difference become possible within and among business enterprises. Like Follett before her, Jane Jacobs saw the potential for self-organizing urban systems based on a combination of proximity and heterogeneity to promote secure and stimulating city living. But the severe stratification of American society due to the voracity of unbridled capitalism, particularly devastating to the urban fabric during the latter third of the twentieth century through suburbanization, destroyed these prospects and transformed hopes to integrate differences in city life into crusades to segregate, whether in the form of commuter suburbanization or gated communities.[100] Most Remarkably, the FOSS movement (along with other Internet experiments like distributed proofreading) demonstrated the potential of Internet-mediated, commons-based peer production to outperform the capitalist organization of knowledge production and dissemination, both in the quality of its results and in the quality of its cooperative–nomadic social relations. But it is under attack from owners of the dominant apparatus of knowledge production, and there is no guarantee that free software—or even a free Internet—will actually be able to resist capitalist expropriation.

Faced with capitalism's dual dynamic of deterritorialization and reterritorialization, the revolutionary strategy of schizoanalysis was to pursue lines-of-flight, to push deterritorialization to the limit, and—if possible—to push it through the limits imposed by capital. The mode of anti-Oedipal social composition projected by schizoanalysis was the subject-group (as distinguished from the Oedipalized subjugated group), derived from Sartre's group-in-fusion; its basic features were these: the anti-Oedipal group would be fluid and inclusive, without a transcendent organizing center and without fixed boundaries. It would act immediately in a situation, continually making, breaking, and remaking connections with society at large rather than folding in on itself and assigning itself long-term goals and thereby deferring the realization of its desired aims. It would refuse the distinction between means and ends, which usually ends up subordinating the former to the latter: instead, process would always be more important than product. Finally, the anti-Oedipal group would have to eschew permanence and accept its necessary transience (accept its own eventual death) rather than strive to become permanent by institutionalizing and thereby degenerating into a subjugated group. Hakim Bey developed this view of group dynamics in his notion of the Temporary Autonomous Zone, although he took pains to classify its thrust as insurrectionary rather than revolutionary. Central to his conception—and most problematic from the perspective of affirmative nomadology—was the explicit impermanence of autonomous zones, despite their desirability and their availability in modern society.[101] "The TAZ is like an uprising which does not engage directly with the State," he suggested, "a guerilla operation which liberates an area (of land, of time, of imagination) and then dissolves itself to re-form elsewhere/elsewhen, before the State can crush it."[102] Bey's view was consonant with the notion of micropolitics that was current in the waning decades of the last century—and indeed he cites the May 1968 uprising as an example—and, more specifically, with the refusal to take power. Power was considered to be monolithic, and the aim was to avoid, circumvent, or subvert rather than take it; in this view, micropolitical action (as insurrection rather than revolution) was to be temporary by design.

Compared to the revolutionary strategy of schizoanalysis, the strategy of affirmative nomadology is more complex and varied. Power is no longer considered monolithically: power-with is to be carefully distinguished from power-over. Questions of the organization of the social field, the type of division of labor, and the composition of social relations come to the forefront, in connection with the protection or constitution and the occupation of smooth space. Instead of the headlong pursuit and intensification of schizorevolutionary lines-of-flight, Deleuze and Guattari now insist that cautious experimentation on specific strata of the social formation is called for:

> This is how it should be done: Lodge yourself on a stratum, experiment with the opportunities it offers, find an advantageous place on it, find potential movements of deterritorialization, . . . experience them, produce flow conjunctions here and there, try out continuums of intensity segment by segment, have a small plot of land at all times.[103]

Have a small plot of land at all times: make at least some autonomous zones long lasting (which is not to say permanent). If a given stratum appears particularly propitious as an alternative to dominant forms of social organization—be it an actual neighborhood or an Internet-mediated community like the FOSS movement—strive to make it self-catalyzing and sustainable. Not permanent revolution but permanent insurrection, insurrection that lasts: a guerilla operation that does not engage directly with the State or with capital but that instead constitutes this or that specific stratum as a durable and enduring (which is still not to say permanent) nomadic alternative. Intensify connections and conjunctions on any propitious strata so that each stratum passes the tipping point into sustainability and so that different strata converge to catalyze one another. For affirmative nomadology, the imperative is not only to struggle *against* capitalism and the State but also, and more important, to struggle *for* a pervasive nomadism by developing, supporting, enhancing, expanding, and, where possible, conjoining the actually existing alternatives to them. Not just fight power-over to take it—presumably with the best intention of eventually having it wither away—but also, and even more, develop immanent power-with, on small as well as large scales, as the crucial alternative to power-over.

If Benjamin, in his "Critique of Violence," is right that in the modern era, wholesale social transformation not predicated on violence is possible by means of the general strike, that is to say, by *walking away* from the old social order rather than trying to confront it directly, it is for affirmative nomadology absolutely crucial, when walking away from that old order, to have something to *walk to,* to have some "small plot of land," some patches of social territory that are sustainable in the medium to long term, to make it possible to walk away from the old order in the first place and—even more important—to walk away from it once and for all. In the next chapter, we will explore further just why the development of small- and large-scale, long-lasting alternatives to capital and the State is so important and what markets may be able to contribute to their emergence, conjunction, and convergence on a new, immanently self-organizing social phase-space.

CHAPTER FOUR

Free-Market Communism

Beyond the developments in enterprise management, neighborhood organization and urban design, and the Internet that we have just examined, the market too represents for affirmative nomadology a potential vehicle for nomadic social organization, especially on scales surpassing the small-scale, face-to-face groups advocated by most anarchist theory. But the main task for the concept of free-market communism will be to draw careful distinctions between markets and capitalism, for the potential benefits of market organization are almost completely offset by the command and control that private capital exercises over them. The suprahuman decision-making abilities of the market as a paragon of collective or distributed intelligence have long been touted, from Adam Smith's invisible hand to Friedrich von Hayek's notion of catallaxy.[1] But insufficient attention is paid by most such champions of the market to the dynamics and effects of capital accumulation, for specifically capitalist markets are not often vehicles for distributed decision making or collective intelligence but rather exercises in collective stupidity, as the effects of advertising, overconsumption, and the looming environmental crisis make patently clear. Affirmative nomadology thus emerges from a close engagement with the works of Marx to gauge the precise relation between markets and capitalism itself. This engagement was initiated by Deleuze and Guattari, whose political philosophy selectively adopts and adapts key concepts from Marx.[2] The key questions for the Problem of free-market communism will be, What are the benefits of truly free free markets, that is to say, nomad markets? What impact does capital have on markets, and what makes capitalist markets different from other markets? Finally, how might markets be protected or freed from the command and control of capital to become nomad markets?

   Deleuze and Guattari draw crucially on two Marxist concepts, although they will, of course, repeat them with a difference—the point of philosophy, once again, being not "to repeat what [earlier philosophers] said [but] to do what they did: create [or re-create] new concepts for problems that necessarily change."[3] These concepts are *mode of production* and *universal history*. Deleuze and Guattari agree with Marx that there is something distinctive about capitalism as a mode of production—although their assessments of just what that something is and of how a mode of production is to be defined differ somewhat from his.[4] For nomadology, two distinctive features of capitalism stand out. First of all, whereas other modes of production are fundamentally conservative and favor the reproduction of existing power relations over the production of the new, capitalism is revolutionary and subordinates political reproduction to economic production: it fosters "constant revolutionizing of production, uninterrupted disturbance of all social conditions, everlasting uncertainty and agitation," as Marx and Engels put it in *The Communist Manifesto*.[5] This first feature is closely tied to the second: by organizing social relations by means of markets instead of politics or directly interpersonal relations, capitalism subordinates the qualitative to the quantitative; whereas other modes of production impose order through meaningful, qualitative codes, capitalism does so through the meaningless quantitative calculus of the cash nexus, which undermines codes and promotes difference over identity.[6] In favoring quantity over quality and economic production over political reproduction, capital constitutes an immensely powerful *difference-engine*.[7] And it is the capitalist difference-engine that makes history universal—although it also remains contingent in a crucial sense that we will examine later. History becomes universal with capitalism both retrospectively and prospectively: retrospectively because of what capitalist oppression reveals about previous forms of oppression in the very process of dissolving them, and prospectively because of the constant revolutionizing of everything that capitalism promotes through its intrinsic production of difference. Only difference is universal. Becoming-different, becoming-minor is the "universal figure [of] everybody-becoming-everything (devenir tout le monde)."[8]

Nomad Markets

Before considering what happens to markets under capitalism, it is important to understand where the potential benefits of free markets lie when they are truly free. For schizoanalysis, the principal benefit of markets involves the process of decoding, which frees desire from capture in illegitimate fixed representations. Indeed, any fixed representation is repressive from the schizoanalytic perspective, inasmuch as desire operates according to a radically free form of semiosis referred to as schizophrenia.[9] Market transactions are based on quantitative comparison (this product is worth that product or a certain amount of money) rather than qualitative evaluation (neither product needs to be "good" in any absolute or concrete sense to nonetheless have economic value). In market societies, exchange-value replaces use-value as the defining feature of things, and monetary value dissolves meaning; "all that is solid melts into air," as Marx and Engels put it.[10] Wherever social relations are mediated primarily by money, the semiotic codes governing meaning weaken, and meanings become free to vary ever more widely according to circumstances,[11] whereas in nonmarket societies, they are more or less strictly controlled from on high.

But we can go further. Money is not only a code-solvent, it is also a power-solvent. Wherever social relations revolve around market transactions, as Marx explains in the *Grundrisse*,[12]

> the power that each individual exercises over the activity of others or over social wealth exists in him as the owner of *exchange values*, of *money*. He carries his social power . . . in his pocket . . . in the form of a thing. *Take away this social power from the thing, and you must give it to persons to exercise over persons* [emphasis added].

It is clear from the immediate context, where market societies are being compared with political societies, that Marx considers the ability to carry social wealth in one's pocket in the form of money to be better than—or at the very least categorically distinct from—the exercise of social power by persons over persons, which he goes on to call in the very next sentence "relations of personal dependence"[13] and on the very next page relations of "natural or political superordination and subordination."[14] Money, in other words, serves to dissolve power relations of command and subordination, for

> the less social power the means of exchange possesses . . .
> the greater must that power of the community still be which
> binds together the individuals, the patriarchal relationship, the
> community of antiquity, feudalism and the guild system. . . . [And
> conversely,] patriarchal conditions and those of antiquity (likewise
> feudal ones) . . . decline with the development of trade, luxury,
> *money, exchange value,* in the same measure in which modern
> society grows with them step by step.[15]

Although Marx is not unequivocal in his support for the power of money in market-mediated social relations, as we shall see, he here considers them clearly preferable to earlier relations of directly interpersonal and political forms of subordination.

There is another set of benefits deriving from the market, however—one that is usually associated with production and the development of productive forces rather than with exchange, although exchange of one kind or another must be involved: this is the expansion of the social division of labor that markets enable. Regardless of the degree of specialization (i.e., the technical division of labor) within any given business enterprise (although usually developing in parallel with it), markets further enhance specialization through the wide-scale social division of labor by coordinating specialized activities taking place in separate firms that may be scattered around the globe.[16] Market society thereby forms what Deleuze and Guattari call a *productive multiplicity,* an assemblage characterized by what Mary Parker Follett would call *immanently related difference*—but now on a scale far beyond the enterprise or neighborhood organizations she had in mind. Market relations are not the only factor involved in the recent emergence of a truly worldwide production system, as we will see later, but they are an important factor, and it is practically impossible to imagine such a system developing otherwise than through the expansion and intensification of the market-mediated social division of labor.[17] Indeed, for nomadology, the expansion of labor specialization is a more important feature of historical development than class struggle (for reasons we will discuss later); as early as *Difference and Repetition,* Deleuze insists (agreeing explicitly with Althusser's reading of Marx) that "in *Capital* the category of differenciation (the differenciation at the heart of a social multiplicity: the division of labor) is substituted for the Hegelian concepts of opposition, contradiction, and alienation."[18] Labor differentiation is crucial for the social multiplicity of market society for two reasons.

The more obvious, and perhaps less Interesting, reason is that the social division of labor is absolutely crucial to and continually increases the development of the productive forces of society. This is already true of the technical division of labor within firms (that it increases productivity), but the technical division of labor alone soon reaches limits imposed by matters of scale: one can only subdivide a productive process so far, without the introduction of special machinery. And it is the social division of labor that enables and fosters the production of such machinery, thereby displacing the limits to the technical division of labor and indeed accelerating labor differentiation within the firm by connecting it to specialization outside the firm, in the social multiplicity at large. In the broadest and most rudimentary terms, social differentiation of labor appears early on as the distinction between the sector producing capital goods and the sector producing consumer goods. But specialization does not end there: engineering differentiates itself from science, on one hand, and handicrafts, on the other, before further differentiating itself into mechanical engineering, electrical engineering, biomedical engineering, and so forth. Science in turn differentiates itself not only by field or discipline but also along lines separating basic from applied sciences and these from technology. And as science, technology, and engineering continue to differentiate, the market is the primary means (though not the only one) by which these many differences get articulated as *related* differences to contribute to the enhanced productivity of the social multiplicity.[19]

The second and, for our purposes, far more Important, distinctive feature of the social division of labor is not the bare fact but the specific mode of articulation that markets can provide. Nomad markets are self-organizing systems of distributed intelligence and collective decision making. Though Marx often distinguishes clearly between markets in general and capitalist markets in particular, as we shall see, he doesn't appear to have foreseen the potential of postcapitalist markets to organize social production immanently. Indeed, on some occasions, he appears to explicitly rule it out. In the account of money as a power-solvent he provides in the *Grundrisse* (quoted earlier), for example, he goes on to posit a third stage of social organization, the first being based on relations of personal–political dependence (patriarchy, feudalism), the second on private property and exchange (capitalism), and the third on the "universal development of . . . individuals and on the subordination of their communal, social productivity, which is their social possession"[20]—in other words, communism. Unlike capitalism, where "individuals are subsumed under social production, which exists outside them as their fate," under communism, social production is to be "subsumed under the individuals who manage it as their common wealth."[21] Remarkably enough, Marx actually acknowledges the Interest of organizing social production via the market:

> It has been said, and may be said, that the beauty and the
> greatness lies precisely in this spontaneously evolved connection,
> in this material and spiritual exchange, which is independent of
> the knowledge and wishes of individuals and presupposes their
> mutual independence and indifference.[22]

But he goes on to critique this view from the perspective of the third, communist stage of historical development, where "social relationships

are their own communal [*gemeinschaftlich*] relations and therefore subjected to their own communal control."²³ And in fact, Marx had already
rejected this positive view of the market two pages earlier: "there can . . .
be nothing more incorrect or more absurd than to assume, on the strength
of *exchange-value,* of *money,* control by the associated individuals of their
collective production."²⁴ And he does so in terms that betray the over-
confident Enlightenment modernism shared by most major Marxisms:
communism, in this view, would represent "knowledge and will derived
from reflection," the "subordination" of social production by "communal control" of the means of production,²⁵ a division of labor based on
exchange-value being replaced by a social (i.e., nonmarket) organization
of labor, "as well as the planned distribution of labor time over the various branches of production."²⁶ It may be possible to read too much into
a turn of phrase or two, but this is a watershed. The beauty and greatness
of immanent self-organization are precisely what affirmative nomadology
will affirm in distinguishing nomad markets from capitalist ones, even
against the grain of a certain (major) Marxism.

Because philosophical concepts are selective as to which components
they adopt from other philosophical sources, which components are not
adopted can be equally Significant. New concepts must be created in relation to Problems that necessarily change. At the same time, the ultimate
value of philosophical concepts is determined not internally (or according to doctrine) but externally, via experimentation in the outside world.
Given an extensive and continually developing social division of labor,
now reaching truly global proportions, the articulation of labor must be
either market mediated or planned. And the results of experimentation
with planned economies of the kind suggested by major Marxism are by
now fairly conclusive—planned economies are inferior to market economies according to the criterion that matters most for schizoanalytic nomadology: the overall development of productive forces.²⁷ In circumstances
that have necessarily changed, the Problem now is not how to subordinate
social production to the conscious mastery of communal control but how
to free from capitalist command the potential of markets to self-organize
social production immanently.²⁸

Although theories of free-market self-organization have a centuries-
long history (dating at least as far back as the sixteenth century) and
have recently been recast in complexity theory terms by the likes of Stuart
Kauffman, Friedrich von Hayek is, for our purposes, the most important
proponent of what he calls decentralized or market planning. To be sure,
invoking the economic theories of von Hayek is almost as problematic as

invoking the political theory of Carl Schmitt: although not himself a Nazi, von Hayek was a severe critic of socialism and (for slightly different reasons) an obdurate foe of organized labor; what's more, ideas of his were championed by the likes of Margaret Thatcher, among others. Yet despite all this, his analysis of the market as a mechanism for distributed decision making is too valuable to dismiss as mere right-wing cant (regardless of how much of this it may have inspired).

Taking up a position made popular centuries earlier by Adam Smith with his image of the providential but invisible hand of the market, von Hayek both updates Smith's notion for the information age and uses it to attack the centralized planning models typical of State socialism. Given the historical context of emerging capitalist hegemony, Smith's model had been aimed against traditional collective or corporatist values such as noblesse oblige: instead of respecting traditional obligations to act for the Common Good of the whole society, Smith's market agents were to act strictly out of self-interest. Michael Perelman has shown how difficult it was to indoctrinate the early modern populace to pursue self-interest and how duplicitous were the means employed by champions of the supposedly free market to coerce people into following its new dictates.[29] But by von Hayek's time, that battle had been won (both culturally and legally). In his view, the main problem for the market in an age of information was therefore not coordinating the activities of self-interested actors but coordinating the activities of relatively ignorant ones in an increasingly complex economy, whatever their motives. Von Hayek argued strenuously against the implicit claims that socialist State planners were or could be in command of sufficient information to run an economy by fiat and that such top-down rule was preferable to letting the economy arrive at its own decisions via the mechanisms of the market. For him, the distributed decision-making mechanisms of the market were far superior—and the historical record of socialist State planning has largely born out this claim, as far as it goes. But we need to look more closely at the details and limits of von Hayek's argument to determine what is nomadic about market decision making and what is not.

Along lines similar to the distinction made earlier between the technical and the social division of labor, von Hayek distinguishes between an economy and what he calls a *catallaxy*.[30] Following classical Greek etymology (οἰκονομία, "management of a household") rather than modern usage, he takes the term *economy* to designate a single household or business enterprise, however large or small, whose members pursue a single shared aim and make individual resource-allocation decisions to that end. A catallaxy, by contrast, comprises a bigger group in which allocation decisions are made by a relatively large number of entities operating independently of one another and pursuing vastly differing ends and where collective decision making is left to an aggregation mechanism such as the market. For von Hayek, two features are crucial to the distinction between a catallaxy and an economy: the relation between means and ends and the relation between information and decision making.

The term catallaxy was important to von Hayek in the first place because, as its cognate *catallactics* (science of exchange) would in effect replace *economics* (management of households), *catallaxy* would be used in place of *economy* "to describe the order brought about by the mutual adjustment of many individual economies [in the etymological sense] in a market . . . [for a] catallaxy is the special kind of spontaneous order produced by the market."[31] But *catallaxy* had an additional advantage: it was derived from an ancient Greek verb, καταλλάσσω, meaning not just "to exchange" but also "to bring into the community" or "to change from enemy into friend."[32] This was important to von Hayek because he considered the aggregation mechanism of the market to be a key component of any free or "liberal" society.[33] For a catallaxy would enable individuals (people, households, firms) to pursue their own particular ends while at the same time providing the means for other members of the community to pursue their own, different ends:

> The important thing about the catallaxy is that it reconciles
> different knowledges and different purposes which . . . will greatly
> differ from one person to another. . . . In the catallaxy men, while
> following their own interests, . . . will further the aims of many
> others, most of whom they will never know.[34]

The catallaxy is fundamental to liberal society, then, in that it presupposes "no common concrete purposes. . . . It is merely means-connected and not ends-connected."[35] And this, in turn, is why the associated meaning of καταλλάσσω, "to change from enemy into friend," matters to von Hayek, for he believes that

> so long as collaboration presupposes common purposes, people
> with different aims are necessarily enemies who may fight each
> other for the same means; only the introduction of barter made
> it possible for the different individuals to be of use to each other
> without agreeing on the ultimate ends.[36]

As suggestive as it is, this assessment is wrong on two counts. First of all, groups of people with different aims are not "necessarily enemies" because each group presupposes a common purpose: people become enemies mainly when the means to realize their aims are scarce, whether they share ultimate ends or not. More important, the introduction of systems of exchange (barter, etc.) does not "change enemy into friend"; it merely makes people pursuing different aims into potentially mutually beneficial trading partners, neither enemies nor friends—for most of them, as von Hayek himself says earlier, remain completely unknown to one another. What the catallaxy does do, however, is *facilitate the emergence and development of a community where agreement on ultimate ends is not required for members' endeavors in pursuit of disparate ends to benefit one another through a network of market exchange.* This is how catallaxy gives rise to the "spontaneous order" that is, for von Hayek, "so superior to any deliberate organization."[37]

Achieving social order without relying on agreed-on ends requires a very particular kind of decision making. What von Hayek calls economies have a fairly clear-cut, vertical authority structure: decision making occurs by command from on high. Catallaxies—like Mary Parker Follett's neighborhoods and Deleuze and Guattari's philosophical Greek agora—have something approaching a horizontal authority structure: decision making occurs by coordination rather than command. Hayekian economies, partly due to their relatively limited size, operate with more or less complete information, which is concentrated at the point of command; catallaxies, by contrast, operate via very limited knowledge, which is distributed among a relatively large number of agents. Von Hayek's main claim—the basis for his critique of government intervention of almost any kind—is that there is simply no way, in any complex modern society (or catallaxy), to concentrate at the point of command (e.g., the socialist State planner) all the information that is dispersed among the multitude of independent agents. The mistake made by socialist State planning—a kind of category mistake, in von Hayek's view—is to transfer the structure and dynamics of command hierarchy from economy to catallaxy, where only distributed decision making via horizontal coordination can succeed.

Like soccer players operating without need of a quarterback, or jazz musicians without a conductor or composer, free-market agents don't need commands from on high to make reasonable decisions based on limited knowledge available to them in situ, on the ground, in their particular time and place. High-speed computer simulations have revealed this to be precisely how birds flock and how fish school: each agent reacts only to its immediate surroundings, adjusting its speed and direction in light of very limited information about the speed and direction of nearby agents. The result is well-nigh perfectly coordinated collective action, with absolutely no need for transcendent command.[38] Von Hayek then takes the model one step further in contrasting command and coordination systems: what matters is not just the *amount* of information but also and even more the *kind* of information relevant for each type.[39] The choice between centralized and decentralized planning, he suggests,

> will . . . largely turn on the relative importance of the different kinds of knowledge: those more likely to be at the disposal of particular individuals and those which we should with greater confidence expect to find in the possession of an authority made up of suitably chosen experts.[40]

Von Hayek then goes on to contrast centralized or universal scientific knowledge with an "unorganized," local knowledge conducive to solving particular problems rather than pronouncing general laws—precisely the kind of knowledge referred to in chapter 1 as minor or nomad science:

> Today it is almost heresy to suggest that scientific knowledge is not the sum of all knowledge. But a little reflection will show that there is beyond question a body of very important but unorganized knowledge which cannot possibly be called scientific in the sense of knowledge of general rules: the knowledge of the particular circumstances of time and place.[41]

Catallaxies work the way they do, von Hayek argues, when particular agents are free to mobilize minor knowledge to reach independent decisions, and then free-market mechanisms aggregate those decisions into a collective result. Much like a flock of birds, the distributed intelligence of a catallaxy arrives at decisions, von Hayek concludes, "not because any of its members survey the whole field, but because their limited individual fields of vision sufficiently overlap so that through many intermediaries the relevant information is communicated to all."[42]

Significantly, the minor knowledge characteristic of catallaxy is incompatible with the royal science of statistics (which operates on what Deleuze and Guattari call *denumerable sets*). The "sort of knowledge with which I have been concerned," von Hayek insists,

> is knowledge of the kind which by its nature cannot enter into statistics and therefore cannot be conveyed to any central

authority in statistical form. The statistics which such a central authority would have to use would have to be arrived at precisely by abstracting from minor differences between the things, by lumping together, as resources of one kind, items which differ as regards location, quality, and other particulars.[43]

So a catallaxy—that is, what is conventionally referred to as a free-market economy—forms a self-organizing multiplicity that operates through the horizontal coordination of multiple agents, each of whom uses minor knowledge to act independently yet in close relation to neighboring agents, and all of whom together form a nondenumerable set of distributed intelligence whose collective actions comprise a functioning whole.

Von Hayek thus offers considerable insight into the dynamics of the nomad market operating as a multiplicity. But it turns out that the limitations of his perspective are equally instructive; they typify much conventional economic thinking about market dynamics. First of all, there is the question of principle: even if a centralized planner were able to compile all the relevant information, would we want society to be programmed from the top down in this way?[44] Far more important, however, is a question concerning information itself: even though von Hayek stresses the importance of using local or minor knowledge in free-market decision making by multiple agents, as we have seen, he ultimately reduces the information involved in such decision making to price alone.[45] The issue for him is always how to overcome local or punctual scarcity by finding the least costly substitute good. So even without subscribing to the self-interest axiom of Smith's invisible hand theory, von Hayek nonetheless reduces market decision making to questions of efficiency and product substitution, for which price information may indeed be sufficient. But the market in fact makes information other than price available to agents and could do even more. At the same time, market agents act on far more than price information alone, and research indicates that consumers would like access to even more information than they have now.[46] What if market agents were expected to act not just out of self-interest and cost consciousness (as per Smith and von Hayek, respectively) but also with regard to the well-being of all? What if, in other words, market agents routinely took into account not just personal desires and price information but information regarding products' circumstances of production, conditions of distribution, environmental impact, and so on? The result of the aggregation mechanism of the market would then be more than mere efficiency: it would be an aggregated version of the Common Good. Like the free, open-source software movement, Wikipedia, or the NASA clickworkers discussed in the previous chapter, a nomad market intentionally oriented to the Common Good in this way would harness what James Surowiecki has called the *wisdom of crowds*.[47] The resultant definition of the Common Good would, of course, always be an approximation, never perfection itself. And it would not constitute the kind of explicitly agreed-on ultimate end that, for von Hayek, signals the death of liberal society. Nomad market agents would be free to pursue their particular ends, as long as this pursuit is coupled with pursuit of their particular versions of the Common Good, with the market producing a continually aggregated and reaggregated approximation of a collective version of the Common Good. So a truly free nomad market would become a novel and additional terrain or vehicle for democratic decision making, alongside the town meeting, the ballot box, and so on.

That the market economy today does not in fact operate this way is testimony not just to the historical reach and cultural force of Smith's injunction to act selfishly, nor merely to the distorting and inflationary influence of advertising on people's desires, but to the impact of capital on the very premises of the market itself. It is for capital's sake—for the sake of ever-increasing private accumulation—that exchange-value takes priority over use-value on the market, that the production of surplus-value takes precedence over production itself, that quantity becomes more important than quality. For all his talk about the importance of a particular or minor knowledge not susceptible to quantitative, statistical treatment, von Hayek adopts a quintessentially major standard for measuring market outcomes: maximum efficiency and optimum resource allocation, quantitatively measured.[48] This, then, is the second major limitation of von Hayek's position, although it is clearly related to the first; for if the information relevant to a market economy is reduced to price, then maximizing exchange-value will be the standard measurement of success—and the market henceforth answers first and foremost and as though by definition to the imperatives of capital accumulation.

The final limitation of von Hayek's position is one he shares with practically the entire tradition, stretching all the way back to Smith. It is the failure to recognize that, from its very beginnings, capitalism would inevitably vitiate the freedoms and virtues ascribed to the market itself.[49] Capitalist markets, in a word, are not and cannot be truly free markets for myriad reasons to which we will turn in a moment. Symptomatic of this failure in von Hayek is his forbearance and half-grudging admiration for business monopolies contrasted with his virulent repudiation of trade unions (which can themselves be considered, in a sense, merely another kind of monopoly). What he refuses to acknowledge is that capital inevitably concentrates and centralizes. It therefore exercises a kind of vertical command over markets that may differ in scale or proportion from that of socialist State planning but does not differ in kind. Centralized, top-down planning is centralized, top-down planning, the antithesis of free-market, distributed decision making—and that there are a small number of business-monopoly centers and just one socialist State center is not decisive. Moreover, any attempt to prevent capital from centralizing or to preclude its exercising power over markets would require precisely the kind of massive State bureaucracy against which so-called free-market advocates inveigh so vociferously. So-called free markets, then, are truly free when and only when they are completely free from capitalist command and control. Truly free nomad markets must therefore be strictly differentiated—conceptually and then actually—from capitalist markets, and it is to that task that we now turn.

Capitalist Markets

That there is serious and long-standing confusion between capitalist markets and free markets is no accident. It is partly due, of course, to the ideological force of the pro-capitalist free-market tradition discussed earlier. Confusion also arises because it was capitalism itself that transformed societies-with-markets into veritable market societies in the first place, by making market exchange the very basis of social relations, even though markets had long preexisted capitalism and can function perfectly well (arguably far better) without it. Finally, and most significant for our purposes, some of Marx's best-known analyses of capitalism have led to considerable misunderstanding about the relations among markets, exchange-value, and capital and about the very nature of capitalism as a mode of production. To understand the impact of capital on market exchange, we need to examine the concepts of primitive accumulation, systematization, and axiomatization from the perspective of nomadology.

Primitive Accumulation

So-called primitive accumulation is a complex and problematic term in Marx's oeuvre and in Marxism more generally. Scare quotes are often placed around the word *primitive* for a number of reasons, the least of which is that it is Marx's German equivalent for Adam Smith's original term, which is simply *previous accumulation*—referring to the stockpiled wealth the capitalist supposedly invested for the first time in means of production to initiate the dynamic of capital accumulation. The term itself thus designates the historical emergence of capitalism as a mode of production and also seems to raise questions about where the "first" stockpile of capital-to-be might have come from. The last part of *Capital,* volume 1 (part VIII, chapters 26–33), sets out to debunk Smith's moral fable according to which the thrifty protocapitalist saves up money until he is in a position to hire the profligate, who have nothing but their labor power to sell. Marx's contrasting account, dripping with sarcasm, emphasizes instead the violence and bloodshed required for capitalism's emergence:

> The discovery of gold and silver in America, the extirpation, enslavement and entombment in mines of the aboriginal population, the beginning of the conquest and looting of the East Indies, the turning of Africa into a warren for the commercial hunting of black-skins, signalized the rosy dawn of the era of capitalist production. These idyllic proceedings are the chief moments of primitive accumulation. On their heels treads the commercial war of the European nations, with the globe for a theatre. It begins with the revolt of the Netherlands from Spain, assumes giant dimensions in England's Anti-Jacobin War, and is still going on in the opium wars against China, &c.[50]

But this richly historical account at the end of volume 1 sits in uneasy relation to the beginning of the same volume, where exchange-value is shown to arise dialectically from use-value, only to find its ideal incarnation in money, out of which, in turn, capital finally arises as the crowning moment of the entire dialectical progression. The dialectical and historical accounts don't quite match—and Marx himself is aware of the disparity. He opens part VIII on primitive accumulation with these remarks:

> We have seen how money is changed into capital; how through capital surplus value is made, and from surplus value more capital. But the accumulation of capital presupposes surplus value; surplus value presupposes capitalistic production; capitalistic production presupposes the pre-existence of considerable masses of capital and of labor-power in the hands of producers of commodities. The whole movement, therefore, seems to turn in a vicious circle, out of which we can only get by supposing a primitive accumulation (previous accumulation of Adam Smith) preceding capitalistic

accumulation; an accumulation not the result of the capitalistic mode of production, but its starting point. . . . This primitive accumulation plays in Political Economy about the same part as original sin in theology.[51]

Such a tension between an apparently seamless, totalizing dialectical account and a detailed, multifaceted historical one in Marx is not limited to the issue of primitive accumulation. Rosa Luxemburg found a similar discrepancy between Marx's painstaking accounts of the simple reproduction of capital and the paucity of his analysis of extended reproduction, that is to say, reproduction involving the ongoing historical accumulation of capital. Indeed, in an important late essay (which explicitly acknowledges its debts to Deleuze, among others), Althusser goes so far as to posit the existence of two different materialist conceptions of the capitalist mode of production in Marx's writings: a historical conception emphasizing contingency (which he calls a "materialism of the encounter" [*das Vorgenfundene*]) and a dialectical conception emphasizing logical necessity and teleology (which he calls "totalitarian" but which could be less pejoratively characterized as "totalizing").[52]

The dialectical account, in brief, presents capital as a self-contained, self-perpetuating closed system. The capitalist mode of production has a single essence, obeys fixed laws, and contains as its telos or finality the seeds of its own destruction (whether in the absolute immiseration of the proletariat or the cataclysmic failure of stagnant class relations of production to contain the explosive power of ever-developing forces of production). The historical account, by contrast, presents capital as the fortuitous result of a chance encounter between, among other things, a critical mass of liquid wealth and a critical mass of labor with no means of subsistence. The encounter happened to have happened but could equally well not have happened at all. Wealth and free labor have existed side by side on other historical occasions, without gelling into a system and becoming a mode of production. According to the one account, capitalism appears as a fait accompli, as Althusser puts it, forever faithfully obeying its set laws of motion; according to the other, capitalism appears as an open question of contingency: how did it emerge as a mode of production, and will it manage to reproduce itself as such? This is not to say that capitalism doesn't obey laws, for once it has become systematic, it certainly does—or rather, it uncertainly does: it obeys laws, but without total certainty. "Rather than thinking of contingency as an exception to the laws of necessity," Althusser suggests, "we must think of necessity as a becoming-necessary arising from the encounter of contingent factors"—a perpetual "becoming-necessary" that never achieves total closure.[53] Lawlike systemic behavior sets in, to be sure, but remains riddled with contingency, like a worm at the core of the apple. We have, then, a major or royal Marxism, which gives a dialectical account of capitalism as a closed, smoothly functioning totality, and a minor or nomad marxism, which emphasizes the complex historical contingency of capitalism's emergence and the uncertainty of its continued reproduction as an open system.[54]

In addition to featuring this minor logic of contingency, Marx's historical account of so-called primitive accumulation lays stress not on the accumulation of capital (as did an entire ideological tradition starting with Adam Smith) but on the "accumulation"—that is to say, the forcible creation and multiplication—of free labor. "In the history of primitive accumulation," Marx says,

> all revolutions are epoch-making that act as levers for the capital
> class in course of formation; but, above all, those moments
> when great masses of men are suddenly and forcibly torn from
> their means of subsistence, and hurled as free and "unattached"
> proletarians on the labor-market.[55]

Hence what the title of the first chapter of part VIII calls the "secret" of so-called primitive accumulation is that it really designates the ruthless destitution of the working poor, not the stockpiling of wealth in liquid form:

> The capitalist system presupposes the complete separation of
> the laborers from all property in the means by which they can
> realize their labor. . . . The process, therefore, that clears the
> way for the capitalist system, can be none other than the process
> which takes away from the laborer the possession of his means of
> production. . . . The so-called primitive accumulation, therefore, is
> nothing else than the historical process of divorcing the producer
> from the means of production.[56]

Indeed, classical political economy was often surprisingly forthright about the conditions required for working people to submit to wage labor (and hence capitalism), as Perelman has shown in his detailed study of "classical political economy and the secret of primitive accumulation" (as his subtitle has it).[57] He quotes one German government minister who acknowledged that when all land has passed into private ownership . . . and capital exerts [its] compulsion on liberated or free workers . . . the command of the slave owner has been replaced by the contract between worker and employer, a contract which is free in form but not really in substance. Hunger makes almost a perfect substitute for the whip, and what was formerly called fodder is now called wages.[58]

In a very similar vein, an eighteenth-century English reverend named Joseph Townsend argued that "[direct] legal constraint [to labor] . . . is attended with too much trouble, violence, and noise, . . . whereas hunger is not only a peaceable, silent, unremitted pressure, but as the most natural motive to industry, it calls forth the most powerful exertions."[59] Having reviewed the "major figures in the pantheon of [classical] political economy," Perelman concludes that they share "an unremitting hostility to self-provisioning of all kinds—at least insofar as it interferes with the recruitment of wage labor."[60] And he likens the impact of primitive accumulation on traditional ways of life to double-bladed scissors, one blade of which "served to undermine the ability of people to provide for themselves," whereas the other comprised a set of "stern measures [designed] to keep people from finding alternative survival strategies outside the system of wage labor."[61]

What's more, although this key separation of producers from their traditional means of subsistence defines so-called primitive accumulation in one important sense (i.e., over and against the accumulation of capital) as "primitive destitution," it does not stop with the consolidation of capitalism as a mode of production; rather, the process of separation-destitution is an ongoing one, a necessary accompaniment to the ongoing expansion of capital itself. Thus even "once capitalist production is standing on its own legs," Marx insists, "it *not only maintains this separation, but reproduces it on a continually expanding scale.*"[62] We will return to the always-ongoing character of so-called primitive accumulation later, in connection with the process of systematization.

For now, it is important to distinguish two modes of enforcing the destitution characteristic of primitive accumulation, one economic and the other extraeconomic.[63] The more dramatic modality is vividly captured in a chapter title from Marx: "Bloody Legislation against the Expropriated, from the End of the 15th Century. Forcing Down of Wages by Acts of Parliament."[64] This is an openly violent mode of enforcement of primitive accumulation, where separation from the means of life is achieved by direct State intervention prohibiting myriad forms of self-provisioning—as in the infamous Enclosure Acts and Game Laws of sixteenth- and seventeenth-century England, which mercilessly stripped the poor of their traditional rights to common lands for grazing, foraging, and hunting.[65] In this early phase, Marx notes, the rising bourgeoisie

> wants and uses the power of the state to "regulate" wages, i.e., to force them within the limits suitable for surplus value making, to lengthen the working day and to keep the laborer himself in the normal degree of dependence. This is an essential element of so-called primitive accumulation.[66]

While this original mode of enforcement never entirely disappears, it gradually gets eclipsed by a second, far less dramatic, indeed well-nigh invisible, mode:

> The advance of capitalist production develops a working class, which by education, tradition, habit, looks upon the conditions of that mode of production as self-evident laws of Nature. The organization of the capitalist process of production, once fully developed, breaks down all resistance. The constant generation of a relative surplus-population keeps the law of supply and demand of labor, and therefore keeps wages, in a rut that corresponds with the wants of capital. The silent compulsion of economic relations completes the subjection of the laborer to the capitalist. Direct force, outside economic conditions, is of course still used, but only exceptionally. In the ordinary run of things, the laborer can be left to the "natural laws of production," i.e., to his dependence on capital, a dependence springing from, and guaranteed in perpetuity by, the conditions of production themselves.[67]

So the historical process of subordinating labor to capital starts with direct political action on the part of the State, but it reaches completion with enforcement by the "silent compulsion" of economic relations themselves, once they have become systematic in fully developed industrial capitalism. As Perelman describes the process at its inception,

> primitive accumulation cut through traditional lifeways like scissors. The first blade served to undermine the ability of people to provide for themselves. The other blade was a system of stern measures required to keep people from finding alternative survival strategies outside the system of wage labor. A host of oftentimes

brutal laws designed to undermine whatever resistance people
maintained against the demands of wage labor accompanied
the dispossession of peasants' rights, even before capitalism had
become a significant economic force.[68]

Once capitalism has become a significant economic force, subordination
to capital by political or blatantly military means tends to get displaced or
remain in effect in the economically underdeveloped regions of the globe,
whereas subordination by economic means tends to prevail in the overdeveloped regions. With the new, neoliberal economic order, however, as
both Naomi Klein and David Harvey have shown,[69] forms of so-called
primitive accumulation reappear in even the most overdeveloped economies—so that in the United States, for example, a regime of expanded accumulation by economic means alternates with a regime of accumulation
by blatantly military means, as we saw in chapter 2.

In any case, the key effect of the enforced destitution characteristic of
so-called primitive accumulation in any of its forms is to render laborers
more and more completely dependent on capital for their very survival.
All the "major figures in the pantheon of political economy," Perelman
explains, express "an unremitting hostility toward self-provisioning—at
least insofar as it interferes with the recruitment of wage labor."[70] Without
alternative means of self-provisioning, labor is first of all forced to sell its
work capacity to owners of the means of production and is then forced
to buy back from those same owners the means of consumption it itself
produced.[71] This is wage slavery, and it is this key dependency that gives
the lie to the myth of the labor contract—for a contract is supposed to
be entered into willingly by both parties. Those who are destitute do not
enter into labor contracts willingly: they literally can't afford not to; they
are prey to the "silent compulsion of economic relations." Just as the social
contract proved to be a screen narrative obscuring citizens' true condition
of dependence on and oppression by the State, the labor contract proves
to be a screen narrative obscuring labor's true condition of dependence
on and exploitation by capital.

But money itself can also represent a kind of screen that obscures dependency and exploitation, as Toni Negri argues in his groundbreaking
reading of the *Grundrisse*.[72] Money must be understood not merely as a
means of circulation or a measure of value, he insists, but as the embodiment of class antagonism and a vehicle for the command of capital over
labor. "The exceptional importance of this attack of the *Grundrisse* on
money," Negri claims, is that in it, "the relation of value is not envisaged

from the point of view of synthesis [of, e.g., use and exchange], but from the point of view of antagonism."[73] Rejecting any Hegelian or dialectical view of the "double face of the commodity, of value," he insists instead that "money has only one face, that of the boss."[74] With value expressed in money, commerce appears to be a free and equal exchange of commodities among individuals; but as Marx says,

> this positing of prices and their circulation etc. appears as the surface process beneath which . . . in the depths, entirely different processes go on, in which the apparent individual equality and liberty disappear. It is forgotten . . . that the *presupposition* of exchange value, as the objective basis of the whole of the system of production, already in itself implies compulsion over the individual, since his immediate product is not a product for him, but only *becomes* such in the social process [of market exchange].[75]

In other words, to simplify and dramatize the point here, under the condition of dependency produced by primitive accumulation (i.e., under the combined compulsions to sell labor power, produce for the market, and buy back the means of life from capital), there can be no such thing as a fair price.[76] For commodity prices always embody yet conceal the struggle over what proportion of the total value produced gets returned to labor, compared to the proportion appropriated by capital.

Now, there is no question that under capitalism, market exchange relations add to the technical and social division of labor we have already discussed a specifically *political* division of labor whereby capital exercises myriad forms of power. The essential question is whether this exercise of power and the struggle it provokes is inherent in money per se, and hence affects or corrupts any and all markets, or is specific to money in its capitalist form. For Negri, money always and everywhere wears the face of the boss; hence communism must eliminate money.[77] This reading of the *Grundrisse* is plausible—though wrong—because Marx's unpolished text is so often imprecise and sometimes even contradictory. Thus, in the paragraph quoted from earlier (about what is "forgotten" by defenders of noncapitalist market exchange), Marx will go on to say that "what is overlooked, finally, is that already the simple forms of exchange value and money *latently contain* the opposition between labor and capital etc."[78] The emphasis on *latently contain* is added to suggest that we are here in the dialectical mode of argumentation characteristic of major Marxism.[79] Yet just a few pages later, Marx will state the opposite: "it is equally clear that the simple movement of exchange values, as it is present in pure circulation, can never realize capital."[80] In this view—expounded via a comparison between commercial or mercantile precapitalism and fully developed, industrial capitalism, and thus hinging once again on the Problem of primitive accumulation—it is the *systematicity* of mature capitalism that makes exchange relations inherently antagonistic, as we shall see in a moment. Examining what makes capitalism a system from the perspective of primitive accumulation will enable us to understand how and why capitalist market exchange differs so dramatically from noncapitalist forms of exchange.

For now, let us note that this minor reading of primitive accumulation constitutes the second theoretical displacement effected by affirmative nomadology. Whereas the major accounts in Marx and Marxism (of the capitalist system as a functional totality; of its simple reproduction) take the existence of capital as a given, or derive it from exchange-value in a self-contained (or "latently contained") dialectical progression, the minor accounts in Marx treat the contingent historical emergence and ongoing reproduction of capitalism as a function of the initially violent yet equally ongoing dispossession of the working poor. Such is the open "secret" of so-called primitive accumulation. This second theoretical displacement is clearly related to the first. There the question of who has the phallus and attempts to possess it was displaced by the problem of overcoming the effects of enforced separation from the Mother as source of the means of life and enjoyment. Here the question of the accumulation of capital and attempts to repossess or expropriate it gets displaced by the problem of overcoming the enforced separation from Mother Earth as source of the means of life and enjoyment.

In light of this theoretical displacement, the pragmatic thrust of a minor or nomad marxism will not be primarily about taking power, or expropriating the expropriators, or reclaiming the wealth extorted from living labor by the dead labor concentrated in capital. Instead, the problem will be to (re-) discover means of self-provisioning that lie outside the orbit of capital, to (re-) connect with social means of subsistence *not* already subsumed by the capitalist system. This is the direction in which the famous lines-of-flight must go—in the direction of that "new earth" to which Deleuze and Guattari cryptically refer throughout their collaborative work. But to map the potential for such lines-of-flight, we must understand what is systematic about capitalism—and even more essential, what isn't.

Systematization

In an important "feminist critique of political economy" (the subtitle of their first book), Katherine Gibson and Julie Graham argue for the deconstruction of essentialist, "unified, singular, and total" conceptions of capitalism.[81] They, too, see the phallus and capital dominating Imaginary representations of the object of social change, and hence of social change itself. They acknowledge the existence of different—essentialist and nonessentialist, major and minor—logics within Marx and Marxism,[82] and they cite Deleuze and Guattari as "difficult and elusive" authors who contribute to the deconstruction of monolithic conceptions of capitalism and allow us a "glimpse of what might lie outside the flows of Capital."[83] They also mention the confusion, both "outside Marxism and within Marxism," of capitalism with the market, implying that careful distinctions should be made between capitalism in particular and markets in general. We need to look closely, then, at what capital does to markets: at how, in what sense, and to what extent it systematizes them—but also at what escapes it.

The work of Rosa Luxemburg is instructive in this regard, largely because of her refusal to take capital as a given in Marx and her subsequent analysis of accumulation—of both so-called primitive accumulation and full-fledged capital accumulation—as an ongoing process that always requires an outside, that continually needs to feed on what lies outside it to survive. Writing at the apogee of imperialism on the eve of World War I (*The Accumulation of Capital,* arguably her greatest work, appeared in 1913), she was understandably most intent on showing how capitalism required military conquest, colonialism, and war to maintain accumulation rates.[84] Alongside this "external" outside, we would emphasize today the importance of an "internal" outside that is also required for continuing capital accumulation, revealed in the intensification of marketing to create and exploit ever-new domestic markets, for example, and in the accelerating adoption of high-tech production and distribution processes to reduce costs and protect profit margins. In this view, capital is not and cannot be a closed system (a "fait accompli" in Althusser's phrase) but comprises instead a process of becoming-systematic that never achieves total unity. Capitalism has strong tendencies to subsume anything and everything in pursuit of continued accumulation, in other words, but it never realizes complete subsumption. And there are equally strong countertendencies. Deleuze and Guattari analyze such tendencies and countertendencies in terms of deterritorialization and reterritorialization, which we will examine later in connection with the processes of axiomatization. Here we will focus on the process of becoming-systematic of capital and its effects on markets.

We have seen that *Capital,* volume 1, contains two very different accounts of the origin of capital—one self-contained and dialectical, the other contingent and historical. In the *Grundrisse,* however, Marx offers a third account situated somewhere between the other two: it is an abstract schema lacking any concrete historical detail, but it charts the transformation of non- or precapitalist monetary assets into capital properly so called. At the same time, it will show that labor power is the sole source of surplus-value (the crux of Marx's "labor theory of value"), even when productivity-enhancing machinery is involved in the process. The account starts out, unfortunately, with a somewhat confusing repetition of the very term, *capital,* that he is trying to define:

> The accumulation of gold and silver, of money, is the first historic appearance of the gathering-together of capital [in a loose sense of the term] . . . but as such it is not yet accumulation of capital [in the proper sense]. For that, the *re-entry into circulation* of what has been accumulated would itself have to be posited as the moment and means of accumulation.[85]

Specifically capitalist circulation, that is to say, differs from mercantilism, but also from barter, in that it comprises a complete or continuous, self-sustaining circuit or system. The merchant buys commodities to sell them: neither their production nor their consumption is of any concern to her. Conversely, barterers acquire goods simply to consume them: the production of those goods and even their exchange-value per se are of minimal concern. Capital becomes capital in the proper sense of the term once it subsumes production and reproduction into its process of self-expansion; this is the moment at which "the commodity-form of the products of labor becomes universal,"[86] as Marx says. This is the moment, in other words, in which capitalism becomes *systematic*:

> Circulation itself is no longer merely the simple process of the exchange of commodities for money [mercantilism] and of money for commodities [consumption] . . . where both appear external to circulation: the final withdrawal of the commodity into consumption, and hence the annihilation of exchange value on the one hand; and on the other, the withdrawal of money, which makes it independent of its substance, and which is again another form of its annihilation.[87]

By contrast,

> exchange value itself [i.e., as capital], and now no longer exchange value in general [e.g., mercantile "precapital" money], . . . has to

appear as a presupposition posited by circulation itself, and, as posited by it, its presupposition. The process of circulation must appear also and equally as the process of production of exchange values.[88]

Capital in the proper sense of the term is thus not only a social relation rather than a thing or an accumulation of things, as Marx affirms elsewhere, but "a *process*," he insists here, "in whose various moments it is always capital."[89] Whereas exchange-value in mercantilism and consumption exists or appears only intermittently and as an intermediary, under capitalism, it becomes a continually self-positing and self-expanding circle or spiral that includes production, consumption–reproduction, realization, investment, renewed production, and so on:

> The first attribute of capital is this: that the exchange value
> deriving from circulation and thus presupposing it, maintains
> itself within it and by means of it; that it does not lose itself when
> it enters into circulation; that circulation is not the movement
> of its vanishing but rather the movement of its real self-positing
> [*Sichsetzen*] as exchange value, its self-realization as exchange
> value.[90]

> Posited in this way, exchange value is *capital,* and circulation is
> simultaneously posited as an act of production.[91]

The specificity of capitalist exchange-value or exchange-value as capital thus entails that circulation itself be considered an act of production, part of an entire system through which value is produced. It is in this sense, according to this understanding of capital as the self-positing and self-realization of exchange-value, that capitalism can be considered a system, as exchange-value takes its capitalist form.

In the chapter in the *Grundrisse* devoted to capital itself (Notebook IV), Marx examines this self-positing circuit of capitalist exchange-value in more detail. In the passages that concern us here, he is interested, for one thing, in what makes capital systematic—circular and self-expanding—in this way but also in how money gets transformed into capital "in the first place." In other words, he is interested, again, in the question of "primitive accumulation," but the treatment here is quite different from that of part VIII of *Capital,* volume 1. Here he is more concerned with the internal dynamics of the transformation of monetary wealth into capital than with the concrete details of the historical emergence of capitalism; he will examine "money in its transition from its determination as [exchange] value to its determination as capital."[92] (One polemical dividend will be to disprove the notion that capitalists "earn" a share of surplus-value by investing their capital in productive enterprise.)

The discussion begins, in a sense, where primitive accumulation leaves off: with a mass of accumulated monetary wealth in private hands confronting a mass of dispossessed workers and proceeding to put these latter to work by providing means of production. In this *first* encounter or cycle of production, the source of the monetary wealth is arbitrary and irrelevant. Marx insists that in the formation of what he calls *surplus capital I* (i.e., capital in the loose sense of the term), the capitalist supplies assets that did not originate from an antecedent capital–labor exchange but from some other process of accumulation:

> It appears as a condition for the formation of *surplus capital I* . . .
> that there be an exchange of values belonging to the capitalist,
> thrown into circulation by him, and supplied to living labor power
> by him—of values which do *not* arise from his *exchange* with
> living labor, or from his relation as *capital* to *labor.*[93]

Once this initial encounter has taken place, however, living labor does indeed become the source of *surplus capital II,* in the process whereby surplus-value is produced (in the form of commodities), realized (through the sale of those commodities), and reinvested in a second cycle of production. Only with this "second appearance of capital,"[94] by capital properly so called, does it function in truly capitalist fashion:

> All moments which confronted living labor power and employed
> it as *alien, external* powers . . . are now posited as *its own product
> and result.* . . . Originally, by contrast, the fact that instruments
> and necessaries were on hand in the amounts which made it
> possible for living labor to realize itself not only as *necessary,* but
> also as *surplus* labor—this appeared alien to living labor itself,
> appeared as an act of capital.[95]

The entire process within which productive labor functions to produce surplus-value therefore requires a *second* cycle of production–consumption–realization–investment–production to constitute itself as such and thereafter reproduce itself on an ever-expanding scale.[96] And Marx's critical insight into the role of labor in the constitution and recurrent valorization of capital depends on understanding the process in its entirety, as a multicycle system.

Lest we get misled by Marx's invocation of the "self-positing and self-realization of exchange-value" once it circulates as capital in such a multicycle system, we should remember the so-called secret of primitive accumulation: that despite appearances and terminology, primitive accumulation is fundamentally about the forcible dispossession of the working poor and their ensuing consignment to the status of wage slaves. In making this point about the relative importance of money and labor to the formation of capital, in one of the few passages in the early chapters of *Capital*, volume 1 (chapter 6) that refers explicitly to history, Marx insists that

> the historical conditions of [capital's] existence are by no means given with the mere circulation of money and commodities. It can spring into life, *only* when the owner of means of production and subsistence finds the free worker available, on the market, as seller of his own labor-power. And this one historical pre-condition comprises a world's history . . . and announces from the outset a new epoch in the process of social production.[97]

In a footnote, Marx adds that this epoch is characterized by the transformation of labor into wage labor and that it is only from this moment that the commodity-form of the products of labor becomes universal: this, in other words, is what makes capitalism a system. The "one historical pre-condition" for systematicity, then, is the commodification of labor—the emergence of the wage relation. "This relation has no natural basis in history," Marx insists a page earlier, "nor is its social basis one that is common to all historical periods."[98] Capitalism is universal, we recall, only in its difference from other social formations. Nor, by interpolation from the passage quoted earlier, is the wage relation intrinsic to or entailed in the circulation of commodities and money in markets. Rather, Marx goes on to conclude, "it is a clearly the result of a past historical development, the product of many economic revolutions, of the extinction of a whole series of older forms of social production"[99]—the result, that is to say, of processes called primitive accumulation. So although money is clearly a precondition for the purchase and sale of labor power, it is a necessary but not a sufficient precondition for capitalism itself. Money and markets are not the principal preconditions of capitalism; wage labor is: no wage labor, no capital.

This analysis of the role of productive labor in the capitalist process of the production of surplus-value has important implications for our understanding of the labor theory of value as a critique, rather than merely an account, of the way capitalism works. Workers don't mysteriously endow the objects of labor with value by muscularly exerting themselves at work; labor time doesn't magically meter the effort or skill applied on the spot during the production of commodities. If, as Marx shows, labor produces surplus-value in a system where "circulation is posited at the same time as an act of production,"[100] it is because the exchange-value in circulation of the goods it produces exceeds the exchange-value paid for the labor power itself—that is, what it costs to produce (or "reproduce") that labor power. (And for the purpose of his analysis, Marx assumes the capitalist always pays this reproduction cost in full; capitalist exploitation, he insists, is categorically distinct from fraud.) Surplus-value is not produced punctually on the shop floor or anywhere else, for it is purely differential, appearing only in the extended context of the multicycle system of capitalist production and circulation.[101]

From this analysis, it is clear why labor power alone, as stipulated by the labor theory of value, and not capital or technology, can produce surplus-value. Surplus-value arises not from cost differentials between inputs and outputs in any single cycle of production but from differences between the values of labor power itself over two or more cycles. For a fair wage (defined as the cost of reproduction of labor power) can only be determined in reference to goods available from a previous cycle of production and exchange, in which labor produces and then buys back from capital its means of subsistence or reproduction. It is from this difference between the value of labor power determined by goods produced in the previous cycle and the value it produces in the current cycle that surplus-value arises. To put the point another way, the reason that machines don't produce surplus-value is that they never purchase means of subsistence on the market, in the way that wage labor must to reproduce labor power. To be sure, Marx will say that value gets transferred from machines to products, but only in the sense that the cost of the machinery is included in (and distributed over) the prices of the goods produced and is recovered or realized when they are sold. So this transfer of value, too, is differential and systematic: it doesn't occur at the point of production but only in the context of cycles of production; machines don't really transfer value unless and until the goods they contribute to producing get sold. From the standpoint of the systematic process of capital's self-expansion, then,

it no longer seems . . . as it still did in the first consideration of the production process [i.e., production initiated by surplus capital I], as if capital . . . brought with it some sort of value from circulation. The objective conditions of labor now [as surplus capitals II, III, . . . , n] appear as labor's product. . . . But if capital thus appears as the product of labor, the product of labor for its part appears as capital—no longer as a simple product, nor as an exchangeable commodity, but as *capital*: objectified labor as dominion, command over living labor.[102]

And not only do the products of labor now appear as capital, but labor itself appears as capital—as *variable* capital, one of the various forms that capital takes in continuous circulation: as means of production (machines and raw materials), as variable capital (labor power), as means of reproduction (consumer goods), as means of circulation (money), and as means of investment (money and nonmonetary financial instruments such as stocks).

From this analysis of capitalism as a system, it should also be clear that capitalist exchange-value differs Significantly from exchange-value in general. In precapitalist exchange, "*circulation . . . does not carry in itself the principle of self-renewal. Its moments are presupposed in it,* not posited by it itself" (as they are in the mature capitalist system); "new commodities must continually be thrown into it from without, like fuel into [a] fire."[103] Until the advent of capitalism, money functioned in simple circulation only intermittently, in its two roles as means of circulation and measure of value, even when it was also a means of accumulation of mercantile precapital, which had yet to internalize production and reproduction–consumption as moments of properly capitalist circulation.[104] With the advent of capitalism, by contrast, "money in its third determination [i.e., as capital] . . . must be not merely the premiss but just as much the result of circulation. And as the premiss of circulation, it must be itself a moment of circulation, something posited by it."[105] The respective roles of money in simple and developed circulation are thus categorically distinct: "it is inherent in the very nature of money itself," Marx concludes, "that it can exist as a developed element of production only where *wage labor* exists."[106] In other words, "*money as capital* is a determination of money that goes beyond its simple determination as money."[107] So although money and just price can always become a matter of negotiation over divergent estimations of value in (precapitalist) systems of simple circulation, money can never express just price and must always embody class antagonism only in the multicycle capitalist system based on wage slavery: money wears the face of the boss, then, only when there is a boss to work for in the first place and when the circulation of exchange-value as capital has become systematic.

The very systematicity of capital, however, makes it all the more exposed to multiple contingencies. No doubt the best known are crises of overproduction or underconsumption, also known as crises of realization. Because surplus-value is regularly deducted from the circuits of circulation, the aggregate value paid to labor in wages is always less than the aggregate value labor produces, so capital always runs the risk of not being able to sell the goods that have been produced and thereby realize in liquid (monetary) form the value incarnated in them so that it can be reinvested. Advertising and marketing attempt to address and avert realization crises by artificially stimulating demand, but they in turn run the risk reducing profit margins by absorbing some (if not all) of the surplus-value to be realized. But there are also crises of reinvestment, when realized value can't find venues for transformation into constant or variable capital. There are also crises of supply such as raw material and labor shortages. Luxemburg sees capitalism's unremitting assault on the social spaces outside itself in pursuit of foreign markets (of all kinds) as a necessary attempt to address these persistent crises, as a necessary continuation of so-called primitive accumulation that is not "previous" at all but in fact strictly contemporaneous with capital, past, present, and future.

Moreover, in addition to capital's ceaseless attempts at the subsumption of foreign markets outside itself, there is a parallel attempt at the subsumption of processes internal to capitalism that is equally unrelenting. Marx's analysis of the real subsumption of labor processes is a well-known example: capitalist production is constantly revolutionized by the introduction of new technologies in the pursuit of relative surplus-value. The regime of relative surplus-value, however, aggravates as much or more than it remedies the tendency of the rate of profit to fall, which constitutes yet another form of endemic crisis. Moreover, the systematic circulation of capital through the form of variable capital leads to the subsumption of reproduction, at least insofar as the consumption of commodities serves to renew labor's capacity for work.[108] There is no guarantee, however, that consumption will serve that end, nor indeed that new technologies will be put to "productive" use (in the sense of producing surplus-value): as we have seen, the Internet has introduced very powerful systems of production (such as free, open-source software development) that now rival those devoted to producing surplus-value. Capital's "totalizing" ambition may be to subsume everything, but it cannot succeed, and the very forces of innovation it unleashes constantly threaten to escape or undermine it, as we will see in connection with axiomatization. Althusser's notion of a Marxist "materialism of the encounter" underscores these risks by suggesting that capitalism is not just originally born of a chance encounter (between free labor and liquid wealth): it must continually reproduce ever larger and more complex sets of encounters or articulations, simply to survive. Instead of taking capitalism as a smoothly functioning whole that automatically reproduces its conditions of existence, then, minor marxism sees capitalism constantly struggling on the verge of dissolution to surmount the multiplicity of contingencies that necessarily expand along with the expansion of capital itself.

Capital's systematicity is thus of a very particular kind. It is best understood, using Althusser's apt phrase, as a perpetual "becoming-necessary" of contingent encounters or articulations. Not only was it born of a chance encounter ("in a single stroke," as Deleuze and Guattari put it[109]), but even once this historical bifurcation point was reached, capitalism must continually rearticulate conditions of existence that are never simply given or entailed: it is not automatically self-perpetuating. Nor does it ever form a totality, despite strong totalizing tendencies toward the subsumption of anything that can be produced by wage labor: not everything is, and not everything can be.[110] It is an open-ended system, in two senses: it must continually seek out and conquer new territories, both external and internal, to sustain the accumulation of capital; and inasmuch as surplus-value is a pure differential, capital accumulation has no substantive limits (neither the immiseration of the proletariat, for example, nor the exhaustion of natural resources). But this does not mean it is necessarily guaranteed to go on forever: its continued existence depends on constantly renewing its myriad contingent articulations; crisis is its standard mode of operation. Finally, the production of surplus-value is dispersed among wide-ranging circuits of circulating capital, yet the source of surplus-value is wage labor alone.

In light of this understanding of the capitalist system, the pragmatic thrust of minor or nomad marxism will not be to eliminate markets or exchange-value or commodification altogether. Instead, the problem will be how to withdraw wage labor itself from the marketplace, how to eliminate the labor market alone, while leaving most other markets intact. With the elimination of wage labor, everything changes—capitalism no longer exists—yet everything else remains the same. The new earth toward which the lines-of-flight will lead is thus not some neoprimitivist world devoid of commerce, commodities, machines, or technology. Its advent hinges on abolishing the domination of markets by capitalist axiomatization to enable the nomadic articulation by free markets (among other institutions) of a global and complex self-organizing social multiplicity.

Axiomatization

Axiomatization is the form of capture specific to the capitalist mode of production. Capture is an abstract social machine that includes the extraction of taxes (or tribute) and rent as well as profit in a variety of different social formations. In the capitalist mode of production, axiomatization predominates in a hierarchy of forms of capture, subordinating the others to itself rather than eliminating them. For nomadology, a mode of production is not unified but multiple: it exists as a contingent assemblage of machinic processes. "We define social formations by *machinic processes* and not by modes of production," Deleuze and Guattari explain, "([for] these on the contrary depend on the processes)."[111] For schizoanalysis, modes of production were already a combination of a specific process of production and a corresponding process of subjectification, called *social production* and *desiring-production,* respectively.[112] To these, nomadology adds regimes of signs, faciality, and war-machines, all of which contribute—along with the form of capture—to defining a given mode of production.

Axiomatization responds to the contingencies outlined earlier—and especially to the endemic crises of overproduction and realization—by adding additional axioms to the original axiom that made capitalism into a self-sustaining and open-ended yet crisis-ridden system: the conjunction of liquid wealth and so-called free labor. Axioms involving production machinery and technology are added, for example, to supplement absolute with relative surplus-value to counteract the tendential fall of the rate of profit; marketing and advertising axioms are added to address crises of realization. *Fordism* designates a set of axioms that combine both of the preceding with, perhaps surprisingly, axioms of State support for trade unions and income redistribution; *post-Fordism* designates yet another (neoliberal) regime of axiomatization that subtracts many of the Fordist axioms while adding others. Whatever works: axiomatization is a flexible, experimental, even innovative process revolving around the core axiom that characterizes capitalism—the capture of surplus-value from capital–labor exchange circuits throughout society.[113] Axiomatization thus emerges from and then revolves around the inaugural conjunction and the ensuing world-historical advent of a society based on abstract labor but is in no way completely determined by it: axiomatization operates by bringing together abstract, quantified factors of production in anticipation of a positive differential return on investment. Anything goes—but not everything succeeds. Once the inaugural conjunction takes, axiomatization takes off—but with no guarantee of success: it tends or tries to totalize but remains as contingent as the initial encounter itself.

It is because axiomatization operates on abstract flows of production factors that Deleuze and Guattari call capitalist capture a surplus-value of flow and distinguish it from the surplus-value of codes characteristic of other modes of production. Axiomatization starts with flow quantities—a certain sum of liquid capital, a certain amount of labor power, marketing power, computer power, and so on—and assigns them qualities ex post facto: liquid capital becomes specific production machines and technologies, labor is selected or trained for certain skills, marketing power takes shape in particular campaigns to program or capture consumer taste for specific commodities, and so forth. Axiomatization is supremely flexible for this reason—but for the very same reason, it captures only a fraction of the flows it produces. This is because axiomatization can only operate on denumerable or striated sets—sets whose members can be homogenized and whose interrelations can be standardized *(logos)*. Nondenumerable sets, by contrast, are contingent assemblages linking nonhomogenous members only with the simple connectives *and, with*, and *among (nomos)*. Now in an increasingly complex society, with both the market and the Internet (among many other institutions) providing countless kinds and instances of encounter or articulation, the ever-growing number of nondenumerable sets far exceeds the number of denumerable sets.[114] It even exceeds the number of sets that can or ever could be denumerated or striated by axiomatization. This is one reason why *capture* is such an apt term for axiomatization: a mode of production based on abstraction fosters all kinds of social connections, only some of which can be turned to account, so to speak, in the production of surplus-value—those are the (unfortunate) ones that get captured. As systematic as capital is, and even despite its rapacious, totalizing tendency to subsume everything it can, it cannot possibly form a total system.

Axiomatization operates, then, through the combined processes of deterritorialization and reterritorialization. In the present context, *deterritorialization* designates the haphazard and spontaneous generation of nondenumerable sets, whereas *reterritorialization* designates the capture and denumeration via axiomatization of a relatively small subset of these sets in the pursuit of accumulation. Drawing on Marx's analyses in *Capital*, volume 3, Deleuze and Guattari outline these two moments of capital's ongoing self-expansion.[115] In the first moment, a wave of new, more productive capital stock transforms the preexisting apparatus of production and consumption in an attempt to forestall or stave off the falling rate of profit. What Marx described as capital's "continual revolution of the means of production" deterritorializes preexisting labor and capital to devote them to newly developed forms of production and consumption.[116] But in the second moment, this creative movement is brought to a halt, and everything gets reterritorialized: the evolving apparatus of production and consumption alike are tied down to what is soon to be obsolete capital stock, solely to valorize it and realize maximum profit on previous investment. A wave of deterritorialization liberates all kinds of creative energies (in consumption as well as in production) at the same time that it revolutionizes and socializes productive forces; but then reterritorialization supervenes, yoking the relations of production and consumption to the dead weight of private surplus appropriation. In Mary Parker Follett's terms, power-with develops continuously with the production of nondenumerable sets, yet succumbs periodically to power-over with the capture of surplus from the successful denumeration of some of those sets; living labor, to paraphrase Marx, continually revolutionizes itself, yet repeatedly succumbs to the dead hand of capital past. Of course, this is an analytic distinction, so the two moments or tendencies do not appear as such in actual historical developments: both tendencies of the process are occurring at any one historical "moment."[117] For affirmative nomadology, nonetheless, this combination of deterritorialization and reterritorialization constitutes the fundamental dynamic of capital's self-expansion.

The State plays a crucial, albeit subordinate, role in capital's reterritorializing tendency. Whereas schizoanalysis focused on the ways family reterritorialization produces Oedipal subjects for capital, as we have seen, for nomadology, it is the State that serves as the main apparatus of reterritorialization and subjectification. In schizoanalytic terms, capital supplanted the body of the State despot as socius or organizing center of the mode of production; for nomadology, capitalist profit has superseded ground rent and despotic tribute as the dominant apparatus of capture, with the subordinate State now serving as point of subjectification and compensatory reterritorialization for the superior deterritorializing power of capitalist axiomatization.[118] Capital depends on the State in two ways, as we saw in chapter 3. For one thing, inasmuch as the relation of free labor to capital is a strictly economic one, the State is required to supplement what Marx calls the *silent compulsion* of the market with force or the threat of force to maintain the political subordination of labor to capital.[119] The State, in other words, serves as an extraeconomic guarantor of the reproduction of capital's conditions of operation. More important, when capital becomes

the dominant apparatus of capture, the transcendent imperial State transforms into a variety of modern States, as we saw, which now serve as so
many different models of realization for worldwide capitalist axiomatization—the socialist model, the liberal model, the dictatorial model, and
so on—by providing concrete substance for the abstractions of capitalist
axiomatization.[120] Axioms can only operate on denumerable sets, as we
said, and so a major contribution of State citizenship is precisely to provide a standard model or models by which to striate its population into
denumerable sets with homogenous members that can be operationalized,
and more generally to provide a framework within which the population
can be managed politically for the sake of ultimately economic ends: capital accumulation. As Althusser saw, the "institutional State apparatus"
of the education system would become central in this regard—but State
legislation and enforcement of labor, banking, and finance laws are also
crucial, among myriad other State functions. Striation, denumeration and
population management, and subjectivation are among the nodes where
axiomatization intersects with biopower as a key feature of modern society identified by Foucault.[121]

Owing in part to this collaboration with the State, and in even larger
part to capital's inexorable tendency (analyzed by Marx) to centralize and
concentrate, axiomatization dominates the market and, in fact, completely
disrupts its capacity for self-organization. Because of their disproportionate size and influence and their near-monopoly or oligopoly status—what
Braudel calls their *antimarket power*—capitalist firms become price makers rather than price takers: they are able to effectively set prices rather
than merely respond to them the way free-market agents (price takers)
do.[122] They thereby contravene the principles of competition, decentralization, and independence on which the proper functioning of free markets
depends, as Surowiecki's analysis suggests. In principle, the free-market
exchange of commodities continually enriches, diversifies, and enlarges human capabilities and sensibilities. Antimarket monopolies and oligopolies,
however, because of their size, wealth, and/or political clout, can control
the market to their own advantage, thereby limiting its self-organizing
dynamics according to the dictates of private accumulation—both quali-
tatively (what gets produced) and quantitatively (how much is left over
for public and private consumption after profits have been extracted).
If we agree, in line with the conclusions of Braudel and Deleuze and
Guattari, that a truly free market would sponsor new social relations of
greater freedom, diversity, and material abundance once the *power-over*
of capitalist antimarket forces is eliminated, then we have a conception of
the material basis and historical possibility for free-market communism:

the world market would become a vehicle for the coordination of difference to enrich and enhance life rather than to exploit and threaten it.

As deleterious as this inevitable tendency toward market domination by sheer size is, axiomatization dominates the market in another, perhaps more insidious way that derives from the machinic process of capture itself: it imposes a single standard of evaluation from on high. As an abstract machinic process, capture in all three of its forms entails a direct comparison (of land, labor, or goods) that simultaneously depends on and enables a monopolistic appropriation (of rent, profit, or tribute), the first moment presupposing an established stock comprising the second moment. In this view, instead of surplus arising from production, as in conventional accounts, production (in the sense of organized labor itself, distinct from work activity in general) arises from surplus—and this is as true of public works labor performed for an emperor as it is of wage labor performed for capital:

> It is by virtue of the stock that activities of the "free action" type come to be compared, linked, and subordinated to a common and homogenous quantity called labor. . . . There is no so-called necessary labor, and beyond that surplus labor. Labor and surplus labor are strictly the same thing; the first term is applied to the quantitative comparison of activities, the second to the monopolistic appropriation of labor by the [emperor or] entrepreneur. Surplus labor is not that which exceeds labor; on the contrary, labor is that which is subtracted from surplus labor and presupposes it.[123]

Here we have another interrogation—perhaps even a reversal—of the notion of so-called primitive accumulation. Marx's major presentation (in *Capital*'s opening chapters) of the relations among exchange, money, and capital can give rise (and has given rise) to the impression that money exchange evolved dialectically from barter and then into capital proper. The historical record, however, shows otherwise: money first arose as a vehicle of the imperial State for imposing and collecting tribute and taxes;[124] it only much later became a medium of commodity exchange and, still later, a medium of wage payments. So whereas the major view sees capitalist surplus-value arising dialectically out of exchange-value and exchange-value out of use-value, we see here that the preaccumulated stock of surplus-value is in fact the basis on which general work activity becomes labor in the first place, takes on abstract comparability and thence exchange-value, and thus acquires use-value for capital.[125] Moreover, what was true of the primitive accumulation of capital at its emergence is equally true of the ongoing accumulation of capital in the present and the foreseeable future: so-called surplus-value originates in the miraculous creation of investment credit, which then proceeds to axiomatize factors of production in anticipation of a return on that investment. Undialectically enough, finance capital precedes and dominates industrial capital. Of course, this miraculous creation of credit capital, perhaps reflecting or revealing the secret affinity of axiomatization for reterritorialization, has determinate conditions of operation: disproportionately large holdings of assets (though never enough to cover the entire amount of credit actually issued) and legal sanction from the State.

Note that the precedence of finance over industrial capital in no way affects the principle of the labor theory of value according to which, in the apparent objective movement of circulating capital, labor power is the source of surplus-value.[126] It is important here to distinguish a precondition from the source. Labor power has value at all because of the (pre-) existence of a stock of exchange-values (so-called primitive accumulation) that renders it abstract and comparable, that makes it into a commodity to begin with—and from then on. Capital assigns value to labor power, as it were, to valorize and expand itself "economically": the source of value from below reflects the standard of value from on high. And capital in fact *must* so assign value to labor because wage labor as variable capital is the sole source of surplus-value, as we have seen: so no wage labor, no capital. A capitalist market—or rather (in the active sense of the term) a *capitalized* market, a market captured and dominated by capital—is, in other words, simply the preexisting terrain on which labor power produces surplus-value for capital. This is the other secret of primitive accumulation, according to minor marxism—and why the Protestant work ethic, as Max Weber clearly saw, is so germane to the culture of capitalism: because labor (as distinct from work) has value only insofar as it repays the infinite debt owed to capital, it represents the penance, undertaken by those in abject dependence, for what Marx called the "original sin" of primitive accumulation, understood, in this light, as the transfer of the infinite debt from the despot to capital.[127]

It is by means of these operations, then, that axiomatization imposes from on high its single standard of evaluation on the market. Because this is a surplus-value of flow, of pure differentials, the standard appears peculiarly devoid of content. As we saw reflected in von Hayek, the only operational criterion of value from the perspective of capital is a positive differential: increase—efficiency, growth, return on investment. In capitalist markets, value is not determined horizontally but vertically, measured solely by the rate of return. Capitalist value, that is to say, is defined by the interest and profit owed at the end of the axiomatization process on the credit miraculously issued at its start. Here we see the final displacement of so-called primitive accumulation: capital accumulation is ultimately not an accumulation of assets at all but an *accumulation of debt*. The infinite debt owed to the despot of the imperial State in the form of tribute has, in the process called primitive accumulation, simply been transferred to capital in the form of interest and profit. So for nomad political economy, capital is not really something you own but something you owe: capital is a social relation rather than a thing, to be sure, but it is not fundamentally a relation of ownership so much as a relation of debt. Here again, we see something like a screen narrative in play: axiomatization appears to dominate the market in the service of capital accumulation, when in fact it does so in repayment of an infinite debt (of which the actual accumulation of capital is merely a by-product or subsidiary effect).

Free-Market Communism

Capital thus captures markets in a kind of pincer movement, attacking both from above and from below: infinite debt, wage slavery. The concept of free-market communism is designed to show how nomad markets free(d) from the command and control of capital operate differently. We know what the potential benefits of free markets are; communism in this context simply designates the elimination of the distortions, constraints, and excesses inflicted on markets by the domination of capital.[128]

Debt

A capital-free, nomad market need not be a debt-free market: credit can serve constructive purposes—but not when it is an infinite debt owed to the demigods of limitless growth, callous efficiency, and private accumulation. Schizoanalysis had already identified an important imperative, based on the parallelism between social production and desiring-production: just as, for Lacanian psychoanalysis, the place of the Other is really empty but gets filled in anyway with Imaginary stand-in authorities like the Father or the subject-supposed-to-know, in much the same way for schizoanalysis, the place of the Creditor under capitalism is really empty: there is no longer any actual god, emperor, or king to whom the infinite debt is owed, just the impersonal stand-ins of efficiency and growth. So just as Lacanian psychoanalysis prescribes an end to Imaginary authority, schizoanalysis prescribes an end to the infinite debt. Social relations are always organized, Deleuze and Guattari insist, around a system of debts. But whereas despotism and capitalism both revolve around *infinite* debt, the type of social formation they call "savagery" is organized by a mobile patchwork of temporary, finite debts that interconnect various families and clans into a tight but flexible network. Nomad financial markets operate along similar lines.

Absent the infinite debt to capital, as coadministered by the State through its central bank (e.g., the Federal Reserve system) and the private banking oligopoly, nomad finance relies on smaller-scale institutions such as credit unions and microfinance. Credit unions pool savings from a specific group of members, most often organized according to locality or occupation, and make loans available to other members at prevailing interest rates. (What rates would prevail without the standard prime rate set by the Federal Reserve, nomad financial markets themselves would decide.) Microfinance or microcredit makes very small loans available to very poor people to jump-start small business enterprises that are routinely ignored by the major banking systems. In both cases, the kind of minor, local knowledge advocated by von Hayek for free markets in general enables financial institutions to make decisions about whether and where investments should be made.

Equally as important as where decisions get made is how—that is, according to what kinds of criteria. Nomad finance no longer makes investment decisions based on returns on investment alone but on a panoply of emphatically extraeconomic criteria. The South Africa divestment movement, for example, called for the end of apartheid through investment decisions. The socially responsible investing movement seeks to balance return on investment with a variety of social goods, including environmental sustainability, workplace democracy and diversity, and product safety, among others. The aptly named (and impossible to translate) *entreprises citoyennes* movement in France and Europe stipulates that investments be directed to firms that are organized democratically, and/or offer employment to the underemployed, and/or provide economic stimulus to underdeveloped regions, and/or sell ecologically sound products from sustainable production and materials-procurement practices.[129] In none of these instances—and there are many others—does nomad finance simply ignore the bottom line. But without the pressure to pay off an infinite debt, the return-on-investment criterion gets incorporated into a larger range of criteria aiming in one way or another at the Common Good. Nomad financial markets, then, provide another venue for aggregated democratic decision making through distributed intelligence of the kind von Hayek (and others) rightfully attribute to free markets. But to be truly free, markets must, of course, be free(d) from the infinite debt to capital.

Value

The potential for nomad retail markets is much the same as that of financial markets, and for much the same reason. Commodity exchange doesn't require socially necessary labor time as a standard of value any more than the availability of credit requires repayment of an infinite debt. From the perspective of nomad political economy, commodity fetishism means, among other things, that the value of goods is determined by price rather than worth (by their exchange-value rather than their use-value), instead of the other way around. But markets don't have to operate that way—capitalist markets do. Absent the imposition of a standard of evaluation from below (socially necessary labor time), the value of commodities is set by market relations themselves, by supply and demand alone operating in the mode of distributed intelligence.[130] In an analogous case, there was something of a panic when, in 1972, Nixon took the U.S. dollar off the gold standard (even though the international gold standard system was only a century old). But it turned out that currency markets, too, can operate perfectly well without a standard of value (although they are subject to volatility when subject to the disproportionate antimarket power of certain players). Here it is crucial to distinguish between money as a means of circulation and as a standard of evaluation.[131] In nomad markets, money functions solely as a means of circulation, and evaluation is not tied to a standard but left to free-market mechanisms of distributed intelligence and the "wisdom of crowds."[132]

Once free from the standard of labor-value, nomad markets evaluate collectively, allocate time and resources, and do the other (in von Hayek's words) "marvelous" things they do, in response to a range of considerations informing aggregate demand and supply. Of course, even capitalist markets must respond in some degree to consumer demand. But the antimarket power of large firms effectively subordinates all other criteria to the anticipated return on investment for which credit was miraculously issued in the first place. Capitalist market power, in other words, captures demand and subverts or diverts it to its own ends, to its infinite, senseless, destructive self-expansion. Nomad markets, by contrast, reverse that hierarchy and then dissolve hierarchy altogether: efficiency, least-cost calculations, and maybe even growth in some sectors remain significant considerations, but they no longer prevail over all others, in the service of capital accumulation. Free-market communism is achieved, finally, when markets freed from the standardized evaluation imposed by capital for the sake of private accumulation simply take as one of the criteria for distributed decision making—not the only one, but one among many—concern for the Common Good.

Multiplicity

With credit free from the infinite debt, and with commodity exchange free from an imposed standard of value, nomad markets become the vehicle not only for distributed intelligence and collective decision making but also for immanently self-organizing social assemblages or multiplicities. Nomad market–mediated multiplicities articulate differences via temporary and local connections rather than the forced conjunctions characterizing axiomatization; their means of articulation are the simple connectives *and, with,* and *among (nomos).*[133] They themselves, in other words, form nondenumerable sets. By contrast, capitalism now deploys two modes of denumeration, which determine two corresponding modes of subjectification: the principal modes of denumeration are what Foucault and Deleuze call *discipline* and *control*; the modes of subjectification are what Deleuze and Guattari call *subjection* and—in what is perhaps an unfortunate choice of terms—*machinic enslavement.* As we saw earlier, discipline denumerates State-citizens with instruments like the census and by means of "ideological State apparatus" such as schools and universities. But this mode of denumeration, although still in force as a kind of baseline denumeration, is too slow and inflexible for the needs of high-speed circulating capital. So disciplinary denumeration is increasingly supplemented with control denumeration, which operates via digitally mediated information feedback or cybernetics. Denumeration via models—the State as model of realization, with its model citizens, parents, students, soldiers, prisoners, and so on, as produced by the ideological State apparatus—is now accompanied and, to some extent, superseded by denumeration via modulation: the practically instantaneous capture of digitized information in the immediate service of axiomatization, bypassing the State, most institutions, and subjectivity itself.[134]

Deleuze and Guattari call this high-speed cybernetic mode of denumeration enslavement because autonomous subjectivity is no longer relevant or even functional: consumer preferences are not measured by opinion polls or focus groups but by galvanic skin response and pupil dilation; book runs are calculated not from book orders placed by professors in advance of each semester but by up-to-the-minute Amazon-dot-com rankings and mass-aggregated consumer feedback (as in Simon and Schuster's "Media-Predict" project[135]); rental car pricing no longer depends on the ad placed weekly in the Sunday paper but on split-second calculations of availability, cost, and profit margins. In so-called machinic enslavement, human bodies and brains become parts of what Lewis Mumford calls a social megamachine. Yet the drawback with calling this mode of denumeration enslavement is that—putting aside for a moment the predominant use to which it is now put—this kind of information feedback is precisely what makes digitally mediated markets so responsive as distributed-intelligence mechanisms for collective decision making. The more information circulating through or alongside markets, the more intelligent those market decisions can be. Now the actual use of most digital information today, it is true, serves the forces arrayed against nomad citizenship and free-market communism: surveillance, in the form of *repressive* State apparatuses; advertising and the antimarket forces of large capitalist firms out to inflame, distort, and/or capture market demand; credit agencies operating in the service of the infinite debt. But that the information is used for the wrong purposes does not diminish the value of the information itself, as a contribution to the distributed decision-making capability of nomad markets: cybernetic information freed from its capture by axiomatization and the State, in effect, boosts these markets' level of intelligence. And what is true for distributed intelligence is also true, in a different way, for embedded intelligence—for what Marx called the "general intellect" that gets embedded in the machinery and technology of fixed capital. "Society's general science, knowledge, has become an immediate productive force," Marx recognizes,[136] but its use, too, is determined by the imperatives of private capital accumulation and the Death-State rather than the Common Good. Free-market communism salvages embedded and distributed intelligence alike from the constraints and distortions of capture by axiomatization.[137]

Labor

Whatever else it may do, free-market communism must, by definition, put an end to capitalism. Conceptually, this is easier than it may sound: "capital creates no surplus-value as long as it employs no living labor."[138] As we have seen, no wage labor, no capital. Freeing credit from the infinite debt, freeing commodity exchange from a standardized valuation, and freeing distributed and embedded intelligence from axiomatization are all invaluable contributions—but ultimately, work activity must be freed from capture as wage labor, which is simultaneously the source of surplus-value, the key effect of primitive accumulation–destitution and the fundamental axiom of capitalism, as we have seen. From the perspective of free-market communism, selling labor services is more noxious than selling sexual favors. With the selling of labor power excluded by definition, production and work free from the reign of standardized value have to be organized differently.

And by extrapolation from chapter 3, we know in principle what that organization will entail: immanently self-organizing work groups, also known in this context as production cooperatives. This means going one or more steps beyond the self-organizing work groups already championed and in some sectors successfully instituted by liberation management advocates of flat hierarchies; beyond worker self-management and workplace democracy, inasmuch as these change only management practices and leave ownership structures intact; beyond even most visions of market socialism, insofar as they call for collective rather than cooperative ownership of the means of production and therefore replace the private capitalist with the socialist State in command of still-alienated labor power. Only self-organizing—that is, self-managed and self-owned—production cooperatives put an end to both the exploitation and the alienation entailed in wage slavery as well as the subordination and alienation entailed in (even socialist) State citizenship.

Free-market communism, then, forms a multiplicity of multiplicities— something like Mary Parker Follett's "group of groups," as it were, but mediated primarily by exchange relations rather than political ones. The groups themselves self-organize immanently, of course, but they also provide an alternative means of self-provisioning outside the circuits of capitalist labor markets and retail markets. These groups are interconnected, then, by truly free—and, where possible, digitally enhanced—nomad markets: markets that are free from the imposed standards of labor value and the infinite debt and that provide distributed-intelligence collective decision-making procedures that arrive at (a continual approximation of) the Common Good horizontally or bottom up rather than top down. They replace the abject vertical dependence of labor on capital with a horizontal interdependence congruent with egalitarian social being. Everyone carries her social power in her pocket in the form of money, but it is power *only* over the social wealth available in products freely offered for exchange, *never* over other people or over labor power itself. At the same time, free-market communism salvages the "general social knowledge" embedded in fixed capital, mobilizing it in the pursuit of the aggregated Common Good rather than for the sake of private capital accumulation.

These, then, are the ideal principles and key components of the virtual concept of free-market communism. It remains to be seen, in conclusion, what kinds of concrete strategies, institutions, and practices can actualize them and how they can together attain critical mass so that they ultimately prevail.

Conclusion

> The real problem of revolution, a revolution without bureaucracy,
> would be the problem of new social relations, where singularities
> come into play, active minorities in nomad space without property
> or enclosure.
>
> —Gilles Deleuze, *Desert Islands and Other Texts*

Bolivia, 1988: The El Ceibo federation of cocoa-growing cooperatives in
the Alto Beni region surpassed the one hundred thousand dollar mark in
exports. Founded in 1977, it drew on centuries-old traditions of Andean
indigenous participatory democracy to organize production cooperatives,
expanding from five to over thirty village cooperatives in its first decade.
The historical conjuncture had not been favorable for such a Remarkable
experiment to succeed. Peasants had been displaced, to begin with, by an
unholy alliance between the Bolivian state and international capital, which
replaced traditional farming with cattle and sheep grazing starting in the
1960s, with disastrous consequences for the environment, the economy,
and indigenous people. Unlike the Enclosure and Game Acts in England
centuries before, however, the Bolivian State's measures did not result in
peasants' total dependence on capital: the production cooperatives became an important alternative source of self-provisioning. But this was
not through subsistence farming: the cocoa growers had to find markets
for their chocolate. The first products were sold locally, but runaway in-
flation (reaching 24,000 percent in the mid-1980s) and State policy that
kept food prices low for urban industrial workers at the expense of rural
farm workers compelled the federation to look elsewhere for markets.[1]

The Netherlands, 1988: A consortium of European import cooperatives established the Max Havelaar fair trade label (named after the hero
of a nineteenth-century novel critical of the Dutch treatment of coffee
growers in Indonesia). This represented the culmination of a decades-
old movement started in the Netherlands in 1959 to remedy third world

underdevelopment through "trade not aid," as the slogan put it. The alternative trade organization movement started by developing so-called World Shops in Europe to sell handicrafts made in the developing world. But as the focus shifted in the 1970s from handicrafts to agricultural goods, starting with coffee, tea, and chocolate, import cooperatives were established in Germany (Gepa), Austria (EZA), and Switzerland (OS3) to arrange purchase agreements with growers throughout the global south. The other key development of the Max Havelaar Foundation was to market goods in regular retail outlets via the fair trade label, rather than exclusively in World Shops, which broadened the market exponentially. The Swiss import cooperative OS3 (later renamed and now doing business as Claro Fair Trade) entered into fair trade agreements with growers throughout Central and South America—including the El Ceibo federation of chocolate growers in Bolivia, starting in 1977.[2]

European markets had different standards for chocolate products than the federation was used to, but rather than succumb to the subordinate position of merely exporting raw material for processing in Europe, the federation invested in its own chocolate-processing plant, which opened in 1985. The timing, in one respect, could not have been worse: the Bolivian state had just embarked on a neoliberal austerity program; the federation would have to rely on international exports for years, until the domestic market rebounded. Support from OS3 in the form of guaranteed European markets was therefore crucial. But the introduction of relatively high-tech machinery into the federation's business plan also required internal adjustments, which threatened the very principles on which the federation cooperatives had been organized and run from the start.

The El Ceibo cooperatives operate entirely on the principles of acephalous egalitarian participatory democracy, one form of nomad citizenship. Everyone participates in decision making, and everyone even receives the exact same wage (the *jornal unica*). Furthermore, much like the Orpheus conductorless orchestra discussed in chapter 1, leadership positions in the El Ceibo cooperatives rotate among the membership so that power does not accrue to any one person or clique. Finally, everyone has equal standing and contributes fully: until the introduction of the high-tech processing machinery, all work tasks were performed by members, and no external wage labor was to be hired. At the point of high-tech machinery's introduction, however, outside expertise had to be hired to run the equipment. But the federation had learned from an earlier experience with hiring outside experts to train members in accounting and management techniques: they were better off training their members themselves because the outside trainers did not adapt their materials to the particulars of the local situation; previously trained members would thenceforth teach newer members. This same principle was then applied to the processing-machinery experts: they were hired on a temporary basis, with the proviso that they would train coop members to replace them as soon as they were able, thereby internalizing the expertise. The federation thus retains the principles of equality and self-sufficiency that are crucial to its success as a self-organizing and self-managed production cooperative completely independent of hired labor and private capital.[3]

Of course, the concept and institution of cooperatives has a long history, dating back to the late eighteenth century. Among the best-known early cooperatives was the Rochdale Equitable Pioneers Society, which was founded in Rochdale, England, in 1844 and whose Rochdale Principles have since become a touchstone for cooperative organizing around the world (including Latin America). Unlike Robert Owen's slightly earlier programs of philanthropy and community development from on high, the Rochdale Society was formed bottom up by a group of destitute weavers who pooled meager resources to establish a consumer cooperative; its success quickly spawned cooperative housing and several manufacturing cooperatives in Rochdale itself and eventually generated an actual cooperative movement throughout the industrializing world.[4] Within two decades, it was already a force to be reckoned with by Marx and Engels and other organizers of the First International. Marx himself saw the immense potential of what he called "these great social experiments," declaring that their "value . . . cannot be overrated" because "they have shown that production on a large scale, and in accord with the behests of modern science, may be carried on without the existence of a class of masters."[5] The enduring success of the Mondragon cooperatives in Spain—which are quite diverse and include a cooperative bank as well as several advanced-industrial and research and development enterprises—testifies to the prescience of Marx's assessment.[6] Yet Marx also foresaw dangers. In his polemic against Lasalle, Marx lambasted any cooperative organization that depended on aid from the State: only independent self-provisioning through cooperative production would represent a lasting threat to capitalist production. More important, Marx recognized that isolated production cooperatives could never prevail over the "geometrical progression of monopoly" in private capital: he therefore insisted that self-organizing cooperatives would have to band together and take the struggle to a higher level:

> The experience of the period from 1848 to 1864 has proved
> beyond doubt that, however excellent in principle and however
> useful in practice, co-operative labor, *if kept within the narrow*

circle of the casual efforts of private workmen, will never be able
to arrest the growth in geometrical progression of monopoly, to
free the masses, nor even to perceptibly lighten the burden of their
miseries. . . . To save the industrious masses, co-operative labor
ought to be developed to national dimensions, and, consequently,
to be fostered by national means.[7]

With this proviso—admittedly a huge one—that cooperative production
self-organize again at an additional level beyond the individual enterprise,
Marx equated such expanded self-organizing cooperative production with
communism itself:

If united co-operative societies [were] to regulate national
production upon a common plan, thus taking it under their own
control . . . —what else, gentlemen, would it be but communism,
"possible" communism?[8]

With additional hindsight, it may now be possible to add that the experience of the period from 1864 to 2004 has strongly suggested, if not proved
beyond a doubt, that the national dimension may not be the best and is
certainly not the only scale on which the expanded self-organization of
production cooperatives may take place, and that the nation-State with a
"common plan" may not be the best and is certainly not the only vehicle
for self-organization beyond the individual firm.[9] Inasmuch as the experience of the El Ceibo cooperatives are any indication, nongovernmental
organizations such as the Max Havelaar Foundation organizing fair trade
on a global scale may be much better for this purpose than centralized
planning by states operating on a national scale.

While the El Ceibo cooperatives embody Important elements of nomad
citizenship, the fair trade movement instantiates Important elements of
free-market communism. From its original incarnation as an import cooperative, the alternative trade organization movement introduced consideration of the Common Good into a set of global market transactions:
instead of paying attention only to price, importers and consumers took the
impact of their market decisions on producers halfway around the world
into consideration.[10] As the movement developed, the Fairtrade Labelling
Organizations International arose to provide the information necessary
for such distributed market decision making to develop and expand. This
enhanced information does not require or entail total transparency of one
social group to all others: only information regarding specific features of

the organization and the remuneration of work is required. As a result of labeling, fair trade sales in 2006 exceeded two billion dollars worldwide and included 569 producer organizations in fifty-eight developing countries.[11] In retrospect, 1988 may someday appear as a historical bifurcation point at which the convergence of fair trade networks, import cooperatives, and production cooperatives throughout the world began to reach critical mass and become self-sustaining and self-replicating, thus leading to the overthrow or gradual displacement of the top-down, capitalist version of globalization by an actual multiplicity of multiplicities.

Then again, it may not. Yet in an important sense, this doesn't matter. For though it is true that there can be no guarantees in nonlinear history, it is equally true that there is no dustbin of nonlinear history: that over the past 150 years or so, cooperative production in industrial economies has been tried (failing in some places, while succeeding in others) but has not (yet) replaced capitalist production in toto the world over does not relegate such experimentation to the dustbin of history—for similar experiments may ultimately prevail at some other time in the future, under other, more propitious circumstances. More important, it's the virtual principles, not just the actual instances, that matter—principles that can be adapted (rather than simply adopted as a model) for use in different situations. And it is the role of affirmative nomadology, of course, to distill such principles from the actual instances of self-organization and fair markets it surveys. The kind of nonlinear argument made here, then, is both structural and conjunctural (or something in between). The paradoxical concepts of nomad citizenship and free-market communism address two of the long-standing myths of liberal–capitalist social thought: the myth of the consensual social contract and the myth of the voluntary labor contract. Yet these concepts are also designed to reflect and reinforce alternative forms of belonging to social groups and interacting through markets that actually exist in the current conjuncture, from neighborhood groups to producer and consumer coops to Internet-mediated affinity groups like Kuro5hin or clickworkers to the global fair trade movement.

The principles of nomad citizenship are laid out by Pierre Clastres and Mary Parker Follett (among others) and instantiated in the Orpheus Chamber Orchestra, the free open-source software movement, and the El Ceibo cocoa growers' cooperatives (among others): they include bottom-up or horizontal self-organization fostering immanent power-with and eschewing transcendent power-over in the formation of nondenumerable groups. Production cooperatives are key, inasmuch as they eliminate the sale of labor power and thereby represent the end of capitalism. But coops occur in a wide variety of different fields, including housing, building, retailing, utilities, and agriculture—in addition to production and consumption. And self-organizing groups are even more widespread, including both face-to-face groups and large-scale virtual communities connected by the Internet and by some (noncapitalist) markets.

The thrust of the concept of nomad citizenship is to redefine citizenship so that it includes and legitimates a wide range of allegiances to such groups—and especially to deprive the State of its claim to any master-allegiance. The nomadic component of the concept is twofold. Nomadism designates, for one thing, a spatial, topographical, or geographical deterritorialization of citizenship that is no longer bounded by State territory but finds loci in groups both larger and smaller in scale than the nation-State, including both face-to-face groups of various kinds and Internet- and market-mediated groups that often span the entire globe. But nomadism also—and perhaps more Importantly—designates the deterritorialization of hierarchy in social groups that self-organize immanently instead of submitting to a transcendent instance of command such as State rule. Fostering multiple allegiances to nondenumerable social groups beneath the level of the State extends the benefits and responsibilities of citizenship throughout social life; in effect, it deconstructs the boundaries separating the State from civil society, and ideally, it encourages the growth of smaller-scale participatory democracy in numerous venues to accompany and inform large-scale representative democracy as we know it. In place of the one lethal master-citizenship along with subordinate slave-citizenships of the kind we have now, nomad citizenship fosters greater parity among many different citizenships. Breaking the State monopoly on affective citizenship is especially Important. Feelings of belonging, commitment, engagement, and enjoyment should be detached from the State—particularly from the Death-State and its grotesque fixation on the Fatherland at the expense of the Motherland. For, practically alone among the various venues for citizenship, Death-State citizenship commands a kind of master-allegiance that requires the sacrifice of life—of self as well as others—a master-allegiance to which the multiple allegiances of nomad citizenship are an Important antidote.

Free-market communism, meanwhile, provides another kind of antidote to the predominance of the Death-State: a citizenship of planetary scope, quite unlike the citizenships available for groups that meet face-to-face or define themselves—however broadly or Imaginarily (in Benedict Anderson's sense)—as "friends" or as somehow "the same." For as we saw, nomad markets freed from domination by capital are able to link far-flung groups and individuals in an immanent social bond that defines them neither as friends nor as enemies but simply as anonymous and temporary trading partners; nomad markets are thereby able to make the most of differences without turning them into enmities. While exchange relations were significant to Marx for their historical tendency to dissolve social formations based on directly personal or political power, for affirmative nomadology, trade also serves to dissolve or deconstruct the binary opposition of friend–enemy on which Schmitt's influential definition of the political depends. For trading partners are neither friends nor enemies. Commercial exchange relations knit social ties that are based neither on immediate proximity and intimacy (one rarely conducts monetary exchanges with family or friends) nor on complete unfamiliarity and the kinds of fear and enmity that produce armed conflict and war.[12] Trade depends instead on mutual consent and promises mutual benefits, yet it can span the globe and link parties that have no firsthand, face-to-face knowledge of one another. One virtue of free-market communism, then—inasmuch as it fosters trade that is voluntary and fair, that is, free from the antimarket power-over of capital—is that it enriches the lives of interested parties by making regional, ethnic, cultural differences available to all. With a global economy freed from the transcendent command of capital, free-market communism in effect enables everyone to become nomad citizens of the world without necessarily leaving home: market exchange does some of the traveling for us. Examples abound that suggest that the virtues of market exchange can indeed be salvaged from the vices of capital and its system of involuntary and inequitable exchange. The fair trade movement is exemplary in this respect, but there are in fact a wide variety of movements—including socially responsible investing, *entreprises citoyennes*, triple-bottom-line accounting, and so forth—that instantiate free-market communism by including consideration of the Common Good among the various criteria informing their market and/or investment decisions.

The concept of free-market communism incorporates two key, interrelated components. One involves freeing markets from antimarket forces that control market dynamics through the exercise of political and/or economic *power-over*. Though political control over markets has been important historically (and to a considerable extent remains in force to this day), it is now the economic power of concentrated capital itself that exerts undue control over markets by actively setting prices unilaterally rather than passively accepting prices set by immanent market self-organization. This is most notoriously (though by no means exclusively) true of the labor market, where the process of primitive accumulation–destitution gives capital undue power-over labor contracts and thus the ability to effectively set wages. Free-market communism therefore targets the labor market specifically for elimination, thereby eventually freeing all other markets from domination by concentrated capital. This in turn enables the other key component of free-market communism to come into play: a renewed but postliberal orientation to the Common Good. Liberalism in effect banished consideration of the Common Good from public life: individuals were to be left free to decide what is Good for themselves rather than having a monolithic notion of it forced on them by a State acting in the name of society. But there is a different way of integrating individual freedom of choice with the welfare of society as a whole, without imposing it from the top down, and that is by taking advantage of the aggregation mechanism of market exchange: an immanent approximation of the Common Good would be continually produced, adjusted, and reproduced through the distributed decision making and collective intelligence of a truly free, communist free market. As a careful reading of Marx and the examples of fair trade, socially responsible investing, and so on, clearly indicate, the Problem to be addressed lies in the capitalist (antimarket) command over markets, not in (free) market dynamics themselves.

These examples are Important not just for the virtual principles they instantiate but also for the very fact of their actual existence. Like capitalism itself, the ongoing process of primitive accumulation–destitution is never complete, and so human life is never entirely dependent on capital for its survival, as important as its variable degree of dependence is for capital's functioning. The fact is that instances of nomad citizenship and free-market communism actually exist and provide important alternative sources for self-provisioning outside or alongside the circuits of capital. Even if 1988 doesn't appear now to have been a key historical bifurcation point, there is no reason to believe that further instances of nomad citizenship and free-market communism can't be brought into being along the lines and principles of the instances already in existence—in which case, 1988 may, in retrospect, become an historical turning point yet.

None of these actual instances of nomad citizenship and free-market communism are utopias in any ideal or perfect sense, but they don't have to be perfect utopias to be utopian nonetheless, for the purposes of affirmative nomadology.[13] The principal utopian aims of affirmative nomadology as an intervention in political philosophy are to highlight the existence of viable alternatives to capital, as a predominant but not all-encompassing form of economy, and to the State, as a predominant but not inevitable form of community, and by conceptualizing the principles underlying these alternatives, to give them expression, strengthen them, and connect them with other actual or potential alternatives to promote widespread social change. Yet in light of our analysis of so-called primitive accumulation–destitution, the actual existence of these alternatives takes on added importance, as resources for imagining—and more important, for actually living—life outside and ultimately beyond capitalism and State rule. The creation of paradoxical concepts as thought experiments within philosophy needs to be connected with experimentation taking place outside philosophy—the essential political relation of philosophy to nonphilosophy, as Deleuze and Guattari conceive it.[14] Concepts of political philosophy are created in response to social problems that are not philosophical; nor will solutions to such problems be philosophical. Moreover, the concepts themselves are not solutions: they are articulations of problems whose solutions can be found only through continuing experimentation in the social field itself. The answers that philosophical concepts propose to the question of what is to be done thus serve not as blueprints for the perfect social order (utopia) but as pragmatic guidelines for conducting such experimentation.

Following the diagnostic concept of the Death-State and the paradoxical concepts of nomad citizenship and free-market communism, the final concept produced by these assays in affirmative nomadology is a pragmatic one: the slow-motion general strike. Following 1640, 1776, 1789, 1848, 1917, and 1949, we have been fixated on the image of revolution—of punctual, violent, wholesale transformation—as the most desirable (and often the only acceptable) mode of social change. But revolution is not the only mode of social transformation: feudalism, for instance, arose piecemeal following the decline of the Roman Empire, in a process that took centuries to complete. Thoroughgoing social change can take place slowly, over countless decades, rather than immediately, in the few months or years of a punctual revolution. For affirmative nomadology, the concept of the slow-motion general strike emerges as a direct response to the Importance assigned by the minor reading of Marx to dispossession as a key feature of the capitalist system—or rather of capital's never-completed tendency toward systematization. For capital never manages to systematize completely; it is only ever becoming-necessary, in Althusser's felicitous phrase.[15] Change therefore doesn't have to happen all at once. Immediate and total social transformation of the revolutionary kind is not absolutely necessary for a number of reasons, not the least of which is that capitalism is not a total system to begin with. Alternatives are not only always possible, they in fact already exist. Inasmuch as the secret of so-called primitive accumulation is that it is actually first and foremost a process of dispossession—ongoing as well as primitive—one answer proposed by affirmative nomadology to the question of what is to be done is thus to initiate a slow-motion general strike. Seek out actually existing alternative modes of self-provisioning—they are out there, in Remarkable number and variety—and also develop new ones; walk away from dependence on capital and the State, one step, one stratum, at a time, while at the same time making sure to have and continually develop alternative practices and institutions to sustain the movement. To effectively replace capitalism and the State, a slow-motion strike must indeed become-general or reach a critical mass or bifurcation point eventually, but it doesn't have to be all encompassing right from the beginning or produce wholesale social change all at once: it can start off small and/or scattered and become-general over time (in much the same way that capitalism starts small and gradually becomes-necessary, in Althusser's view).

Social transformation conceived of in this way renounces what Richard Day has shrewdly identified as the "hegemony of hegemony"—the idea that truly important social change "can only be achieved simultaneously and en masse, across an entire national or supranational space."[16] Hegemonic thinking (i.e., thinking that social change is always and only a matter of hegemony), Day argues, leads to the double impasse of "revolution or reform": given its totalizing view of society, one must either seek the total and utter demolition of that society through revolution or settle for piecemeal reforms that ultimately have no decisive effect on it. But society is not a totality: it is a contingent assemblage, or assemblage of assemblages. Nomad citizenship thus proposes, in Day's terms, a variety of "small-scale experiments in the construction of alternative modes of social, political and economic organization [as] a way to avoid both waiting forever for the Revolution to come and perpetuating existing structures through reformist demands."[17] For Day, finally, as for affirmative nomadology, what is Important is to create alternatives to abject dependency on capital and the State. "There does need to be a leave-taking," he agrees, but "those who leave must have somewhere to go . . . [and some way] to survive materially over the long term."[18] Beyond Gramsci and hegemony, then, there are three rather than two alternatives to simply accepting the status quo: struggle against the axiomatic (revolution); struggle within the axiomatic (reform); and struggle (to get) outside the axiomatic, which we are calling the slow-motion general strike. Pace Day, none of these three forms of struggle are to be ruled out once and for all or considered dead or passé, but their relative promise and risks can and should be weighed.

The idea of a punctual, wholesale, and violent overthrow of the capitalist State by direct action against the axiomatic is a gratifying and compelling one, inspired by a number of heroic and since-canonical historical events such as 1848 and 1914. And were it to occur, revolution would by definition produce the maximum amount of change (total transformation) in the minimum amount of time. This major model of change has two Significant drawbacks, however. The first derives from the dialectical, confrontational nature of revolutionary change: armed struggle challenges but also for that very reason reinforces the State's proclivity for violence and its overdevelopment of the means of violence. Revolutionary struggle therefore reproduces the binary, us-versus-them structure of Fatherland politics, as Carl Schmitt conceives it, and thus ultimately strengthens the State, instead of abolishing it—unless its defeat could somehow be guaranteed in advance. To the degree that revolutionary success could be assured, the risk of reinforcing State power would thereby be diminished, leaving only the problem of how to guarantee the dismantling afterward of the very means of violence amassed to overthrow the capitalist State in the first place. It is in this context that Benjamin's insights into the nonviolence of the general strike are so constructive: the general strike promises widespread social change, but by means of disengagement and the avoidance of violence rather than direct confrontation or expropriation and the perpetuation of violence. The second drawback of the major model of change derives from the very impossibility of obtaining guarantees regarding the first: given the extreme difficulty of predicting when the time is ripe for revolution and the fatally counterproductive consequences of miscalculating such a prediction, the prudent strategy is to wait. Ironically, the very mode of struggle promising the most rapid social change leads to near-total inaction in anticipation of a dramatic event that gets indefinitely postponed.

This quandary is visible throughout the recent and very important work of Michael Hardt and Toni Negri. Although their perspective is in most ways quite close to our own, direct confrontation with the power of Empire and rapt anticipation of a history-shattering event remain central to their strategic thinking. When they ask, in *Empire,* "How can the actions of the multitude become political?" "the only response [they] can give . . . is that the action of the multitude becomes political primarily when it begins to confront directly and with an adequate consciousness the central repressive operations of Empire."[19] But even if the stipulation of an adequate consciousness were met, they acknowledge a further precondition for success in any direct confrontation with the power of Empire:

> We are still awaiting . . . the construction, or rather the insurgence, of a powerful organization. The genetic chain is formed and established in ontology, the scaffolding is continuously constructed

and renewed by the new cooperative productivity, and thus we await only the maturation of the political development of the posse.[20]

That might be a long wait. For affirmative nomadology, however, there is no need to wait: alternative nomadic groups, practices, and institutions already exist, and the imperative is to sustain and develop them directly and without delay, invent new ones along similar lines, and knit stronger and broader relations among them so that they eventually reach a critical mass and come to displace rather than overthrow the existing social order.

Hardt and Negri's faith in the transformative power of a "strong event" is even clearer in *Multitude*.[21] Although they recognize that the "new possibilities for economic self-management . . . political and social self-organization" mean that "instead of an external authority imposing order on society from above, the various elements present in society are able collaboratively to organize society themselves,"[22] the "question of time" remains for them "essential"—by which they mean the time of Kairos, the time of sudden, wholesale change:

> When does the moment of rupture come? . . . not [from] the linear accumulation of Chronos and the monotonous ticking of its clocks but the sudden expression of Kairos. Kairos is the moment when the arrow is shot by the bowstring, the moment when a decision of action is made. Revolutionary politics must grasp . . . the moment of rupture or *clinamen* that can create a new world.[23]

No doubt such a moment of revolutionary rupture is devoutly to be wished for, but that is not sufficient reason in the meantime to reject the accumulation of slow-motion minor changes occurring in chronological time. It may indeed be the case, to echo Hardt and Negri's elegiac prose, that "today time is split between a present that is already dead and a future that is already living"—but for affirmative nomadology, there is no "yawning abyss between them [that] is becoming enormous."[24] On the contrary, the dead present and the living future coexist side by side, and the path to social change starts with a short step from one to the other, provided that step is a long-lasting and irreversible one.

The strategy of social change through reform within the axiomatic has a different set of benefits and drawbacks. Two advantages of reform correspond to the two major drawbacks of revolutionary social change discussed earlier: reform is nonviolent and therefore does not produce binary political structures nor provoke retaliatory and escalating violence on the part of the State, and it operates in chronological rather than kairotic time and therefore does not have to be indefinitely postponed. Compared to revolution, reform may not be as dramatic or total, but it can be enacted immediately, at almost any time. Despite the enormous recuperative power of what Deleuze later characterized as advanced-capitalist "control society," Deleuze and Guattari conclude that "it would be an error to take a disinterested stance toward struggle on the level of the axioms"[25] (contrasted with revolutionary struggle against the axiomatic). On the contrary,

> the pressure of the living flows, and of the problems they pose and impose, must be exerted inside the axiomatic . . . [for] it is decisive (at the most diverse levels: women's struggle for the vote, for abortion, for jobs; the struggle of the regions for autonomy; the struggle of the Third World; the struggle of the oppressed masses and minorities in the East or West . . .).[26]

It is not the case, in other words, that "every axiom, in capitalism or in one of its States, constitutes a 'recuperation'": inasmuch as capitalism's continual process of becoming-necessary or remaining-necessary requires "constant readjustments of the . . . axiomatic,"[27] those readjustments become the object of legitimate struggle. Indeed, reform proposals operating on the level of the axioms are legion.

Best known among them, no doubt, are struggles to win recognition of rights from the State and struggles to win higher wages from capital. The struggle for recognition involves masses and minorities identifying themselves and making themselves visible or countable in the eyes of the State as a particular kind of group to be able to claim rights from the State in the name of that identity. The struggle for high wages, similarly (and even if it could be generalized to apply equally throughout the workforce, rather than invidiously, as has usually been the case), involves workers reclaiming (through self-valorization) the value of a portion of their work activity that would otherwise valorize capital and generate privately appropriated surplus-value. The major drawbacks of both these struggles, and of reform in general, are that they do not challenge or reduce the abject dependency of workers and masses on capital and the State and that they in fact reinforce or even increase the power of the State and capital, whether by increasing the scope of the State (multiplying rights axioms) and thereby enlarging the territory of rights it ultimately defines and administers itself or by stabilizing and expanding the commodification of reproduction (so that enhanced purchasing power merely buys more goods and realizes greater profits), thereby securing the continued subordination of labor to capitalist command.

These drawbacks are shared, surprisingly, by the practical measures Hardt and Negri propose at the end of *Empire,* despite the revolutionary thrust of much of their rhetoric (as we saw earlier). Acknowledging that "confront[ing] [Empire] directly . . . although . . . clear at a conceptual level, remains rather abstract," they ask "what specific and concrete practices will animate [their] political project."[28] Having no answer to this question ("We cannot say at this point"), they nonetheless propose a political program consisting of three demands. The first is a demand for "global citizenship" for everyone, by which the authors mean in the first place people's "full rights of citizenship in the country where they live and work."[29] This is unobjectionable as far as it goes and is clearly of significant benefit to displaced workers—but it doesn't go very far. Global citizenship in this sense (i.e., as citizenship in whatever country one works in), unlike nomad citizenship, does nothing to eliminate or even mitigate the dominion that any and every State exercises over its citizens, as we have seen. And it only improves displaced workers' conditions relatively—granting them eligibility for rates of exploitation by capital that are no longer greater than those of indigenous workers but are nonetheless on par with them. Perhaps because of the limitations of this first component of their demand for global citizenship, Hardt and Negri add a second component: "the general right to control its own movement is the multitude's ultimate demand for global citizenship."[30] But as our analysis of primitive accumulation–destitution has shown, the Important issue is not the *right* to "move or stay still" but rather the *ability* and the desirability of doing so: unlike Hardt and Negri's global citizenship and its rights claims, nomad citizenship entails the ability of groups to sustain an autonomous form of life on their own terms and hence in a place (or places) of their own choosing.

The second demand is equally reasonable but ultimately suffers from similar limitations: this is the demand for a social wage and a guaranteed income for all. Replacing the family wage with a social wage has the huge advantages of reducing the power exercised by male wage earners over nonwaged others and the social prejudice favoring wage labor over nonwaged (e.g., household) work. A guaranteed income for all, furthermore, would partially counteract destitution-dependency by dramatically reducing capital's ability to use labor market competition to suppress wages and thereby vastly increase the prospects for workers' self-valorization. (Fredric Jameson's "utopian" demand for full employment would promise similar benefits.[31]) But these demands do nothing to challenge the wage relation itself. Workers—and indeed everyone, if there were a guaranteed income—would still be dependent on capital for the means of life purchased with that social wage or guaranteed income and would still contribute to the realization and private appropriation of surplus value. The radical alternative to wage increases, income guarantees, and full employment—as salutary as these would be in their own (limited) way—is self-provisioning, which is both one of the prime objectives and one of the preconditions for success of the slow-motion general strike.

Both of Hardt and Negri's first two demands, then, fall short of addressing the one feature of contemporary social life singled out by schizoanalysis, minor marxism, and affirmative nomadology as the most Problematic: abject dependency on the State and on capital. Their third demand is no doubt intended to address this Problem: "the right to reappropriation [or the] right to self-control and autonomous self-production."[32] The perfect solution to the Problem of dependency is, of course, precisely autonomy. What is not clear, however, is to whom such a demand would be addressed. Who would grant the multitude such a right? The only rights that ultimately matter to capital are the right to hire wage labor, the right to own means of production, and the right to privately appropriate the surplus-value generated by their conjunction. Any and all other rights are of tangential concern (and perfectly permissible) to capital, as long as they don't threaten these three. A truly socialist State might conceivably substitute workers' and citizens' rights for the three axiomatic rights of capital—thereby ending capitalism with the stroke of a pen—but no State could grant its citizens the rights to full-fledged autonomy and self-determination without thereby ceasing to exist as a State. Nothing is intrinsically wrong with or undesirable about these hypothetical rights scenarios—except their extrinsic implausibility and the (related) lack of any addressee for the demand for such rights itself. That even such advanced and often revolutionary thinkers as Hardt and Negri still formulate a political program in terms of demands suggests how much we remain in thrall to conceptions of power and freedom dating from the age of sovereignty.[33] But the fundamental Problems today, as our analysis of the Importance of primitive accumulation–destitution has shown, involve not just what we do or don't have the *right* to do but what we are *able* to do. (And so Spinoza and Nietzsche inevitably eclipse Kant and Hegel as primary points of reference.) This is what is distinctive about the slow-motion general strike: its basic thrust is to enable, not to demand. And as Benjamin was among the first to note, the key difference between every ordinary strike and the general strike is that while the former makes demands on capitalist employers, the latter simply steps away from capital altogether and—if it is to succeed—moves in the direction of other form(s) of self-provisioning, enabling the emergence of other form(s) of social life—for example, nomad citizenship and free-market communism.

As a strategy for social change working outside the axiomatic, the slow-motion general strike is, in an Important sense, neither reformist nor revolutionary. It does not employ violence in direct confrontation with the capitalist State and is therefore unlikely to provoke State violence in return, yet neither does it rely on and thereby reinforce the existing practices and institutions of capital and the State. By directing the investment of energy outside the axiomatic, the slow-motion general strike avoids both the retaliatory violence of the State and the extraordinary recuperative capacities of capital. The concept of the slow-motion general strike builds on key insights from Benjamin, as we have seen, and on the minor marxism of Deleuze and Guattari; it also bears a strong resemblance to the theory of exodus propounded by Paolo Virno, on which Hardt and Negri have also drawn.

As Benjamin's analysis shows, the general strike is itself neither revolutionary nor reformist. Yet in the refusal to work for capital, it represents a categorical and indeed terminal repudiation of wage slavery. It does not engage in armed conflict and does not make demands: it entails a disengagement from direct confrontation and a refusal of dependency and entreaties, while pointing society in the direction of fundamental social change, nevertheless. But fundamental social change does not have to happen all at once: the general strike as an increasingly widespread movement away from capital and the State toward other forms of self-organization and self-provisioning can take place over an extended period of time—in slow motion, as it were, in a long-term process of the becoming-general of the general strike. Vital to the success of a slow-motion general strike is its sustainability: the unrelenting process of dispossession by capital known as *primitive accumulation* must actually be reversed. For a minor marxism, this does not entail the "expropriation of the expropriators" via direct confrontation and violent seizure of the means of production or the State apparatus but rather the identification, exploration, and further development of alternative ways of producing and accessing means of life. Providing access to alternative means of life puts an end to abject dependency on capital, ensuring that the daring step away from capital that initiates the general strike is a sustainable step toward and onto something else. Deleuze and Guattari's lines-of-flight, in other words, must have someplace to land so as not to go spinning off into the void or end up in a black hole. They must be brought into convergence or interconnection on a "new earth" understood—and practiced and instituted—as a self-organizing plane of consistency rather than a plane of top-down organization, "via a pure becoming of minorities," as Deleuze and Guattari put it in *A Thousand Plateaus.*[34] The category of "minority," for Deleuze and Guattari, refers not primarily to specific ethnic or other identity groups but to multiplicities or nondenumerable sets of what Mary Parker Follett called *related difference* that cannot be homogenized and counted, and hence exploited and commanded, by the axioms of capital or the State. And if "struggle on the level of axioms" remains of paramount importance to them, as we have seen, it is partly because struggle within the axiomatic always tends to lead outside and away from it:

> These struggles [within the axiomatic] are the index of another,
> coexistent combat. . . . The struggle around axioms is most
> important when it manifests, itself opens, the gap between
> two types of propositions, [minority] propositions of flow and
> [majority] propositions of axioms. . . . The power of . . . minorities
> is [ultimately] measured not by their capacity to enter and make
> themselves felt within the majority system . . . but to bring to
> bear the force of the nondenumerable sets, however small they
> may be, against the denumerable sets. . . . The issue is not at all
> anarchy versus organization . . . but a calculus or conception of
> the problems of nondenumerable sets, against the axiomatic of
> denumerable sets.[35]

Deleuze and Guattari thus refer to the "undecidability" of the relation between minority propositions of flow and majority propositions of axioms, not primarily because the outcome of struggle between them is uncertain (which is true, but also "necessarily a part of every system," they say) but because both flows are produced by capitalism:

> At the same time as capitalism is effectuated in the
> denumerable sets serving as its models, it necessarily constitutes
> nondenumerable sets that cut across and disrupt those models. It
> does not effect the "conjugation" of deterritorialized and decoded
> flows without those flows forging farther ahead; without their
> escaping both the [capitalist] axiomatic that conjugates them and
> the [State] models that reterritorialize them; without their tending

to enter into "connections" that delineate a new Land; without
their constituting a war machine whose aim is neither the [Bush–
neo-Conservative] war of extermination nor the [Clinton–neo-
Liberal] peace of generalized terror but revolutionary movement
(the connection of flows, the composition of nondenumerable sets,
the becoming-minoritarian of everybody/everything).[36]

The Problem for nondenumerable minorities, to follow and extend Deleuze and Guattari's line of thought, is that of "smashing capitalism [and]
of redefining socialism"[37] as free-market communism, of constituting a
multiplicity of war-machines composed of nomad citizens that become
"capable of countering the world war machine by other means"[38]—which
is to say, for affirmative nomadology, means other than war. For beyond
the dialectic of violent confrontation, as we have seen, the nomad war-
machine (as both end and means) "is in its essence the constitutive element of smooth space, the occupation of this space, displacement within
this space, and the corresponding composition of people: this is its sole
and veritable positive object *(nomos)*."[39] In other words, lines-of-flight
or becoming-minorities must intersect and interconnect on—and thereby
form—a plane of consistency located elsewhere in relation to both "the
plane of organization and development of capital and the bureaucratic
socialist plane" of the planning State.[40]

Virno's theory of exodus provides another rationale for seeking and constituting such an elsewhere.[41] Arguing against Hannah Arendt (and by im-
plication, an entire Aristotelian tradition), Virno claims that the relations
among work, action, and thought have changed dramatically with the extensive incorporation of what Marx called *general intellect* into processes
of production requiring high levels of both advanced technology and cooperation among workers. The Problem as Virno sees it is that this general intellect-based cooperation is alienated under capitalism and takes the
form of top-down bureaucratic administration instead, in State and capitalist bureaucracies alike. The solution he proposes is to extract thought,
work, and action from State and capitalist administration and render
them truly public. And the strategy to accomplish this he calls *exodus*—
that is to say, a

> mass defection from the State, [based on] the alliance between
> general intellect and political Action, and a movement toward
> a public sphere of Intellect. . . . Today . . . a realm of common
> affairs has to be defined from scratch. Any such definition must

draw out the opportunities for liberation that are to be found in taking command of this novel interweaving among Work, Action, and Intellect, which up until now we have only suffered. . . . The political action of the Exodus consists, therefore, in an engaged withdrawal.[42]

The strategy of *engaged withdrawal* is based on a concept of radical civil disobedience that Virno develops via a critique of Hobbes. At the dawn of modern social contract theory, Hobbes recognized that obedience to any particular State law necessarily presupposed a tacit acceptance of obedience to the State as a matter of principle. (This predisposition to obedience to the State before obeying any of its particular laws corresponds precisely to—and in Hobbes, effectively obscures—the prelegitimate act of violence necessary for founding the State, identified, as we saw, by Benjamin and Derrida, that precedes the exercise of its monopoly on legitimate violence.) Whereas liberal civil disobedience is designed to contest the legitimacy of particular laws, Virno points out, radical civil disobedience denies the legitimacy of the State itself, "inasmuch as it not only violates the laws, but also challenges the very foundation of their validity."[43] It therefore operates not in the mode of confrontational protest and demand vis-à-vis the State but by withdrawing from engagement with the State altogether.

Even more important than denying the legitimacy of the State, the strategy of defection, like the slow-motion general strike, opens up new territories for exploration and experimentation. It "changes the rules of the game," Virno insists, instead of merely playing along, and thereby alters the kind of Problems that are posed to thought. Political philosophy adopts a mode of "free-thinking inventiveness" whereby actual constraints on thought and action are abandoned in favor of exploring virtual possibilities lying outside the axiomatic. For Virno, such exploration is predicated on "a latent wealth, on an abundance of possibilities," but this "virtual abundance" for him is primarily an "abundance of knowledge, communication . . . [and] collective imagination."[44] For affirmative nomadology, the abundance lying outside the axiomatic includes not just Common knowledges and collective imaginings but also actual instances of nomadic self-organizing cooperation and the material self-provisioning they afford. The slow-motion general strike as a form of exodus both presupposes and further develops this pragmatic basis of and counterpart to the abundance of the general intellect and the widespread sharing of Common knowledges and collective intelligence. It proceeds as a growing network or assemblage of self-organizing groups that Virno calls "acting minorities, none of which . . . aspires to transform itself into a majority";

instead, each develops power as power-with rather than power-over and hence "refuses to become government."[45] These groups of nomad citizens self-organize—both internally and externally, in relation to one another—in the mode of "related difference" and serve as what Virno calls the "organs of nonrepresentative democracy."[46] "Democracy today," he insists, "has to be framed in terms of the construction and experimentation of forms of nonrepresentative and extraparliamentary democracy."[47] Just as self-organizing groups don't need to project the principle of their unity onto a transcendent leader (e.g., the orchestra conductor), a movement of exodus or a slow-motion general strike doesn't need to project its unity onto a sovereign, nor onto capital, nor onto even a socialist planning state, inasmuch as it self-organizes in the mode of related difference through the operations of general intellect, Common knowledges, Internet groups, cooperatives, fair markets, neighborhoods, and so on, as we have seen.

Largely because they seek to open up new territories and invent new forms of life, calls for and examples of struggle (to get) outside the axiomatic tend to appear apolitical or even antipolitical; the problems to which they respond transcend social crises of democracy and economic decline. So although the strategies they propound may be similar to the slow-motion general strike, their tone tends toward the apocalyptic. Such is the case with the now-famous pamphlet anonymously authored by an Invisible Committee called *The Coming Insurrection,* which first appeared in print in 2007, inspired in part by the riots that started in Paris in November 2005 and continued throughout Europe for weeks thereafter.[48] "The sphere of political representation is closed," the pamphlet declares on its first page. "From left to right, it's the same nothingness."[49] The real problem lies elsewhere: "what we're faced with is not the crisis of a society, but the extinction of a civilization,"[50] which is dramatically pronounced "clinically dead";[51] in the same vein, the tract declares that "it isn't the economy that's in crisis; the economy is itself the crisis."[52] The only appropriate strategy in such a dire situation is to "collectively desert the regime,"[53] to refuse both work in the capitalist economy and political engagement in representative democracy. This strategy of what Virno calls exodus, or *mass defection* in general, is accompanied in *The Coming Insurrection,* however, by two more specific tactics.

One amounts to a kind of direct attack on the regime but is more a provocation than an attempt to take power: it consists of sabotage and blockades. Despite the claim that modern civilization is brain-dead already, the Invisible Committee seeks to hasten its complete collapse by disrupting its networks, waging a "guerrilla war"[54] not only by sabotaging the machinery of production but also by blockading the entire technical infrastructure of circulation (of people, goods, capital, information, etc.) required for global capitalism. This tactic does not involve a frontal assault on capital or the State: it is not a prelude to reappropriating the means of production or seizing the reins of government. Anonymity and invisibility are the recommended modes of operation, with the aim of "avoid[ing] direct confrontation as much as possible."[55] Indeed, the tract maintains a quite cautious position on the use of violence: armed struggle is necessary, but the point of bearing arms is to become a strong enough force to "make their use unnecessary";[56] insurrection can only triumph politically, because its militarization would mean certain defeat. Yet from the perspective of the slow-motion general strike, even the degree of provocation entailed in sabotage and blockades is unwarranted and seems likely to prove self-defeating. (And in fact, the French state arrested and jailed members of a food coop in the small village of Tarnac, accusing some of them of terrorism and the sabotage of a French rail line and others of authoring *The Coming Insurrection* itself.)

The international Transitions movement provides a useful contrast in this respect.[57] Started in Ireland in 2005, but now operating in most of the English-speaking world as well as Japan and South America, the Transitions Network shares some of the presuppositions and organizational philosophy propounded in *The Coming Insurrection*. Although far less apocalyptic in tone, Transitions, too, constitutes a response to what it considers the crisis of modern civilization: in this case, the imminence of peak oil and potentially catastrophic climate change, aggravated more recently by the financial collapse of 2008 and the general failure of the economic model of perpetual growth. Owing to the inability of "industrial society" and representative democracy to address the crisis, steps had to be taken to do so autonomously, outside the usual channels of big business and government. The Transitions movement comprises a plethora of local groups dedicated to preparing for *energy descent* (the move toward a lower-energy, carbon-free economy), in which authority and decision making are distributed and situation-specific: the aim is to "help people access good information and trust them to make good decisions":

> the intention of the Transition model is not to centralize or control decision making, but rather to work with everyone so that it is practiced at the most appropriate, practical and empowering level, and in such a way that it models the ability of natural systems to self organize.[58]

Local groups are thus linked in an international network whose main purpose is not to command or even coordinate action but simply to share examples of and information about fostering community resilience in the face of climate change, peak oil, and the inevitability of energy descent. Although the means it employs are entirely peaceful, in contrast to those of *The Coming Insurrection*, the Transitions Network envisions social change on a similarly global scale, implemented via similarly distributed decision making and action taking by small groups.

The other tactic that distinguishes *The Coming Insurrection* from Virno's strategy of exodus is its insistence on the importance of organizing the defectors in communes and of assuring that these communes are not only immanently self-organizing but materially self-sufficient or self-provisioning as well. Within the group, authority and decision making are distributed and situation-specific, as recommended by Mary Parker Follett and practiced by the Orpheus Chamber Orchestra: "each person should do their own reconnaissance, the information would then be put together, and the decision will occur to us, rather than being made by us."[59] Coordination among groups, in turn, also involves immanent self-organization, inasmuch as "proliferating horizontal communication is . . . the best form of coordination among different communes, the best way to put an end to hegemony."[60] Equally important, though, is overcoming all forms of dependency on a social order that has effectively collapsed: "a commune tends by its nature towards self-sufficiency"[61] to "ensure the viability of an insurrection beyond its first stages"[62]—which is one reason why "taking over Rungis [the enormous wholesale food market serving the entire Paris metropolitan area] would certainly be more effective than taking over the Elysée Palace [the seat of the French State]."[63] The material requirements of sustainability for the long-term success of the strategy of mass desertion are considered far more important than the symbolic value of occupying the central site of State hegemony. As it is in the slow-motion general strike, self-provisioning is here recognized as crucial to the objective of being able to operate independently of the axiomatic and to gradually develop new forms of social life.

The strategy of the slow-motion general strike, with its aim of creating and sustaining new forms of social life outside the axiomatic, is not intended and does not need to rule out or completely replace strategies of reform or revolution. If a revolutionary conjuncture or Hardt and Negri's kairotic "moment of rupture" ever materializes, it should be seized on and exploited to the full. Indeed, the existence of a multiplicity of self-sufficient local groups would no doubt make it far easier to mobilize people in large numbers to attack the axiomatic from the outside, precisely to make the best of such a long-awaited opportunity whenever it arises. But for affirmative nomadology, the essential thing is not to wait for it. The dazzling promise of a total revolution that never comes does us little good: it is better to act now. The advantage of reforms within the axiomatic, correlatively, is that they can be pursued immediately—and should be. Rights for all oppressed groups should be defended and extended as much as possible through major struggles with the State; exploitation of labor should be contested and mitigated as much as possible through major struggles against capital, by trade unions and political formations alike. It is Important to acknowledge, however, that these major struggles on behalf of denumerated sets—as indispensable as they may be—risk reinforcing the scope and power-over of the very institutions they seek to transform and are inevitably conducted from a bite-the-hand-that-feeds-you position of inferiority (lesser force), subordination, and dependence. Pressures exerted within the axiomatic are brought to bear against countervailing pressures from capital and/or the State, from which any gains must be won. Energy exerted outside the axiomatic, by contrast, simply and directly produces or enhances access to alternative means of life. Such is the advantage of the slow-motion general strike. It constitutes a kind of globally distributed nomad war-machine, *"capable of countering the [capitalist] world war machine by other means,"* as Deleuze and Guattari suggest in *A Thousand Plateaus,*[64] but of the kind that does not have war itself as its object. Rather it is the kind that has as "its essence the constitutive element of smooth space, the occupation of this space . . . and the corresponding composition of people: this is its sole and veritable positive object *(nomos)."*[65] Thus the sole and positive object of the slow-motion general strike is the convergence of nomad citizenships with free-market communism and Internet-facilitated collective intelligence to produce a gradual but irreversible, and ultimately definitive, becoming-unnecessary of our abject dependence on both capital and the State, coupled with the becoming-common of greater freedom and shared enjoyment.

Nomadological and Dialectical Utopianism

To be truly radical is to make hope possible rather than despair convincing.

—Raymond Williams, *Resources of Hope*

For Deleuze and Guattari, as we have seen, "the word utopia . . . designates [the] conjunction of philosophy, or of the concept, with the present milieu—political philosophy," but they go on to say that "in view of the mutilated meaning public opinion has given to it, perhaps utopia is not the best word."[1] Affirmative nomadology, I have argued here, involves a more specific form of utopianism than Deleuze and Guattari attribute to political philosophy in general, so it's worth contrasting the utopian vocation of affirmative nomadology with better-known dialectical views by considering issues of representation, historicity, and negation. We take as our initial point of comparison Fredric Jameson's magisterial work on utopia, *Archaeologies of the Future*.[2]

Representation

It is in one sense unfair to take a study devoted primarily to utopian fiction as the exemplar of dialectical thinking about utopia in general, for the very object of the study (literature) tends to (perhaps inevitably) favor textual utopias over what Jameson (quoting Ernst Bloch) calls the *utopian impulse* and thereby necessarily foregrounds the issue of representation.[3] But Jameson's treatment of utopianism is so thorough that most of the important questions get raised despite the gravitational pull of his object of study. Thus he will invoke Coleridge's distinction between Fancy and Imagination to characterize the tension between utopian impulses and the completed vision or blueprint of utopia as they register in utopian texts, ultimately assimilating pluralizing Fancy with anarchism and totalizing Imagination with Marxism as the two dominant poles of left-leaning political thought.[4] The central issue for us, however, remains the extent to which features specific to textual utopias bleed back into considerations of the utopian impulse itself and color the view he presents of it.

As a dialectician, Jameson construes the relation between utopian impulse and utopian text in terms of the relation of content to form. It may well be that representational form of any kind will inevitably fail in its mission to adequately capture its supposed content—yet in the case of utopian texts, representation fails for a very specific reason: even though the utopian text is allowed to evade a realistic narrative account of how utopian society is supposed to have come about, it is nonetheless obliged to provide a realistic description of what the resulting utopian society looks like as a whole, that is to say, as a totality. Yet we actually have no idea, Jameson insists, what utopian society as a whole will really look like. A flaw or feature inherent in the genre of utopian fiction—the requirement to represent society as a totality—shades over into a failure of utopian imagination in general: Jameson indeed defines utopia at one point as "a necessary failure of imagination"[5] and insists from the start that "the best Utopias are those that fail the most comprehensively."[6]

The best utopias fail most comprehensively, Jameson argues (drawing on the work of Louis Marin), by neutralizing rather than synthesizing key social contradictions, in a process very much like a negative dialectics.[7] Any positive, mock-Hegelian synthesis of the contradictory terms in a utopian text would be "precisely a bad Utopianism, founded on the illusions of representation and of affirmative content,"[8] and "any positive or substantive terms in which Utopia is thematized [would merely] . . . reflect the class ideology of its deviser (and its public)."[9] It is thus no wonder that Jameson is sensitive to criticisms of his "perversely formalist approach"[10] and a "stubborn negativity"[11] that may appear "depressingly self-defeating if not indeed positively defeatist"[12]—for utopia has in his hands slid back into satire, which was supposed to be its generic complementary opposite. In the terms of Robert Elliott's well-known genre study, satire presents an explicit negative critique of our actual society based on social ideals that remain implicit, whereas utopia presents an explicit positive ideal for society whose critique of our actual society remains implicit.[13] But for Jameson, "all ostensible Utopian content [is] ideological, and . . . the proper function of its themes [lies] in critical negativity, that is in their function to demystify their opposite numbers."[14] In fact, Jameson takes Elliott one step further, with the help of Marin, by removing even the implicit ideals of his satirical ex-utopias via the "neither one nor the other" procedure of neutralization.[15] This is indeed a bleak view of utopia, as Jameson is well aware.

Yet if we focus instead on the utopian impulses themselves rather than on fictional utopia as final product, on Fancy and the partiality and vagaries of content rather than on Imagination and the formal requirement of totality and closure, the picture may look very different. For the critique of representation applies to social theory as well as utopian fiction (as Gibson-Graham have shown): the picture of a single and totally unified mode of production is "founded on the illusions of representation" in social theory just as much as the depiction of a singular and totally perfect society is founded on the illusions of representation in utopian fiction.[16] So unless we conceive of a mode of production as total(izing) and all inclusive, there is no reason to automatically dismiss all positive content as a mere reflection of class ideology or to decide in advance that "our imaginations are hostages to our own mode of production"—to which Jameson adds, parenthetically, "(and perhaps to whatever remnants of past ones it has preserved)."[17] Surprisingly, nothing is said here, even parenthetically, about future ones—for one familiar way (well known to Jameson himself) to correct for the propensity of a concept like the mode of production to overtotalize and simplify complex historical realities is to distinguish among dominant, residual, and emergent tendencies within a mode of production at a given time;[18] though this solution (which Jameson does not deploy here) has distinct advantages over a monolithic conception of the mode of production, it poses other problems, to which we return in the next section.

What Jameson does recognize, in the last chapter of the long theoretical essay that opens the book, is that the grip of totalizing thought and absolute formal closure on utopian fiction begins to relax in the waning decades of the twentieth century, as a new mode of utopian thinking appears, both in fiction (he cites Kim Stanley Robinson's great *Mars* trilogy) and in theory (where he cites Robert Nozick from *Anarchy, the State, and Utopia* and Yona Friedman's *Utopies réalisables*). Rather than the "obsessive search for a simple, single-shot solution to all our ills"[19] that characterizes the Imagination of classic utopian texts, more recent utopian thought and fiction acknowledge and emphasize Fancy and the plurality of possible utopias instead. Friedman, for example, depicts a plethora of distinct utopian societies scattered across the globe, each embodying its own unique set of ideals uncontaminated by contact with the others.[20] Robinson's sprawling novels, similarly, portray a wide range of different utopian experiments and communities in the course of his account of the colonization of Mars.[21] The significance of this recent direction taken in utopian thought and fiction is the departure from singularity and totality that had seemed inherent in, if not indeed definitive of, the genre: the plurality of utopian impulses and ideals defies the singular perfection of utopia. From here it is but one step—albeit a significant one—to the vocation of affirmative nomadology to detect and reinforce utopian ideals in actually existing institutions of whatever scale, from neighborhoods to virtual Internet communities to production cooperatives to far-flung global trade arrangements.[22] The utopian character of these institutions remains completely distinct from any singular utopia conceived as a total, self-contained community, for they are interwoven transversally with one another and constitute something like a meshwork rather than a unified whole.

Jameson is no doubt correct to correlate this formal development within utopian thought and fiction with the eclipse of the nation-State and the emergence of what he calls "federalism" in political theory (which, at the same time, however, leaves the singular-totality of the mode of production pretty much intact). Here he cites Fernand Braudel's vision of the Mediterranean as an example of a new kind of utopian archipelago replacing the singular island Utopia (and he could have equally well cited Edouard Glissant's utopian paean to the Caribbean archipelago).[23] However, Jameson is on the whole rather pessimistic about this development, for reasons that reveal further significant differences between dialectical and nomadological utopianism.

The first reason is that, for Jameson, utopianism must pass through what Lacan called the *defiles of representation*: "the failure of federalism to become completely utopian lies . . . above all in the absence from it of representation, that is, of the possibility of any powerful libidinal cathexis."[24] This is not the place to rehearse the entire argument, but schizoanalysis (and hence affirmative nomadology) is based squarely on the principle that the most powerful (schizophrenic) libidinal cathexes are precisely those that do not pass through representation but rather index the Real more directly and productively, in ways that defy conventional codification and the kind of totalizing closure Jameson (correctly) associates with classical utopian texts themselves.[25] It thus becomes possible, and indeed indispensable, to distinguish between two modes of referential relation: *representational* and *indexical*. Representational reference operates via recognition and some form of correspondence between image and reality; in this mode, textual utopias would serve as a kind of blueprint for the ideal society we then seek in reality or seek to construct in reality, or at the very least (e.g., via the process of neutralization) as a kind of negative yardstick against which to measure and critique existing society. Indexical reference operates as a kind of relay between thought and reality, serving as a provisional guide to practical operations without making any definitive claims; in this mode, as we have seen with affirmative nomadology, utopian thought distills selected principles from existing social practices to inspire further practical experimentation, which might then adduce additional or other principles, and so forth. The choice is between utopian thought conceived of either as a mode of connection with or as a representation of the forces of beneficial social change. And the question, then, is which is more likely to produce powerful libidinal cathexes in the interest of change: a representational view that entails either impossible, false-positive syntheses dismissed as comfortably simplistic and ideologically suspect or relentless negative critique of everything in actual existence, on one hand, or an indexical view that involves the tentative affirmation of principles informing actual social practices to reinforce positive elements of existing institutions and experiment with extending them further into additional institutions and practices, on the other? Rather than the stubborn negativity and depressing defeatism of a dialectical approach, affirmative nomadology insists on carefully selected, positive libidinal cathexes that work to restore our capacity to "believe in this world."[26]

The second reason Jameson is less than hopeful about the prospects of federalism for the future of utopia also derives from his commitment to totality. What the "federal" utopias lack, he insists,[27] is the capacity to portray or generate a "genuinely radical disruption" of the present, the ability to produce a "radical and systemic break."[28] But the requirement of such a radical systemic break is necessary only when you conceive of a society or mode of production as a total system in the first place. Here again, a fatal flaw of utopian form—the need to present the ideal society as a totality—similarly affects social theory. For if society is actually composed of truly heterogeneous elements that don't form a total system, then a radical systemic break may not be necessary (and may indeed not even be possible, almost by definition). Construing such elements in terms of dominant, residual, and emergent improves utopian prospects considerably, inasmuch as there would presumably be positive elements to affirm (the "emergent" ones) alongside the negative ones to critique and reject (presumably all the "dominant" ones)—but this solution, as we have already suggested, entails a mode of temporality and an understanding of history that are incompatible with affirmative nomadology.

Historicity

For only on the basis of a linear understanding of history is it possible to distinguish among the emergent, dominant, and residual elements of a given historical conjuncture. Under ordinary or close-to-equilibrium conditions, it may be possible to project the dominance and limits of historical tendencies with some degree of confidence. When such confidence is high, linear history becomes teleological. This is the view expressed by Hardt and Negri in *Empire*.[29] For despite some borrowings from Deleuze and Guattari, *Empire*'s grand narrative remains an essentially linear and dialectical one, in which subject and object tend toward mutual correlation in an auspicious future. The inherent inclinations of the multitude providentially correspond to and realize the objective tendencies of the historical passage from imperialism to Empire. This is similar to the stance of that other great proponent of dialectical utopianism, Ernst Bloch, for whom "the revolutionary decision of the proletariat" amounts to a commitment to "the final struggle of liberation, a decision of the subjective factor in alliance with the objective factors of economic–material tendency."[30] In the same vein, Hardt and Negri's self-proclaimed goal is to "construct an apparatus for bringing together the subject (the multitude) and the object (cosmopolitical liberation)."[31] As it turns out, that apparatus focuses on the subjective pole of the dialectic, which is "the primary site of struggle,"[32] according to Hardt and Negri, and entails "at the most basic and elemental level . . . *the will to be against*."[33] And although they acknowledge the objection that a subjectivity defined from the start as a will-to-be-against may not provide a "properly political subject" for a philosophy of history, they insist that "this objection does not present an insuperable obstacle because the revolutionary past and the contemporary cooperative productive capacities . . . of the multitude . . . *cannot help revealing a telos*, a material affirmation of liberation."[34] At this level of confidence, essential questions about the historical process seem to have been settled in advance, as if close-to-equilibrium conditions, linearity, and teleology could be taken for granted.

But as conditions move far from equilibrium and historical tendencies approach their limits, questions of dominance and emergence become radically uncertain: a tendency that appeared dominant under equilibrium conditions may unexpectedly yield to some other tendency, or an emergent tendency may suddenly become dominant. What's more, on a nonlinear view of history, where the magnitude of effects can be utterly disproportionate to that of causes, it is impossible to project at any given moment how close a tendency may be to its limits and thus how close the system itself may be to a bifurcation point. On the nonlinear view of history, time is utterly asymmetrical, and the future is radically unpredictable: assigning it a certain direction, much less an ultimate end, becomes entirely impracticable. This is the view presented by Marge Piercy in *Woman on the Edge of Time* (and quoted by Jameson at the very end of his introductory essay!) when the utopian visitors from "the future" explain their predicament to Connie, the protagonist of the present—for they and that future will not even exist if Connie and the people of her time do not succeed in their struggles: "We must fight to exist," the visitors explain, "to remain in existence, to be the future that happens."[35] For an emergent element to actually emerge and prevail, in other words, it must be actively affirmed. Connie's visitors are asking her for the same kind of libidinal cathexis that Piercy is arguably asking of her readers—the same kind of libidinal cathexis that affirmative nomadology provokes in us by effectively distilling commendable utopian principles from actual social practices, movements, and institutions.

Like Hardt and Negri's dialectical view, then, the nonlinear view of affirmative nomadology stresses the role of subjective agency in history, but for a very different reason: it is not that a will-to-be-against can simply be assumed but rather that historical change is, practically speaking, entirely up to us because the future of history itself is so radically unknowable. What's more, the unpredictability of bifurcation points means that the social-change experiments proposed by affirmative nomadology must not only be potential contributors to an eventual phase transition leading beyond capitalism and the State but must also be of immediate value in and of themselves, in the here and now—and not a dialectical negation or militant–ascetic sacrifice made for the sake of some wished-for but uncertain future. That bifurcation points are unpredictable does not mean, however, that careful assessment of actual historical circumstances isn't important. For affirmative nomadology, as we have seen, the point of creating philosophical concepts is precisely to map the lines-of-flight and virtual potential for beneficial social change residing in or alongside actual states of affairs; and the point of those concepts, in turn, is to encourage future experimentation along those lines-of-flight rather than merely to diagnose the ills of the present. The will-to-experiment of affirmative nomadology may ultimately require more utopian enthusiasm than Jameson is willing to allow.[36]

Negation

For Piercy's utopian visitors, the struggle for "their" future must be affirmed in the present for them to come into being. For Deleuze (drawing here on Nietzsche's notion of the eternal return), any being whatsoever must be affirmed for it to emerge from becoming and take on the consistency of actual existence. Affirmation, it is true, is not in itself a sufficient condition for actual emergence; it is only a necessary one. The other conditions for emergence compose the domain of the virtual, which is always richer in determinations and potentialities than the actual—hence the utopian vocation of political philosophy, as we have said, to map the virtual for the real potential it harbors to alleviate suffering and improve the prospects for life on earth.

When actually existing society is conceived of as a seamless and all-embracing totality, then unremitting radical critique and wholesale revolutionary transformation appear to be the only possible solutions, and their realization requires systematic negation. The dialectical leap of faith is that this first negation will itself undergo negation in turn and that this negation of the negation will produce a positive result. Nomadology does not harbor that kind of faith in linear or dialectical historical progress. Wholesale revolutionary transformation is a too-distant hope, and radical critique—even if it were totally successful—would merely cancel out all that is bad and produce precisely nothing as a result. This would be so, I hasten to add, unless the critique of society were conducted from the standpoint of certain ideals—whether implicit, as in satire, or explicit, as in utopia: in this case, the explicit affirmation of ideals may actually become more productive than a critique conducted implicitly in their name—as long as the ideals are instantiated in actually existing institutions and therefore compose part of the real–virtual conditions of existence of the society in question. This presupposes, of course, that society is not in fact a seamless totality but rather contains at least some positive instances that are worthy of affirmation, among all that is negative. In a similar way, the construction of philosophical concepts involves the selection of components that are to be affirmed rather than the negation of those to be rejected. The task of nomadological utopianism is then to detect and reinforce such alternative instances, distill and express the ideals informing them, then relay and propagate those ideals in additional institutions and practices throughout social life, in anticipation of pushing society to a tipping point beyond which they actually come to prevail.

Nomadological utopianism is not opposed to dialectical utopianism, just different. And nomadology does not require a critique of the dialectic, from which it would derive: it comes into being on its own account, through affirmation rather than negation—although it no doubt benefits from comparison with the more established mode of thought. To promote difference instead of opposition, comparison instead of critique: one aim of nomadology and one reason for this appendix.

Introduction

1. Deleuze and Guattari, *What Is Philosophy?*, 82, 52. In what follows, I retain Deleuze and Guattari's capitalization of *Important, Remarkable, Interesting,* and *Problem* to highlight the selective and nonrepresentational relation of the philosophical concept to problems in its sociohistorical milieu; I also capitalize *Intolerable* for much the same reason: what strikes a given philosophy as Intolerable or Significant in its milieu depends on its image of thought, which is highly selective. I capitalize *State* for a different reason, following standard usage in much political theory (including Deleuze and Guattari's): the State is a basic form of social organization, an ideal type; when I refer to particular states, the term is not capitalized.

2. As Massumi, *Parables for the Virtual*, 88, suggests, "belonging per se has emerged as a problem of global proportions. Perhaps *the* planetary problem."

3. For a survey of the range of citizenship venues with an interest similar to ours in extending citizenship beyond the nation-state, see Hanagan and Tilly, *Extending Citizenship, Reconfiguring States*.

4. Appadurai, "Patriotism and Its Futures," 421.

5. Ibid., 411.

6. Ibid., 413–14.

7. Ibid., 421.

8. Ibid., 428.

9. Letter, Thomas Jefferson to Henry Lee, August 10, 1824, as cited in Cooper, *An Ethic of Citizenship for Public Administration*, 81.

10. On schizoanalysis, see Deleuze and Guattari, *Anti-Oedipus*, and my *Deleuze and Guattari's Anti-Oedipus*. On affective citizenship, see my "Affective Citizenship and the Death-State." See also the groundbreaking work of Rose, *States of Fantasy*, and of Berlant, including *Anatomy of National Fantasy* and *Queen of America Goes to Washington City*; see also the more recent work of Pease, *New American Exceptionalism*.

11. Derrida, *Politics of Friendship,* 104.

12. Ibid., 158–59; he is no doubt trying to avoid choice and decision as an anti-Schmittian tactic, among other reasons.

13. Derrida, ibid., 105, wants to "think and live a politics, a friendship, a justice which *begin* by breaking with their naturalness or their homogeneity, with their alleged place of origin"—to which we here add thinking and living a citizenship that begins, or that has already begun, by breaking with its naturalized State form and that place or space of foundation.

14. For in modernity, the nation-State was supposed to have replaced religion as the prime focal point for personal identity and social belonging, partly by claiming a monopoly on legitimated violence. One index of the asymmetry between modernity and postmodernity is that there is not, and probably cannot be, a "religious citizenship." For a sense of the panic this asymmetry provokes among State theorists, see Schmitt, "Theory of the Partisan," 63, who will do his best to assure that "the partisan's irregularity remains dependent on the sense and content of a concrete regularity" and that the real, i.e., State-defined, enemy does not become an "absolute" enemy—although it must be said that the "new partisanship" about which Schmitt was concerned at the time was revolutionary communism rather than religious fundamentalism. See also Watson, "Oil Wars."

15. On fascist tendencies in the Bush regime, see my "Schizoanalysis, Nomadology, Fascism"; Pease, *New American Exceptionalism;* Hedges, *American Fascists;* Dean, *Conservatives without Conscience;* and Altemeyer, *Authoritarian Specter.*

16. On the importance of this kind of enduring or systemic violence, see Žižek, *Violence.*

17. On primitive accumulation in Marx, see esp. *Capital,* vol. 1, part VIII, chapters 26–33, in Marx and Engels, *Collected Works;* on the "secret history" of primitive accumulation in English political economy, see Perelman, *Invention of Capitalism.*

18. A major resource here is, of course, the entire anarchist tradition; among recent works, I have found the following most useful: Holloway, *Change the World without Taking Power;* Knowles, *Political Economy from Below;* Purkis and Bowen, *Changing Anarchism;* Ward, *Anarchism;* Meltzer, *Anarchism;* and Taylor, *Possibility of Cooperation.* On the relations between anarchism and the poststructuralist theory on which we draw here, see Koch, "Poststructuralism and the Epistemological Basis of Anarchism," and esp. the excellent work of May, including "Is Poststructuralist Political Theory Anarchist?" and *Political Philosophy of Poststructuralist Anarchism.* See also, from a quite different perspective, Cassirer, *Myth of the State.*

19. See Young, *Justice and the Politics of Difference* and *Inclusion and Democracy.* I hasten to add that anarchism can be considered a pitfall only insofar as it restricts itself exclusively to small-scale, face-to-face groups, as most anarchist theory tends to do; the concept of free-market communism is designed to overcome this limitation, among other things.

20. See Rosanvallon, *L'âge de l'autogestion* and *Democracy Past and Future.*

21. See, e.g., Archer, *Economic Democracy*; Dow, *Governing the Firm*; and Ellerman, *Democratic Worker-Owned Firm.*

22. See Follett, *Freedom and Coordination, Dynamic Administration, Mary Parker Follett,* and *New State.*

23. Deleuze and Guattari, *What Is Philosophy?,* 28.

24. See my *Deleuze and Guattari's Anti-Oedipus,* esp. xi–xii; "Studies in Applied Nomadology"; and "Jazz Improvisation." More recently, Eagleton has gone as far as to take jazz group improvisation as an image of the "good life"; see the concluding pages of his *Meaning of Life,* 171–74. For Deleuze and Guattari's presentation of nomadism, see their "Treatise on Nomadology," Plateau 12 of *A Thousand Plateaus.*

25. Brian Massumi, Manuel DeLanda and John Protevi have all emphasized this aspect of Deleuze and Guattari's thought: see Massumi, *User's Guide to Capitalism and Schizophrenia*; DeLanda, *A Thousand Years of Nonlinear History* and *Intensive Science and Virtual Philosophy*; Protevi, *Political Affect* and *Political Physics*; and Protevi and Bonta, *Deleuze and Geophilosophy.* See the appendix for further discussion of the relevance of complexity and nonlinearity to affirmative nomadology.

26. See Kauffman, *Origins of Order* and *At Home in the Universe.* For more general accounts, see Mainzer, *Thinking in Complexity*; Taylor, *Moment of Complexity*; and Johnson, *Emergence.*

27. Deleuze and Guattari, *What Is Philosophy?,* 52.

28. In addition to Derrida's *Politics of Friendship,* see, e.g., Archibugi et al., *Re-imagining Political Community*; Beiner, *Theorizing Citizenship*; Agamben, *Coming Community*; Nancy, *Inoperative Community*; and Miami Theory Collective, *Community at Loose Ends.*

29. Van Gunsteren, *A Theory of Citizenship,* 10. See also Taylor's notion of *partial communities* (although given his philosophical commitments, they are destined for eventual unification) in *Hegel and Modern Society,* esp. 111–18.

30. Van Gunsteren, *A Theory of Citizenship,* 26.

31. Ibid.

32. See Nancy, *Inoperative Community;* he revisits the term in "Around the Notion of Literary Communism," in *Multiple Arts,* 22–34.

33. Nancy and Deleuze and Guattari also have very different—even opposed—senses of the term *immanent.*

34. Nancy, *Inoperative Community,* 78.

35. Deleuze and Guattari, *Anti-Oedipus,* 25.

36. Nancy, *Experience of Freedom,* 95.

37. For a serviceable though uncritical historical survey of European accounts of self-organizing social systems, both political and economic, see Barry, "Tradition of Spontaneous Order."

38. Braudel, *Capitalism and Material Life: 1400–1800;* for a useful review, see

DeLanda, "Markets and Antimarkets in the World Economy" and "Meshworks, Hierarchies, and Interfaces."

39. See my *Introduction to Schizoanalysis,* 59–60, 80–82, and *Studies in Applied Nomadology,* 30–31.

40. Surowiecki, *Wisdom of Crowds.* See also, for a more enthusiastic but less rigorous account, Rheingold, *Smart Mobs.* For a similar view rooted in insect ethology and artificial intelligence, see Kennedy et al., *Swarm Intelligence.*

41. Or is it the other way around? Perelman, *Invention of Capitalism,* shows that State power was essential in the initial establishment of capitalism, and it may be only recently that economic antimarket forces have ultimately prevailed over political ones.

42. Deleuze, *Foucault.*

43. Deleuze, "Five Propositions on Psychoanalysis," in *Desert Islands and Other Texts,* 274–80. He goes on to explain that "for that very reason, we no longer want to talk about schizoanalysis, because that would amount to protecting a particular type of escape, schizophrenic escape" (280).

44. On the concept of the war-machine and its relations to earlier concepts from *Anti-Oedipus,* see my "Schizoanalysis, Nomadology, Fascism" and "Affirmative Nomadology and the War Machine."

45. Deleuze and Guattari, *A Thousand Plateaus,* 43.

46. On the relations between schizoanalysis and pragmatics, see also ibid., 146, 227.

47. There is reason to suppose that such a denial of any master allegiance to the State might be linked to the critique of monotheism, particularly given the recent recognition of the inseparability of religion and nationalism, but making the argument lies well beyond the scope of this book.

48. See my *Introduction to Schizoanalysis.*

49. For the feminist uptake of Follett's work, see Allen, "Rethinking Power," esp. 33–37; Starhawk, *Truth or Dare,* esp. 9–19; Hartsock, "Political Change"; and Carroll, "Peace Research." As Allen notes, Hannah Ardent's notion that power is intrinsically related to groups rather than individuals is very similar to (if not influenced by) Follett's views; for Arendt's definition of *power,* see *On Revolution,* esp. 170–75, and *On Violence,* esp. 44, where she writes that "power corresponds to the human ability not just to act but to act in concert. Power is never the property of an individual; it belongs to a group and remains in existence only so long as the group keeps together."

50. Holland, "Utopian Dimension of Thought in Deleuze and Guattari," esp. 218–20.

51. For a similar challenge to the State form and orthodox Marxism, see Hardt and Negri, *Labor of Dionysus.*

52. See Federici, *Caliban and the Witch,* and Mies, *Patriarchy and Accumulation on a World Scale.*

53. Important contributions to a Deleuzian feminism, if not a feminist nomadology per se, include the following: Braidotti, *Metamorphoses*, "Becoming-Woman," "Toward a New Nomadism," and *Nomadic Subjects*; Grosz, *Time Travels*, "A Thousand Tiny Sexes," and *Volatile Bodies*; Colebrook and Buchanan, *Deleuze and Feminist Theory*; and Buchanan, "Becoming-Woman and the World-Historical." At a slightly greater remove, but still consonant with many aspects of Deleuze and Guattari's thought, see Gibson-Graham, *End of Capitalism* and *A Postcapitalist Politics*; Keller, *Making Sense of Life*; Haraway, *Simians, Cyborgs, and Women*; and Fuss, *Essentially Speaking*.

54. On minor or "ambulant" science as problem posing rather than problem solving, see the "Treatise on Nomadology" in Deleuze and Guattari, *A Thousand Plateaus*, esp. 361–80: "the ambulant sciences quickly overstep the possibility of calculation [by means of which one would solve a problem]: they inhabit that 'more' that exceeds the space of reproduction and soon run into problems that are insurmountable from that point of view; they eventually resolve them by means of a real-life operation. . . . The ambulant sciences confine themselves to *inventing problems* whose solution is tied to a whole set of collective, non-scientific activities" (374).

55. Ibid., 374.

56. Deleuze and Foucault, "Intellectuals and Power," 206.

1. From Political Philosophy to Affirmative Nomadology

1. Deleuze and Guattari, *What Is Philosophy?*, 85.

2. Ibid., 64.

3. Ibid., 110.

4. Ibid., 95.

5. On geophilosophy, see Deleuze and Guattari, *What Is Philosophy?*, 85–113; on geohistory, see Braudel, *Mediterranean and the Mediterranean World in the Age of Philip II*, *On History*, and *Capitalism and Material Life*.

6. Deleuze and Guattari, *What Is Philosophy?*, 96.

7. Thought as a response to chaos is by no means limited to philosophy; in fact, Deleuze and Guattari discuss the relations of thinking philosophically to thinking through religion, science, and the arts at length in *What Is Philosophy?*, 8. I limit myself mostly to philosophical thought here for reasons of expediency and clarity of exposition.

8. Deleuze and Guattari, *What Is Philosophy?*, 42.

9. Ibid., 48.

10. Ibid., 38.

11. Ibid., 47.

12. Deleuze and Guattari's plane of immanence thus bears comparison with Derrida's notion of *différance* (free play in a structure of differences without a

transcendent center) and with Foucault's concept of *episteme*. Althusser's wrestling with the idea of "determination by the economy in the last instance" whose "lonely hour never comes" (and which, if it ever arrived, would stop thought at a final determination) is another contemporary illustration, and it is not clear whether having the economic determine which instance is dominant rather than being itself the dominant instance rescues his structural causality model from transcendence; see Althusser, "Contradiction and Overdetermination" and "On the Materialist Dialectic" in *For Marx*, 87–128 and 161–218. In *Difference and Repetition*, 186, Deleuze suggests that "'the economic [instance]' is never given properly speaking, but rather designates a differential virtuality to be interpreted, always covered over by its forms of actualization."

13. Deleuze and Guattari, *What Is Philosophy?*, 37–42.

14. Ibid., 61–83.

15. Ibid., 64.

16. Ibid., 70.

17. Deleuze, *Difference and Repetition*, 227.

18. Deleuze, *Logic of Sense*, xiii.

19. Deleuze and Guattari, *What Is Philosophy?*, 16.

20. Ibid., 103.

21. Ibid., 28.

22. Ibid., 99–100.

23. Although they do allow that "in view of the mutilated meaning public opinion has given to it, perhaps *utopia* is not the best word"; ibid., 100.

24. Ibid., 99.

25. Ibid., 99–100.

26. Ibid., 108.

27. Ibid., 110.

28. Ibid., 100.

29. To put the question in terms of another distinction that Deleuze and Guattari make in the "Treatise on Nomadology" in *A Thousand Plateaus*, 351–423, is philosophy to be considered work or free action? "The two ideal models of the motor are those of work and *free action*. Work is a motor cause that meets resistance, operates on the exterior, is consumed and spent in its effect, and must be renewed from one moment to the next. Free action is also a motor cause, but one that has no resistance to overcome, operates only upon the mobile body itself, is not consumed in its effect, and continues from one moment to the next" (397). Here Deleuze and Guattari rejoin Nancy, provided we are able to rescue the concept of production from that of work (see the introduction).

30. Deleuze, *Nietzsche and Philosophy*.

31. Deleuze and Guattari, *What Is Philosophy?*, 97–99. Geophilosophy: "From the point of view of philosophy's development, there is no necessary continuity passing from Greece to Europe through the intermediary of Christianity; there is

the contingent recommencement of a same contingent process, in different conditions" (98). "The birth of philosophy required the conjunction of two very different movements of deterritorialization, the relative and the absolute, the first already at work in immanence. Absolute deterritorialization of the plane of thought had to be aligned or directly connected with the relative deterritorialization of Greek society" (92).

32. Ibid., 98.

33. Goux, *Symbolic Economies*, and Sohn-Rethel, *Intellectual and Manual Labor.*

34. See Deleuze, *Difference and Repetition*, 1, on the importance of and relation between "the quantitative order of equivalences" and "the qualitative order of resemblances" as the two principal antagonists of difference.

35. Deleuze and Guattari, *What Is Philosophy?*, 101.

36. On thought or theory as a relay between one practical orientation and the next, see Deleuze and Foucault, "Intellectuals and Power."

37. Deleuze and Guattari, *What Is Philosophy?*, 108, 218.

38. Ibid., 72.

39. Ibid., 18.

40. Deleuze and Guattari, *A Thousand Plateaus*, 22. In the same vein, they assert that "the book is not an image of the world. It forms a rhizome with the world" (11). See also Deleuze and Guattari, *What Is Philosophy?*, esp. 22, "The [philosophical] concept is defined by its consistency . . . but it has no *reference*: it is self-referential," and 79, "Since [philosophical] concepts are not propositional, they cannot refer to problems concerning the extensional conditions of propositions assimilable to those of science"; see also 82.

41. See esp. Deleuze and Guattari, *What Is Philosophy?*, chapter 5, "Functives and Concepts," 117–33; but see also 23–24, 33, 42, 79–80. Deleuze and Guattari draw a similar distinction in the opening pages of *A Thousand Plateaus* between (scientific) tracing and (philosophical) mapping: "What distinguishes the map from the tracing is that it [the map] is entirely oriented toward an experimentation in contact with the real" (13). Later in *A Thousand Plateaus*, however, they present a far more complex view of science and distinguish between royal and nomad science, as we shall see.

42. "Philosophy invents modes of existence or possibilities of life"; Deleuze and Guattari, *What Is Philosophy?*, 72. Such invention is clearly not representational. See Patton's excellent account of Deleuze and Guattari's philosophical endeavors in *Deleuze and the Political*, in which he observes, regarding precisely the issue of nomadism, that Deleuze and Guattari "are engaged in the invention of a concept rather than empirical social science" (117).

43. Deleuze and Guattari, *What Is Philosophy?*, 66, 65.

44. And despite that Guattari treated schizophrenics at the LaBorde Clinic he codirected; see Deleuze and Guattari, *Anti-Oedipus*, 380.

45. Deleuze and Guattari, *What Is Philosophy?*, 70. The relations between conceptual personae and psychosocial types are complex: "The features of conceptual personae have relationships with the epoch or historical milieu in which they appear that only psychosocial types enable us to assess. But, conversely, the physical and mental movements of psychosocial types, their pathological symptoms, their relational attributes, their existential modes, and their legal status, become susceptible to a determination of thinking and thought that wrests them from both the historical state of affairs of a society and the lived experience of individuals, in order to turn them into the features of conceptual personae, or *thought-events* on the plane [of immanence] laid out by thought or under the concepts it creates. Conceptual personae and psychosocial types refer to each other . . . without ever merging" (70).

46. Ibid., 16; see also 79.

47. Ibid., 82.

48. Deleuze and Guattari, *A Thousand Plateaus*, 11–15.

49. Deleuze and Guattari, *What Is Philosophy?*, 50, 52, 69.

50. Ibid., 52.

51. See Deleuze, *Difference and Repetition*, 212: "The virtual possesses the reality of a task to be performed or a problem to be solved: it is the problem which orientates, conditions and engenders [actual] solutions."

52. Deleuze and Guattari, *What Is Philosophy?*, 156.

53. Ibid., 118.

54. Ibid., 122.

55. Deleuze, *Difference and Repetition*, xx, 287. In the preface, Deleuze explains that one of the two lines of research underlying the book is "a concept of repetition in which physical, mechanical or bare repetitions (repetition of the Same) would find their *raison d'être* in the more profound structures of a hidden repetition in which a 'differential' is disguised and displaced" (xx).

56. On "clothed" or "covered" or "disguised" repetition, see ibid., 18, 24, 84, 287, 302.

57. Deleuze and Guattari, *What Is Philosophy?*, 71–72.

58. On smooth vs. striated space, see Plateau 14, "1440: The Smooth and the Striated," in Deleuze and Guattari, *A Thousand Plateaus*, 474–500.

59. Ibid., 380.

60. See the introduction, n. 25.

61. See Bell, "Of the Rise and Progress of Historical Concepts," *Deleuze's Hume*, and *Philosophy at the Edge of Chaos*.

62. Hjelmslev, *Prolegomena to a Theory of Language*, and Hjelmslev and Uldall, *Outline of Glossematics*. For the critique of hylomorphism accompanying the replacement of Saussure with Hjelmslev, see Deleuze and Guattari, *A Thousand Plateaus*, 408–9, and Simondon, *Du mode d'existence des objets techniques*.

63. As Deleuze and Guattari say in the "Treatise on Nomadology," in *A Thou-*

sand Plateaus, 408, "it is a question of surrendering to the wood, then following where it leads by connecting operations to a materiality, instead of imposing a form on matter: what one addresses is less a matter submitted to laws than a materiality possessing a *nomos.*" In a similar vein, Cage (in "Music for Carillon") writes a musical score on a piece of wood so that the wood grain becomes part of the musical notation; cited in Herzogenrath, "The 'Weather of Music,'" 22.

64. Deleuze and Guattari, *What Is Philosophy?,* 177–84.

65. Ibid., 166. In a similar vein, jazz guitarist Bailey will argue in *Musical Improvisation,* 117–18, that "although some improvisers employ a high level of technical skill in their playing, to speak of 'mastering' the instrument in improvisation is misleading. The instrument is not just a tool but an ally. It is not only a means to an end, it is a source of material, and technique for the improviser is often an exploitation of the natural resources of the instrument. . . . Almost any aspect of playing an instrument can reveal music. . . . The instrument's responsiveness to its acoustic environment, how it reacts to other instruments and how it reacts to the physical aspects of performing, can vary enormously. The accidental can be exploited through the amount of control exercised over the instrument, from complete—producing exactly what the player dictates—to none at all—letting the instrument have its say."

66. Deleuze and Guattari, *A Thousand Plateaus,* 361.

67. Gould, *Structure of Evolutionary Theory* and *Wonderful Life;* for further implications, see Kauffman, *At Home in the Universe.*

68. In this connection, Deleuze and Guattari, *A Thousand Plateaus,* 372, insist that "a distinction must be made between two types of science, or scientific procedures: one consists in 'reproducing,' the other in 'following.' The first involves reproduction, iteration, and reiteration; the other, involving itineration is the sum of the itinerant, ambulant sciences. . . . The ideal of reproduction, deduction, or induction is part of royal science, at all times and in all places, and treats differences in time and place as so many variables, the constant form of which is extracted precisely by the law: for the same phenomena to recur in a gravitational and striated space it is sufficient for the same conditions to obtain. . . . Reproducing implies the permanence of a fixed point of *view* that is external to what is reproduced: watching the flow from the bank. But following is something different. . . . One is obliged to follow when one is in search of the 'singularities' of a matter, or rather of a material, and not out to discover a form; when one escapes the force of gravity to enter a field of celerity . . . when one engages in a continuous variation of variables, instead of extracting constants from them."

69. Ibid., 462; translation modified.

70. Ibid., 368.

71. On the relations between prestige or power and the intellectual capital that may be necessary to perform skilled vs. unskilled labor, see Sohn-Rethel, *Intellectual and Manual Labor.*

72. Deleuze and Guattari, *A Thousand Plateaus*, 456.

73. Ibid., 463.

74. Bacon, *Advancement of Learning*.

75. Deleuze and Guattari, *A Thousand Plateaus*, 456.

76. This is a key conclusion of Simondon, *Du mode d'existence des objets techniques*.

77. Deleuze and Guattari, *A Thousand Plateaus*, 456; emphasis added.

78. I am in what follows intentionally using a fairly broad construction of what counts as jazz, a topic that lends itself to considerable controversy. I am not concerned, for example, with distinguishing European and African components within or contributions to jazz; nor am I claiming that jazz is the only musical genre in which improvisation occurs or that it always occurs there; nor I am taking into account either jazz composition or solo jazz performance, both of which certainly merit the name "jazz." By jazz here I mean live group jazz improvisation, which involves musicians (1) working at most from a chord chart (not a score), if not from nothing at all, and (2) trading solos (usually of unpredictable length) between choruses or engaging in call-and-response-style conversations among individuals within the group. (Group jazz improvisation can, of course, be recorded, but the fleeting event of interactive creativity thereby gets frozen for eternity.)

79. On the distinctions in various games between smooth and striated space, nomad and State movement, *nomos* and *polis,* see the beginning of the "Treatise on Nomadology" plateau of Deleuze and Guattari, *A Thousand Plateaus,* 352–53.

80. Holland, "Introduction to the Non-Fascist Life"; "Studies in Applied Nomadology"; and "Jazz Improvisation."

81. For an extended analysis of soccer, but without the focus on team dynamics, see chapter 3, "The Political Economy of Belonging and the Logic of Relation," in Massumi, *Parables for the Virtual,* esp. 71–79.

82. Of course, there is always a—comparatively—small margin of "artistic interpretation" in classical music performance (compared, that is, to improvisational jazz, where that margin moves to the center), and individual improvisation has been and is important in musical genres other than jazz—in the early baroque period and in Indian ragas, for example—but these important exceptions do not alter the basic distinction between the forms of social organization and interaction of the jazz group and the modern symphony orchestra: in one, coordination is strictly immanent to the group process, whereas in the other, coordination is imposed from above by a transcendent instance of command.

83. Deleuze and Guattari, *A Thousand Plateaus*, 397.

84. Canneti, *Crowds and Power*.

85. Ibid., 394.

86. Ibid., 395–96.

87. Ibid., 395.

88. Ibid.

89. Compare what Bailey, *Musical Improvisation,* 116, has to say about the difference between improvising and performing from a precomposed score: "One reason why the standard Western instrumental training produces non-improvisers (and it doesn't just produce violinists, pianists, cellists, etcetera: it produces specifically non-improvisers, musicians rendered incapable of attempting improvisation) is that not only does it teach how to play an instrument, it teaches that the creation of music is a separate activity from playing that instrument. Learning how to create music is a separate study totally divorced from playing an instrument. Music for the instrumentalist is a set of written symbols which he interprets as best he can. They, the symbols, are the music, and the man who wrote them, the composer, is the music-maker. The instrument is the medium through which the composer finally transmits his ideas. The instrumentalist is not required to make music. He can assist with his 'interpretation' perhaps, but, judging from most reported remarks on the subject, composers prefer the instrumentalist to limit his contribution to providing the instrument, keeping it in tune and being able to use it to carry out, as accurately as possible, any instructions which might be given to him. The improviser's view of the instrument is totally different."

90. Of course, those rules *(nomoi)* themselves vary, as does therefore the degree of improvisation—so, for example, big bands, where discrete individual solos punctuate an otherwise composed piece, would lie at one end of a spectrum, on the other end of which would be free jazz, where at the limit everyone is improvising all the time.

91. Deleuze and Guattari, *A Thousand Plateaus,* 416.

92. Ibid., 417.

93. Ibid.

94. Ibid., 422.

95. Ibid., 417.

96. Ibid., 366. For an analysis of the relations between nomadism and the war-machine, see my "Affirmative Nomadology and the War Machine." Because war-machines have such a variable relation to war itself, Patton, *Deleuze and the Political,* 110–20, cogently argues for calling them "metamorphosis-machines" instead. Deleuze and Guattari, *A Thousand Plateaus,* 360, themselves explain that "the war machine's form of exteriority is such that it exists only in its own metamorphoses; it exists in an industrial innovation as well as in a technological invention, in a commercial circuit as well as in a religious creation, in all flows and currents that only secondarily allow themselves to be appropriated by the State," and then they contrast "war machines of metaphorphosis" with "State apparatuses of identity" (361).

97. De Certeau, *Practice of Everyday Life.*

98. Deleuze and Guattari, *A Thousand Plateaus,* 473.

99. Ibid., 473; see also 220, 464.

100. Von Clausewitz, cited in ibid., 467.

101. Ibid., 467.

102. Ibid., 423.

103. Deleuze, *Foucault,* 89: "the final word is that *resistance comes first.*"

104. In a long note surveying the agreements between Foucault's positions and their own in the "Several Regimes of Signs" plateau (111–48), Deleuze and Guattari, *A Thousand Plateaus,* end by saying that "our only points of disagreement with Foucault are [that] (1) to us the assemblages seem fundamentally to be assemblages not of power but of desire (desire is always assembled), and power seems to be a stratified dimension of the assemblage; (2) the diagram and the abstract machine have lines of flight that are primary, which are not phenomena of resistance or counter-attack in an assemblage, but cutting edges of creation and deterritorialization" (530–31n39).

105. Deleuze and Guattari, *A Thousand Plateaus,* 417; emphasis added.

106. Ibid., 423.

107. Ibid., 499.

108. Ibid., 377.

109. Deleuze and Guattari, *What Is Philosophy?,* 71.

110. On surfing as an image of nomadic thought, where entering into an existing wave replaces occupying points of leverage or absolute origin, see Deleuze, "Mediators," in *Negotiations,* 121–34, esp. 121.

111. Deleuze and Guattari, *What Is Philosophy?,* 106.

112. Ibid., 102.

113. Ibid., 104.

114. Ibid., 110.

115. Ibid., 28.

116. Ibid., 107.

117. Ibid.

2. Death-State Citizenship

1. Deleuze and Guattari, *Anti-Oedipus* and *A Thousand Plateaus.*

2. Deleuze and Guattari, *Anti-Oedipus,* 217–22

3. For the argument against "evolutionism" (according to which a State would have evolved smoothly from pre-State societies), see Deleuze and Guattari, *A Thousand Plateaus,* 427–35.

4. This transfer is accomplished through the process often called *primitive accumulation,* discussed at length in chapter 4.

5. While the content of civil law in the liberal State may be up for negotiation between citizens and the State, the obligation to obey is not; as the great theorist of State power, Thomas Hobbes, *De Cive,* 181, put it, "[The] obligation to civill obedience, by virtue whereof the civill Laws are valid, is before all civill Law."

6. On the enduring relation between biopower and death, see Mbembe, "Necropolitics," and, esp., Braidotti, "Biomacht und nekro-Politik."

7. The key work is Clastres, *Society against the State*; but see also his *Archaeology of Violence,* esp. chapter 6, "Power in Primitive Societies," 87–92.

8. Clastres, *Society against the State, 213–18.*

9. As in the potlatch ceremonies analyzed by Marcel Mauss, this form of redistribution of wealth also serves to ward off the accumulation of power on the part of the chief.

10. For Deleuze and Guattari's debate with Clastres, see *A Thousand Plateaus,* 357–59. They will conclude that "the State seems to rise up in a single stroke, in an imperial form, and does not depend on progressive factors. Its on-the-spot emergence is like a stroke of genius, the birth of Athena" (359). In both volumes of *Capitalism and Schizophrenia,* Deleuze and Guattari quote from Nietzsche *(The Genealogy of Morals)* and Kafka ("The Great Wall of China") to evoke the sense of rupture or absolute discontinuity that characterizes the violent imposition of State rule. The quotation from Nietzsche reads as follows: "They came like fate, without reason, consideration, or pretext. . . . They appear as lightning appears, too terrible, too sudden." The quotation from Kafka reads as follows: "They have pushed right into the capital, although it is a long way from the frontier. At any rate, here they are; it seems every morning there are more of them. . . . Speech with the [conquering] nomads is impossible. They do not know our own language." See Deleuze and Guattari, *Anti-Oedipus,* 195, and *A Thousand Plateaus,* 265, 353.

11. Derrida, "Force of Law," and Benjamin, "Critique of Violence." See also Hamacher, "Afformative, Strike."

12. See Schmitt, *Concept of the Political,* 45.

13. Clastres, *Society against the State,* 2; and on the internal function of war waging, see his *Archeology of Violence,* esp. 139–95.

14. For a recent examination of the variability of policing in the "police state," see Foucault, *Birth of Biopolitics,* esp. 51–60.

15. See his famous essay on the three stages of citizenship: Marshall, "Citizenship and Social Class."

16. Delegation of the enforcement of labor contracts to the State involves a refunctioning of the imperial State, which merely appropriated surpluses arising from preexisting political relations among the conquered peoples; we return to the contrast between direct (political) subordination and indirect (economic) subordination through exploitation in chapter 4.

17. On the State's appropriation or encastment of the war-machine, see the Nomadology plateau of Deleuze and Guattari, *A Thousand Plateaus,* 351–423, esp. 386, 418–21.

18. Buber, "Society and the State."

19. Hegel, *Philosophy of Right;* Fichte, *Addresses to the German Nation,* esp. 101–41, 223–24.

20. Derrida, *Politics of Friendship.*

21. Weber, *Politics as a Vocation;* the classic formulation is found in Weber, *Theory of Social and Economic Organization:* an entity is a "'state' if and insofar

as its administrative staff successfully upholds a claim on the monopoly of the legitimate use of violence in the enforcement of its order" (154).

22. Appadurai, "Full Attachment," 445.

23. Ibid., 447.

24. Ibid., 445.

25. Deleuze and Guattari, *Anti-Oedipus,* 264.

26. Brown, *Life against Death.*

27. On the historical variability of family forms and their effects on psychic structure and dynamics, see, in addition to Deleuze and Guattari, *Anti-Oedipus,* Poster, *Critical Theory of the Family.*

28. Brown, *Life against Death,* 19.

29. On the transformation of death into an instinct, see Deleuze and Guattari, *Anti-Oedipus,* 184, 199, 213, 223, 262, 329–37; see also my *Deleuze and Guattari's Anti-Oedipus,* 95–96, and "Infinite Subjective Representation and the Perversion of Death."

30. Bataille, *Accursed Share.*

31. Lacan may have been the first to highlight the significance of *nachträglichkeit,* which he translated as *"après coup,"* in "Function and Field of Speech and Language in Psychoanalysis." Laplanche and Pontalis then developed the concept, first in "Fantasy and the Origins of Sexuality," and then in *Language of Psychoanalysis.*

32. On states as models of realization of the capitalist axiomatic, see Deleuze and Guattari, *A Thousand Plateaus,* 454–65.

33. Anderson, *Imagined Communities.*

34. For a similar view, but expressed in terms of "welfare rewards" rather than power rewards, see Wallerstein, "Global Possibilities," 226–43, esp. 234–36, 239–42.

35. We will have occasion to distinguish between the quality of power felt in these two instances: protection from excluded others involves what we will call *power-over,* whereas provision for those included within the nation involves *power-with*; see chapter 3.

36. Fichte, *Addresses to the German Nation.* For more on fantasies of Motherland and Fatherland, see Hage, *Against Paranoid Nationalism,* and Davis, *Deracination.* At the dawn of the modern age, Rousseau detected with characteristic clarity the growing gap between Motherland and Fatherland—see his *Confessions,* esp. vol. 1. Note how Motherland and Fatherland take up the protection–mediation–provision functions outlined by Clastres, with the Motherland offering provisions, the Fatherland offering protection, and "mediation" falling in between the two: establishing harmony is a function of the Motherland (customs, mores, culture as shared expectations), whereas attempting to resolve conflict from on high when harmony breaks down is a feature of the Fatherland.

37. Lakoff, *Moral Politics.*

38. Ibid., 108. On the family metaphor as it resonates throughout American political rhetoric, see ibid., 153–61, 322–31.

39. Oddly enough, Lakoff, ibid., himself avoids calling this second ideal the Nurturant Mother worldview, as symmetry would lead one to expect, claiming that "[al]though this model of the family seems to have begun as a woman's model, it has now become widespread in America among both sexes" (108); but of course, the Strict Father ideal is also widespread among both sexes, so we retain the term *Nuturant Mother* to accentuate the degree to which, like Fichte's Motherland and Fatherland, political rhetoric resonates with the positions and dynamics of the nuclear family. There may be reason to speculate that Benedict Anderson's nation, as an imagined or Imaginary community comprising nurturing horizontal affiliations, resonates with ideals of the Motherland, with the strict Fatherland tied more closely to the Symbolic order.

40. Ibid., 33–34, 65–140.

41. Young, "Responsibility and Global Justice."

42. The individual–retributive model is deeply ingrained in our culture and resonates powerfully with (in the narrowly Schmittian sense) political distinctions between friend and enemy and religious distinctions between the saved and the damned. With respect to the latter, Connolly proposes a model of collective responsibility opposed to much Christian ethics and akin to Young's; see his *Identity/Difference*, esp. chapter 4.

43. Federal taxes paid by corporations paid for about 25 percent of federal government expenditures in the 1950s; in the 1960s, that portion fell to 20 percent; by the early years of the presidency of George W. Bush (2002–3), the portion of government expenditures paid for by corporate taxes had fallen to 6 percent. Likewise, while the amount of corporate taxes paid in 1960 was about 4 percent of gross domestic product, it had dropped to about 1 percent by 2003. See McIntyre and Nguyen, "Corporate Income Taxes in the Bush Years," 8. See also the Center for Budget and Policy Priorities, "Decline of Corporate Income Tax Revenues," http://www.cbpp.org/files/10-16-03tax.pdf.

44. Marshall, "Citizenship and Social Class."

45. That war is the fundamental raison d'être of the State is a favorite theme of anarchist critique. See, e.g., Bourne, *War and the Intellectuals*, 69–70: "War is essentially the health of the state. . . . The State is the organization of the herd to act offensively or defensively against another herd similarly organized. War sends the current of purpose and activity flowing down to the lowest level of the herd, and to its most remote branches. All the activities of society are linked together as fast as possible to this central purpose of making a military offensive or military defense, and the State [finally] becomes what in peacetime it has vainly struggled to become. . . . The slack is taken up, cross-currents fade out, and the nation moves lumberingly and slowly, but with ever accelerated speed and integration, towards the great end, . . . that *peacefulness of being at war.*" For a historical analysis coming to much the same conclusion, see Tilly, *Coercion, Capital, and European States.* But see also, from a very different perspective, using war as a heuristic, Foucault, *Society Must Be Defended,* 18, who considers "the extent to which the binary

schema of war and struggle, of the clash between forces, can really be identified as the basis of civil society, as both the principle and motor of the exercise of political power."

46. This is not as surprising as it may at first sound: for according to schizoanalysis, the nuclear family structure reproduces in domesticated form the libidinal dynamics of the despotic State, with the Father taking on the position of the Despot; see Deleuze and Guattari, *Anti-Oedipus*, esp. chapter 3. What Deleuze and Guattari fail to note is that the segregation of the modern nuclear family from all other social and extended-family relations foregrounds the binary pair, mother–father, and henceforth provides a resonating chamber for affective political dynamics revolving around the Motherland–Fatherland binary.

47. Buber, "Society and the State."

48. For an extended meditation on this dependency, see Brown, *States of Injury*.

49. Marcuse, *Eros and Civilization*.

50. Foucault, *History of Sexuality*, esp. 1:140–41: "there was an explosion of numerous and diverse techniques for achieving the subjugation of bodies and the control of populations, marking the beginning of an era of 'bio-power.' . . . This bio-power was without question an indispensable element in the development of capitalism; the latter would not have been possible without the controlled insertion of bodies into the machinery of production and the adjustment of the phenomena of population to economic processes. But this was not all it required; it also needed the growth of both these factors, their reinforcement as well as their availability and docility; it had to have methods of power capable of optimizing forces, aptitudes, and life in general without at the same time making them more difficult to govern. . . . The adjustment of the accumulation of men to that of capital, the joining of the growth of human groups to the expansion of productive forces and the differential allocation of profit, were made possible in part by the exercise of bio-power in its many forms and modes of application."

51. Holland, *Baudelaire and Schizoanalysis*.

52. President George W. Bush is mentioned twice in a meta-analysis of the psychology of conservatism that identifies these key features of the cognitive style and motivational needs of conservatives: fear of death and of system instability, intolerance of ambiguity (closed-mindedness), need for order, inability to manage integrative complexity, and lower self-esteem. See Jost et al., "Political Conservatism as Motivated Social Cognition."

53. For a thorough study of the born-again or Christian fundamentalist personality, based on extensive interviews, see Strozier, *Apocalypse*; for some implications and cultural manifestations, see Davis, *Death's Dream Kingdom*.

54. President Bush notoriously asserted, "I don't do nuance." See Jost et al., "Political Conservatism as Motivated Social Cognition," 353n8.

55. Lakoff, *Moral Politics,* 73, 97.

56. See also ibid., 71–73.

57. For extended treatments of narcissism as a schizoanalytic category, see my

Baudelaire and Schizoanalysis and "Narcissism from Baudelaire to Sartre."

58. For more on political repercussions of imbalanced investments between Mother and Father, see my "Schizoanalysis, Nomadology, Fascism," and Theweleit, *Male Fantasies.*

59. In connection with this sense of self-righteousness, it is worth recalling that ten times more Iraqi civilians died in the three years following the U.S. invasion than American citizens who died on 9/11, each year bringing on more deaths than the last.

60. Deleuze and Guattari, *A Thousand Plateaus*, are well aware of this ambiguity; in fact, they adopt it explicitly from von Clausewitz himself: "It is . . . true that total war remains subordinated to State political aims and merely realizes the *maximal conditions* of the appropriation of the war machine by the State apparatus. But it is also true that when total war becomes the object of the appropriated war machine, . . . the object and the aim enter into new relations that can reach the point of contradiction. This explains Clausewitz's vacillation when he asserts at one point that total war remains a war conditioned by the political aims of States, and at another that it tends to effectuate the Idea of unconditional war" (421).

61. Ibid., 467.

62. In his infamous "Telegram 71," issued as the Third Reich was collapsing, Hitler said, "If the war be lost, let the nation perish!" Speaking of everything from infrastructure to the basic necessities of life, he added that in the face of advancing Allied troops, "it would be better to destroy [all of] that, and to destroy it ourselves." See Bullock, *Hitler,* 774–75.

63. This realignment in the American case started with the New Deal, contemporaneous with the rise of Nazism in Germany, though in a quite different mode; for a comparison of this realignment in the United States, Italy, and Germany, see Schivelbusch, *Three New Deals.*

64. Deleuze and Guattari, *A Thousand Plateaus*, 466.

65. Ibid., 427; see also 460.

66. The adjective *neo-Liberal,* as used here to characterize the Clinton regime, is not to be confused with *neoliberalism,* which is a much broader term (encompassing both the Bush and Clinton regimes). On neoliberalism as a mode of production, see Harvey, *Brief History of Neoliberalism*; on neoliberalism as a mode of subjectivation, see Foucault, *Birth of Biopolitics.*

67. Deleuze and Guattari, *A Thousand Plateaus*, 466; see also 421. In chapter 4, the rhythm of capital formation is described in terms of deterritorialization and reterritorialization; see n. 115 of that chapter.

68. We are, for the most part, no longer discussing the nomadic war-machine but rather relations between State and capitalist war-machines. For more on the relation between militarism and the post–cold war State, see Buchanan, "Treatise on Militarism."

69. Deleuze and Guattari, *A Thousand Plateaus*, 467.

70. Ibid., 466.

71. Ibid., 467.

72. On the Trilateral Commission's impatience with democracy, see Crozier et al., *Crisis of Democracy,* esp. 113.

73. In this connection, president-elect Gore represented an even greater threat to the neoconservatives than Clinton, for not only did he obviously represent continuity with Clinton's successful economic policies but he also knew all about the environmental dangers of big oil and, worse yet, offered no easy "culturalist" targets to the fundamentalist Christian smear campaigns.

74. For an account of the long twentieth century in terms of these two basins of attraction, see my "Schizoanalysis, Nomadology, Fascism."

75. For an extended analysis of the centrality of this kind of sacrifice to nationalism, see Marvin and Ingle, *Blood Sacrifice and the Nation.*

76. There is, in principle, nothing wrong with violence per se, but violent confrontation with the Death-State today might well be suicidal.

3. Nomad Citizenship

1. For a full account of the Orpheus Chamber Orchestra, see Seifter and Economy, *Leadership Ensemble*; quotation is from 4.

2. Kozinn, "Orpheus Group to Do without Director, Too."

3. Follett, *Mary Parker Follett—Prophet of Management,* 160.

4. Seifter and Economy, *Leadership Ensemble,* 29–36, 75–81, 152–56, 194–99.

5. Republication of Follett's work started in the 1970s and accelerated through the end of the century, when she also became very influential in Japan. The main collection of her work in management theory is *Mary Parker Follett—Prophet of Management.*

6. Ibid., 213–26.

7. Follett, *Dynamic Administration,* 30.

8. Follett, *Freedom and Coordination,* 5.

9. Follett, *New State,* 75. Follett's standpoint of "depersonalization" and her corresponding focus on the group align her perspective closely with that of Deleuze and Guattari.

10. Ibid., 7, 33.

11. Ibid., 34. This notion of common thought clearly bears strong resemblance to Spinoza's idea of common notions—and indeed, much of what Follett says about society has strong Spinozan resonance. She is careful to distinguish her view of the integration of differences into an articulated whole in group dynamics from the Hegelian synthesis of contradictions (see *New State,* 300, and *Mary Parker Follett—Prophet of Management,* 115–18); in her view, contradictions are fruitless because they result from mere short-sightedness, whereas differences are inherent and productive (as they are for Deleuze).

12. Ibid.

13. Ibid., 63–64.

14. Likeness and obedience are, of course, the central features of the Oedipus complex: the child internalizes and reproduces Oedipal authority by both identifying with the father and obeying his prohibition. Deleuze and Guattari's critique of Oedipus thus dovetails nicely with Follett's critique of crowd dynamics; Deleuze and Guattari draw on Sartre's *Critique of Dialectical Reason* for extending their critique of the Oedipus to group dynamics; see my *Deleuze and Guattari's Anti-Oedipus,* esp. 103–6, 122.

15. Follett, *New State,* 154.

16. Ibid., 230.

17. For this all-important distinction, see Follett, *Mary Parker Follett—Prophet of Management,* esp. 97–119.

18. Follett's categories align closely with the distinction between *potentia* and *potestas* elaborated by Antonio Negri in his reading of Spinoza: power-with represents the power to create, whereas power-over represents the power of command over others and their activity; see his *Savage Anomaly.* There is no evidence either way whether Follett was familiar with Spinoza, but her distance from Hegel and her very insistence on power-with and the importance of thought in common suggests she may have been. For a biographical sketch of Follett (albeit one that exaggerates her debt to Hegel), see Kevin Mattson, "Reading Follett: An Introduction to the New State," in Follett, *New State,* xxix–lix.

19. On the concept of "power-to," see Connolly, *Terms of Political Discourse,* esp. chapter 3, "Power and Responsibility," 85–138.

20. Follett, *Dynamic Administration,* 82. For a similar view, see Shotter, "Psychology and Citizenship." Shotter argues (invoking Anderson's "imagined community" [125], among other things) that self-realization depends not on internal capacities but on resources deriving from being/feeling at home in a group or community: "in this approach, instead of treating the phenomena of mind and identity as structured identities *within* and *central* to the being of a person, they are treated as continually reproduced stabilities (that is, imaginary objects) 'subsisting' in the dynamic relations *between* people. In other words, all the powers we now attribute to individuals, and locate 'inside' them, as personal powers, must be seen in this view as social powers, sustained 'in' the individual only in virtue of his or her embedding within a particular 'region' or 'locus' of social activity" (127).

21. See Taylor's *Principles of Scientific Management,* 4, in which he states that "the development of [management] science . . . involves the establishment of many rules, laws, and formulae which replace the judgment of the individual workman."

22. Ibid., 13.

23. Ibid., 23; emphasis original. See also p. 8: "there is a science of handling pig iron, and . . . this science amounts to so much that the man who is suited to handle pig iron cannot possibly understand it, nor even work in accordance with the laws of this science, without the help of those who are over him."

24. Boltanski and Chapello, *New Spirit of Capitalism.*

25. Follett, *New State,* 120.

26. See Hardt and Negri, *Labor of Dionysus.*

27. Ibid., 130, 129, 134.

28. Follett, *New State,* 202, 142.

29. Ibid., 197.

30. Ibid., 196.

31. Ibid., 228.

32. Could there be a more dramatic illustration of the forced assimilation of nomad social relations to the State war-machine? On the collapse of Follett's movement with the onset of World War I, see Mattson, "Reading Follett," esp. liv–lvii. For a broader history of the neighborhood association movement, see Williams, *Neighborhood Organization.*

33. Williams, *Neighborhood Organization,* 72.

34. Young, "City Life and Difference."

35. See her "City Life and Difference," 258–59, where she says that the "ideal of the immediate copresence of subjects, however, is a metaphysical illusion. Even face-to-face relations between two people is [*sic*] mediated by voice and gesture, spacing and temporality. As soon as a third person enters the interaction the possibility arises of the relations between the first two being mediated through the third, and so on. The mediation of relations among persons by the speech and actions of other persons is a fundamental condition of sociality. The richness, creativity, diversity, and potential of a society expand with growth in the scope and means of its media, linking persons across time and distance. The greater the time and distance, however, the greater the number of persons who stand between other persons."

36. Ibid., 251.

37. Van Gunsteren, *Theory of Citizenship,* 26–27.

38. In addition to Follett and van Gunsteren, this is a view of city life shared by Henri Lefebvre; see his *Urban Revolution.*

39. This is the argument of Richard Sennett (among others); see his *Fall of Public Man,* esp. chapter 2.

40. Young, "City Life and Difference," 268.

41. The two were related, of course. Whereas in Europe, World War II had laid waste to vast areas of cities, which then had to be rebuilt, this had to be accomplished in the United States by willfully razing slums; only then could a new city (or part of one) be built in place of the old. See Jacobs, *Death and Life of Great American Cities.*

42. Le Corbusier, *City of To-morrow and Its Planning*: "WE MUST BUILD ON A CLEAR SITE. The city of today is dying because it is not constructed geometrically. To build on a clear site is to replace the 'accidental' layout of the ground, the only one that exists today, by the formal layout. Otherwise nothing can save us" (220).

43. Which does not mean Jacobs's understanding of urban complexity was incompatible with planning; indeed, city planners and urban activists have both drawn on her work in attempts to salvage and improve city life.

44. As Jacobs, "Use of Sidewalks," in Kasinitz, *Metropolis,* 111–29, puts it, "you can't make people use streets they have no reason to use. You can't make people watch streets they do not want to watch. Safety on the streets by surveillance and mutual policing of one another sounds grim, but in real life it is not grim. The safety of the street works best, most casually, and with least frequent taint of hostility or suspicion precisely where people are using and most enjoying the city streets voluntarily and are least conscious, normally, that they are policing" (45, 118).

45. Ibid., 129.

46. Ibid., 113.

47. See Taylor, *Moment of Complexity,* esp. chapter 1, in which he opposes Mies van der Rohe and Frank Gehry in the same spirit (simple grid vs. complexity) as I have opposed Le Corbusier and Jane Jacobs.

48. Jacobs, "Use of Sidewalks," 125.

49. Berman, *All That Is Solid Melts into Air,* esp. 314–38.

50. Follett, *New State,* 193–94.

51. Ibid., 285.

52. Ibid., 289.

53. Ibid., 75.

54. Ibid., 289–90; emphasis added.

55. Ibid., 288.

56. Ibid.; emphasis added.

57. Ibid.

58. Ibid., 291.

59. Ibid., 77.

60. Ibid., 291.

61. Ibid., 301.

62. Ibid., 265.

63. Ibid., 266.

64. Ibid., 267.

65. Ibid., 266.

66. Ibid., 313.

67. It is no doubt symptomatic of Schmitt's androcentrism that there is no mention of or allusion to the figure of woman anywhere in *Concept of the Political,* as Derrida observes in *Politics of Friendship,* 156.

68. Follett, *New State,* 283.

69. Ibid., 271.

70. Ibid.

71. Ibid., 138. Follett recognizes that this is an ideal: "to obey the group which we have helped to make and of which we are an integral part is to be free because we are obeying ourself. Ideally the state is such a group, actually it is not, but it depends upon us to make it more and more so" (138).

72. Thus, for Hegel, *Philosophy of Right* , ¶ 348, "all actions, including world-historical actions, culminate with individuals as subjects giving actuality to the

substantial. They are the living instruments of what is in substance the deed of the world mind and they are therefore directly at one with that deed though it is concealed from them and is not their aim and object."

73. Schmitt, *Concept of the Political,* 53.

74. Ibid., 41.

75. Ibid.

76. Ibid., 45.

77. Ibid., 44.

78. Ibid., 47.

79. Appadurai, "Patriotism and Its Futures," 421.

80. Ibid., 427.

81. Galloway, *Protocol.*

82. Follett, *New State,* 34.

83. See http://en.wikipedia.org/wiki/WP:NPOV.

84. Giles, "Internet Encyclopaedias Go Head to Head."

85. McHenry called Wikipedia a "faith-based" encyclopedia in his online article, http://www.ideasinactiontv.com/tcs_daily/2004/11/the-faith-based-encyclopedia.html.

86. Follett, *New State,* 34.

87. It is true that the webmaster–editor positions are an exception to the rule of equality and that they can in emergencies serve as referees—but this is more for process than for content.

88. Although some rifts have developed between those who emphasize *free* (as a parameter of distribution and use) and those who emphasize *open source* (as a method of development), there is enough common ground to consider them part of one movement. See both http://www.gnu.org/ and http://www.opensource.org/; see also Moglen, "Free Software Matters."

89. See http://dawn.jpl.nasa.gov/clickworkers and http://marsoweb.nas.nasa.gov/HiRISE/.

90. See http://www.pgdp.net/c/stats/stats_central.php.

91. Benkler, "From Consumers to Users," "Coase's Penguin," "Sharing Nicely," and *Wealth of Networks*; Moglen, "Anarchism Triumphant," "dotCommunist Manifesto," and "Freeing the Mind."

92. Moglen, "Anarchism Triumphant."

93. Indeed, most capitalist software development firms have adopted "flat-hierarchy" team-production models of the kind described by Follett, Seifter and Economy, Drucker, Peters, and others—yet they still cannot match the efficiency and power of Internet-mediated commons-based peer production; see Drucker, *Landmarks of Tomorrow,* and Peters, *Liberation Management.*

94. See also, e.g., http://savannah.gnu.org/.

95. This so-called new institutional economics movement represented a huge advance over the implausible assumptions made by traditional economics. The classic

works are Coase, *The Firm, the Market, and the Law,* which includes his famous 1937 essay "Nature of the Firm," and Williamson, *Markets and Hierarchies.* See also Williamson and Winter, *Nature of the Firm*; Ménard, *Institutions, Contracts, and Organizations*; and Furubotn and Richter, *Institutions and Economic Theory.*

96. Benkler, *Wealth of Networks,* 105.

97. Benkler, "From Consumers to Users," and Moglen, "Anarchism Triumphant."

98. See Boyle, "The Second Enclosure Movement," one of whose examples is the attempt to patent liver cells.

99. See ibid. and Moglen, "dotCommunist Manifesto."

100. See Davis, *City of Quartz.*

101. See Bey, *T.A.Z.,* esp. the section titled "The Will to Power as Disappearance," 128–32.

102. See Bey, "Temporary Autonomous Zone"; the quotation is from 404 and the reference to May 1968 is on 427.

103. Deleuze and Guattari, *A Thousand Plateaus,* 161.

4. Free-Market Communism

1. For a historical survey of Western views of the market as distributed intelligence, see Barry, "Tradition of Spontaneous Order." From a very different perspective, see Foucault, *Birth of Biopolitics.*

2. For fuller accounts of Deleuze and Guattari's debts to Marx, see Thoburn's excellent *Deleuze, Marx, and Politics* and my "Karl Marx."

3. Deleuze and Guattari, *What Is Philosophy?,* 28.

4. See my "Karl Marx," esp. 150–53.

5. Marx and Engels, *Collected Works,* 6:487.

6. For more on decoding, difference, and the cash nexus, see my *Deleuze and Guattari's Anti-Oedipus,* 11–13, 20–21.

7. On capitalism as one difference-engine in relation to two others, evolution and expression, see my "Utopian Dimension of Thought in Deleuze and Guattari," esp. 219–21. See also Ansell-Pearson, *Deleuze and Philosophy,* esp. 1–24, 180–210.

8. Deleuze and Guattari, *A Thousand Plateaus,* 470; translation modified. The French original is "*Minorité comme figure universelle, ou devenir tout le monde*" (Deleuze and Guattari, *Mille Plateaux,* 588), which Massumi translates as "becoming-everybody/everything." Two pages later, Deleuze and Guattari offer a slightly different formulation (somewhat easier to translate, perhaps) as an explication of revolutionary movement: "*le mouvement révolutionnaire (connexion des flux, composition des ensembles non dénombrables, devenir-minoritaire de tout le monde)*" (Deleuze and Guattari, *Mille Plateaux,* 590), which Massumi translates as "the becoming-minoritarian of everybody/everything" (Deleuze and Guattari, *A Thousand Plateaus,* 473).

9. For a fuller explanation of how Deleuze and Guattari use the term *schizo-phrenia*, see my *Deleuze and Guattari's Anti-Oedipus*, esp. 2–3, 93–96.

10. Marx and Engels, *Communist Manifesto*, in Marx and Engels, *Collected Works*, 6:487.

11. Or in a Wittgensteinian idiom, meaning is not fixed but rather varies according to "use" and, ultimately, according to "forms of life"; see his *Philosophical Investigations*.

12. Marx and Engels, *Collected Works*, 28:94–95.

13. Ibid., 28:95.

14. Ibid., 28:96.

15. Ibid., 28:94–95.

16. In addition to the important distinction between the technical and the social division of labor (the latter receiving relatively little explicit attention in mainstream economics until recently, particularly from the so-called new institutional economics movement), there is also the political division of labor, between command and execution or intellectual and manual labor. There can be a political division of labor transecting the technical division of labor in any enterprise divided by class as well as specialization per se, and there can be a political division of labor transecting the social division of labor, to the extent that exchange relations are not relatively equal, voluntary, and fair, as we will see later. See Sohn-Rethel, *Intellectual and Manual Labor*, and Gorz, *Division of Labor*.

17. The other major factor is the accumulation imperative; see the later discussion.

18. Deleuze, *Difference and Repetition*, 207. In his footnote to this passage, Deleuze cites Althusser and Balibar, *Reading Capital*, but the relevant essays (by Rancière, Macherey, and Balibar) are not included in the English translation; see 327n21. In *Difference and Repetition*, Deleuze draws an important technical distinction between *differenciation* (the term used here) and *differentiation*, but the distinction is not crucial for us, so we retain the standard spelling of *differentiation* throughout.

19. Although currently under threat by the privatization of research and the patenting of scientific discoveries (a kind of enclosure of the knowledge commons), the academic circulation of information also forms a social multiplicity where related difference can be extremely productive. For an analysis of academic research as knowledge commons, see Harvie, "Commons and Communities in the University."

20. Marx, *Grundrisse*, in Marx and Engels, *Collected Works*, 28:95.

21. Ibid., 28:96. In orthodox Marxism, such management is understood to depend on the "common appropriation and control of the means of production" (96); the Problem we are addressing here is what role markets may play in both the appropriation and the "communal control" (99) of socially produced wealth.

22. Ibid., 28:98.

23. Ibid., 28:99.

24. Ibid., 28:96. One of the difficulties of reading the notebooks of the *Grundrisse* is knowing whether, in a given passage, Marx is presupposing capitalist market relations (i.e., developed or simple circulation, as we will see later); in this case, he clearly is: the paragraph starts, "The very necessity to transform the product or activity of the individuals first into exchange value . . . [proves that] individuals now produce only for society" (95), i.e., for the market—thus presupposing the condition of market dependency produced by so-called primitive accumulation.

25. Ibid., 28:98–99.

26. Ibid., 28:98–99, 109.

27. For a dialectical version of historical materialism opposing subject and object (humankind and nature), such an emphasis on the development of productive forces raises legitimate environmental concerns. But the nonlinear historical materialism of schizoanalytic nomadology, based on the Spinozan view that humankind is part of nature (Nature = History = Industry, as Deleuze and Guattari put it in *Anti-Oedipus*, 25), would not count as development of productive forces anything that would damage the environment and thereby reduce its part of productive forces.

28. One Important question in the interpretation of Marx is whether production cooperatives coordinated by self-organizing markets would together count as "communal control" of the means of production; this chapter and the conclusion will argue in the affirmative.

29. Perelman, *Invention of Capitalism*.

30. For the derivation and development of the term *catallaxy*, see von Hayek, "Market Order and Catallaxy," in *Law, Legislation, and Liberty*, vol. 2, *Mirage of Social Justice*, 107–32.

31. Ibid., 108.

32. Ibid.

33. Although (correctly) associated today with neoliberalism, von Hayek considered himself more of a classical liberal; see "Why I Am Not a Conservative."

34. Von Hayek, "Market Order," 110.

35. Ibid.

36. Ibid.

37. Ibid.

38. This is, of course, precisely the way Deleuze and Guattari define *rhizomatic organization*: "acentered systems [are] finite networks of automata in which communication runs from any neighbor to any other, the . . . channels [of communication] do not preexist, and all individuals are interchangeable, defined only by their *state* at a given moment—such that the local operations are coordinated and the final, global result synchronized without a central agency"; see *A Thousand Plateaus*, 17. Wolf packs operate in a somewhat similar way when hunting, despite the much-touted existence of the alpha male or breeding pair. Like

Clastres's acephalous groups, the alpha function in wolf packs is sporadic and has to do mostly with matters of distribution and reproduction (who eats first, who mates) rather than production: hunting itself is conducted by wolves operating as a pack, via coordination rather than command. Deleuze and Guattari sometimes use packs to illustrate nomadic group organization; see, e.g., *A Thousand Plateaus*, 355–61. Fish schooling and bird flocking are other examples of rhizomatic organization, albeit in simpler form.

39. Von Hayek, "Use of Knowledge in Society." There may be a family resemblance (in the strong, Wittgensteinian sense) between von Hayek's rejection of socialist planning and fellow-Viennese Wittgenstein's rejection of logical positivism; von Hayek says, "I fear that our theoretical habits of approaching the problem with the assumption of more or less perfect knowledge on the part of almost everyone has made us somewhat blind to the true function of the price mechanism and led us to apply rather misleading standards in judging its efficiency" (527).

40. Ibid., 521.

41. Ibid.

42. Ibid., 526.

43. Ibid., 524.

44. The end of Asimov's *I, Robot* poses exactly this question, but the issue also arises in Plato's *Republic* and Zamyatin's *We*.

45. Von Hayek, "Use of Knowledge in Society," 525–27.

46. In addition to the voluminous literature on the fair trade movement, see Howard, "Central Coast Consumers Want More Food-Related Information"; Howard and Allen, "Consumer Willingness to Pay for Domestic 'Fair Trade'" and "Beyond Organic and Fair Trade?"; Stolle et al., "Politics in the Supermarket"; and Miller, *Acknowledging Consumption*, esp. Miller, "Consumption as the Vanguard of History," 1–57, and Fine, "From Political Economy to Consumption," 127–63.

47. Surowiecki, *Wisdom of Crowds*.

48. Von Hayek, "Use of Knowledge in Society," 521, 527.

49. To be fair, Adam Smith himself may have recognized this danger but gave it too little weight; his latter-day champions give it practically none.

50. Marx, *Capital*, vol. 1, in Marx and Engels, *Collected Works*, 35:739.

51. Ibid., 35:704.

52. A tension between these two conceptions replaces for the mature Althusser the historical "break" the young Althusser posited between the writings of a younger and older Marx; see Althusser, "Underground Current of the Materialism of the Encounter," in *Philosophy of the Encounter*, 163–207, esp. 197: "in fact, we find two different conceptions of the mode of production in Marx which have nothing to do with one another" (translation modified). Althusser characterizes what we are calling the "major" conception of the mode of production as "totalitarian, teleological, and philosophical" (200)—as opposed to open, contingent, and historical.

53. Ibid., 194.

54. For more on this, see Read, "Primitive Accumulation," and my "Nonlinear Historical Materialism and Postmodern Marxism."

55. Marx, *Capital*, 35:707.

56. Ibid., 35:705–6.

57. See Perelman, *Invention of Capitalism*.

58. Ibid., 103. "Free in form but not really in substance"—for an account of the important shift in American contract law across the nineteenth century regarding how "voluntary" agreements between employers and employees had to be to count as legally binding contracts, see Horwitz, *Transformation of American Law*, esp. chapter 6, 160–210: "only in the nineteenth century did judges and jurists finally reject the longstanding belief that the justification of contractual obligation is derived from the inherent fairness or justice of an exchange. In its place they asserted for the first time that the source of obligation of contract is the convergence of the wills of the contracting party" (160). Horwitz has been criticized for representing economics as the linear cause of changes in contract law; they are no doubt better understood as mutually codetermining and reinforcing. See also Sandel, *Democracy's Discontent,* esp. part 2.

59. Perelman, *Invention of Capitalism*, 102.

60. Ibid., 125.

61. Ibid., 14.

62. Marx, *Capital*, 35:705; translation modified and emphasis added.

63. See Holloway and Picciotto, *State and Capital*.

64. Marx, *Capital*, 35:723.

65. For an extensive examination of this process, see Perelman, *Invention of Capitalism*.

66. Marx, *Capital*, 35:726.

67. Ibid.; translation modified.

68. Perelman, *Invention of Capitalism*, 14.

69. The more dramatic account is provided by Klein, *Shock Doctrine*; a more thorough account of contemporary primitive accumulation as destitution is provided by Harvey, *Brief History of Neoliberalism*.

70. Perelman, *Invention of Capitalism*, 125.

71. Eventually, certain forms of self-provisioning can become a kind of subsidy to capital, once the wage relation is firmly established. As Perelman, ibid., says, as soon as "primitive accumulation was . . . successful . . . [and] industrial technology became substantially more productive than self-provisioning, the household economy became even less of a threat to the capitalist sector of the economy. At that point, capital could take advantage of the economies of self-provisioning, so long as household labor would not interfere with the commitment to wage labor"(103). The point was "to make sure that workers would be able to be self-sufficient enough to raise the rate of surplus without making them so independent that they would or could resist wage labor" (107). We thus see how mostly female

household labor becomes subordinate through its dependency on mostly male wage labor, as primitive accumulation changes the conditions and institution of patriarchy; see Federici, *Caliban and the Witch*. See also Malos, *Politics of Housework*, esp. Freeman, "When Is a Wage not a Wage?" 142–48; Federici, "Wages against Housework," 187–94; and Landes, "Wages for Housework," 195–205.

72. See Negri, *Marx beyond Marx*. For a similar view, see also Reddy, *Money and Liberty in Modern Europe*, who shows how "the notion of monetary exchange asymmetry clarifies the relation between money and power" (199).

73. Negri, *Marx beyond Marx*, 24.

74. Ibid., 23.

75. Marx, *Grundrisse*, 28:179; translation modified.

76. To put the point another way, under capitalism, even a commodity's "fair" price as set by the market cannot be a just price, given the power asymmetry embodied in and concealed by monetary exchange relations. On the categorical distinction between capitalist exploitation and fraud, see the later discussion.

77. Thus Negri, *Marx beyond Marx*, will claim that "there is no revolution without a destruction of bourgeois society, and of wage labor, as a producer of value, and of money as an instrument of the circulation of value and of command" (27) and conclude that since "value is money, is . . . shit, . . . there is no alternative but destruction: the suppression of money" (29). But this conclusion is based on a passage from the *Grundrisse* in which the "fundamental question" Marx is raising (in his critique of Proudhon) is whether monetary reform *in and of itself* is sufficient to produce revolutionary change: "can the existing relations of production . . . be revolutionized by a change in the instrument of circulation, in the organization of circulation?" (*Grundrisse*, as cited by Negri, *Marx beyond Marx*, 28). My claim is not that monetary reform can effectuate revolutionary change in the relations of production all by itself but that money as an instrument of circulation may survive the revolutionary transformation of social relations to end capitalism, which requires the elimination of wage labor rather than of money.

78. Marx, *Grundrisse*, 28:179–80; translation modified, emphasis added.

79. Even more dramatically, on the next page, Marx insists that "it is an aspiration as pious as it is stupid to wish that exchange value would not develop into capital" (Marx, *Grundrisse*, 28:180).

80. Ibid., 28:185.

81. See Gibson-Graham, *End of Capitalism*, 253–59.

82. Ibid., 259.

83. Ibid., 89.

84. See Luxemburg, *Accumulation of Capital*.

85. Marx, *Grundrisse*, 28:165–66; translation modified.

86. Ibid., 28:180n1.

87. Ibid., 28:167.

88. Ibid.; translation modified.

89. Ibid., 28:189; translation modified.

90. Ibid., 28:190; translation modified.

91. Ibid., 28:168; emphasis added.

92. Ibid., 28:379.

93. Ibid., 28:385.

94. Ibid., 28:379.

95. Ibid., 28:380; translation modified.

96. Thus, like the legitimization of the State according to Benjamin and Derrida, the capitalization of capital according to Marx occurs *après coup* (Lacan) or through *nachtraglichkeit* (Freud).

97. Marx, *Capital*, 35:181; translation modified, emphasis added.

98. Ibid., 35:179.

99. Ibid.

100. Marx, *Grundrisse*, 28:168.

101. For a more technical and thoroughgoing development of this line of analysis, see Harvey, *Limits to Capital*.

102. Marx, *Grundrisse*, 28:382.

103. Ibid., 28:186.

104. See ibid., 28:184–85: "commercial [mercantile] capital is only circulating capital, and circulating capital is the first form of capital; in which it has *as yet by no means become the basis of production*."

105. Ibid., 28:156.

106. Ibid.; emphasis original.

107. Ibid., 28:182; emphasis original.

108. See Federici's account of the nuclearization of the family as part of the process of primitive accumulation in *Caliban and the Witch*.

109. Deleuze and Guattari, *A Thousand Plateaus*, 453.

110. Gibson-Graham argues this point extensively in *End of Capitalism*, whereas Deleuze and Guattari take it more or less for granted.

111. Deleuze and Guattari, *A Thousand Plateaus*, 435.

112. For more on the relation between desiring production and social production, see my *Deleuze and Guattari's Anti-Oedipus*, 18–24. For another development of this view, see Balibar, "Infinite Contradiction."

113. For a complexity-theory account of axiomatization as a self-catalyzing system operating by drift and probe head exploration, see my "Nonlinear Historical Materialism and Postmodern Marxism."

114. In his "Control Societies" essay, Deleuze shows that the capitalist apparatus of capture takes a quantum leap forward in striating heretofore nondenumerable sets, with the advent of the likes of computer surveillance. But capital still can't capture everything. See Deleuze, "Postscript on Control Societies," in *Negotiations*, 177–82.

115. Deleuze and Guattari, *Anti-Oedipus*, 259–60; Marx, *Capital*, vol. 3,

37:239–49; Marx, *Grundrisse,* 29:7–12. See also my *Deleuze and Guattari's Anti-Oedipus,* esp. 80–81.

116. Marx and Engels, *Communist Manifesto,* 6:487.

117. For a discussion of the mobilization of the analytic distinction for historical study, see my *Baudelaire and Schizoanalysis,* esp. xi–xvi. The distinction is nonetheless crucial inasmuch as it highlights the difference between power-with (the formation of nondenumerable sets) and power-over (as the capture of surplus from the demuneration of some of those sets) as two conflicting moments or components of capitalist development.

118. "It is thus proper to State deterritorialization to moderate the superior deterritorialization of capital and to provide the latter with compensatory reterritorializations" (Deleuze and Guattari, *A Thousand Plateaus,* 455).

119. In chapter 28 of *Capital,* vol. 1, Marx refers to the "silent compulsion of economic relations [that] completes the subjection of the laborer to the capitalist" inasmuch as the "constant generation of a relative surplus population keeps the law of supply and demand of labour, and therefore keeps wages, in a rut that corresponds with the wants of capital." But he goes on to say that in exceptional circumstances, "direct force, outside economic conditions, is of course still used" (726; translation modified). On the modern State's relation to capital, see Holloway, *Change the World without Taking Power,* esp. 29–35.

120. On modern states as models of realization for capitalist axiomatics, see Deleuze and Guattari, *A Thousand Plateaus,* 454–55.

121. Foucault, *Society Must Be Defended,* esp. 239–44.

122. In addition to the work of Braudel and DeLanda (introduction, n. 38), see Wallerstein, "Bourgeois(ie) as Concept and Reality," esp. 147–50, and Baran and Sweezy, *Monopoly Capital.*

123. Deleuze and Guattari, *A Thousand Plateaus,* 442.

124. Ibid., 427–28, 443.

125. This is one respect in which Jean Baudrillard was right that use-value is a product of exchange-value rather than the other way around (see his *Mirror of Production*); the conclusions he draws, however, are very different.

126. On the pertinence of Marx's labor theory of value to the distinction Deleuze and Guattari will draw between striated and smooth capital, see *A Thousand Plateaus,* 391–92.

127. Thus abject dependence of subjects on the despot trifurcates into abject dependence of "citizens" on (1) parents, who in the segregated nuclear family, represent the only source of personal sustenance; (2) the State, which becomes the sole legitimate arbiter of larger and larger domains of social life; and (3) capital, which, following primitive accumulation as destitution, is the only source of social sustenance.

128. Of course, there are a variety of different but equally Important ways of defining *communism* (such as the distribution principle, "to each according to

need"), which would call for concepts other than free-market communism for their delineation.

129. On *entreprises citoyennes*, see Rouille d'Orfeuil, *Economie, le réveil des citoyens*.

130. Toward the end of the *Grundrisse*, Marx muses that once "the workers . . . themselves appropriate their own surplus labour . . . the measure of wealth is then not any longer, in any way, labour time, but rather disposable time" (see Marx and Engels, *Collected Works,* vol. 28, 708).

131. There are generally understood to be three functions of money: medium of exchange, unit of accounting, and store of value. Inasmuch as money stores value, it enables commodity exchange to develop from barter into true markets. At this point, it becomes a unit of accounting, inasmuch as goods are no longer evaluated directly in terms of other goods but in terms of monetary units instead. The key distinction is whether the value of money as unit of accounting needs to be grounded in some external standard, such as gold or socially necessary labor time, or remains immanent to the exchange process, as reflected in the value of the goods whose exchange it mediates. In nomad markets, money takes the latter form. See Goux, *Symbolic Economies,* esp. 88–121.

132. See Postone, *Time, Labor, and Social Domination,* 27: "overcoming capitalism involves the abolition of value as the social form of wealth."

133. Hence one formulation for political struggle given in Deleuze and Guattari, *A Thousand Plateaus*: to "bring connections to bear against the great conjunction of the apparatuses of capture and domination" (423).

134. Developing the analysis of political struggle adumbrated earlier (n. 133), Deleuze and Guattari, ibid., assert that "every struggle . . . constructs *revolutionary connections* in opposition to the *conjugations of the axiomatic*" (473).

135. Surowiecki, "Science of Success."

136. Marx, *Grundrisse,* 29:92.

137. Compare the older formulation of Sohn-Rethel, *Intellectual and Manual Labor*, 177: "the achievement of socialism does not necessitate scrapping the means of capitalist production to replace them with socialist means. To recognise, with Marx, the potentialities of emancipation in . . . capitalist machinery means, however much this machinery incorporates the rule of capital over labor, it can be transformed into means of production for socialism once the revolutionary power of the working class has broken the power of capital."

138. Marx, *Grundrisse,* 29:60.

Conclusion

1. Healy, *Llamas, Weaving, and Organic Chocolate.* See also http://www. elceibo.org/.

2. Roozen and van der Hoff, *L'Aventure du Commerce Equitable.* The year

1959 marks the incorporation of the Komitee SOS (the Stichting Steun voor Onderontwikkelde Streken, "Support for Underdeveloped Regions Foundation"), later renamed the Stichting SOS (Steun Ontwikkelings Streken, "Support of Development Regions Foundation"). See also http://www.claro.ch/.

3. Healy, *Llamas, Weaving, and Organic Chocolate*, chapter 6.

4. On the history of the Rochdale pioneers, see Brown, *Rochdale Pioneers*, and Holyoake, *History of the Rochdale Pioneers*. On the cooperative movement and workers cooperatives more generally, see Adams, *Putting Democracy to Work*, esp. 11–14 on the Rochdale principles, and Dow, *Governing the Firm*.

5. Indeed, Marx claimed that the cooperative movement constituted a "greater victory of the political economy of labor over the political economy of property [than the Ten Hours Bill]" limiting the legal length of the working day. See Marx, "Inaugural Address of the International Working Men's Association (The First International)," in Marx and Engels, *Collected Works*, 20: 5–13; quotation is from 10.

6. Although probably the best-known and largest cooperative enterprise in the world, Mondragon is far from perfect or free from controversy. Critics have argued that labor is just as alienated at Mondragon as elsewhere, for example, and it may be that something like a class hierarchy is developing, as Mondragon has employed casual labor to work alongside worker–owners. For critical perspectives, see Kasmir, *Myth of Mondragón*, and Cheney, *Values at Work*. See also Bradley and Gelb, *Cooperation at Work*; Whyte and Whyte, *Making Mondragon*; and Gibson-Graham, "Surplus Possibilities: The Intentional Economy of Mondragón," in *A Postcapitalist Politics*, 101–26.

7. Marx, "Inaugural Address," 11–12.

8. Marx, "Third Address to the International Working Men's Association (May 1871) on the Paris Commune"; included as part of "The Civil War in France," in Marx and Engels, *Collected Works*, 22:307–55; quotation is from 335.

9. On the contradiction between the global scale of economic organization and the State-bound scale of political organization, see Wallerstein, *Politics of the World-Economy*, esp. 9–10.

10. From early on, one of the slogans of the Fair Trade movement was "You don't just buy a product, you buy it from someone." See Roozen and van der Hoff, *L'Aventure du Commerce Equitable*, 104.

11. Fairtrade Labelling Organizations International, http://www.fairtrade.net/. Fairtrade sales grew another 15 percent in 2009, despite the worldwide recession.

12. Provided, of course, that these exchange relations are completely voluntary—a crucial proviso to which we return later. (Exchange relations also presuppose mutual recognition of ownership rights to the goods exchanged.)

13. See the appendix for more on the distinction between *utopia* and *utopian*.

14. Deleuze and Guattari, *A Thousand Plateaus*, 374.

15. See chapter 4, nn. 52–53.

16. See Day, *Gramsci Is Dead,* 8.

17. Ibid., 16.

18. Ibid., 210.

19. See Hardt and Negri, *Empire,* 339.

20. Ibid., 411.

21. See Hardt and Negri, *Multitude,* 358.

22. Ibid., 336–37.

23. Ibid., 357.

24. Ibid., 358.

25. Deleuze and Guattari, *A Thousand Plateaus,* 463.

26. Ibid., 471; translation modified.

27. Ibid., 463.

28. Hardt and Negri, *Empire,* 399–400.

29. Ibid., 400.

30. Ibid.

31. Jameson, *Archaeologies of the Future,* 147–48.

32. Hardt and Negri, *Empire,* 407.

33. Ben Trott had proposed an Interesting distinction between what he calls *transitional* demands and *directional* demands, the former resembling traditional major Marxist demands and the latter being explicitly likened to Deleuze and Guattari's *lines-of-flight.* But it still remains unclear to whom or what institution(s) such demands are to be made and why they would be granted. See his "Walking in the Right Direction?" at http://turbulence.org.uk/turbulence-1/walking-in-the-right-direction/.

34. Deleuze and Guattari, *A Thousand Plateaus,* 471.

35. Ibid.; translation modified.

36. Ibid., 472–73.

37. Ibid., 472.

38. Ibid.

39. Ibid., 417.

40. Ibid., 473.

41. See Virno, "Virtuosity and Revolution."

42. Ibid., 197.

43. Ibid., 198.

44. Ibid., 199.

45. Ibid., 201.

46. Ibid., 203.

47. Ibid., 202.

48. See The Invisible Committee, *Coming Insurrection.*

49. Ibid., 23.

50. Ibid., 94.

51. Ibid., 92.

52. Ibid., 63.

53. Ibid., 51.

54. Ibid., 110.

55. Ibid., 126.

56. Ibid., 128.

57. Although Transition Initiatives are under way in Australia, Canada, England, Germany, Ireland, Italy, the Netherlands, New Zealand, Scotland, South Africa, Spain, Sweden, the United States, and Wales, the movement is, not surprisingly, loosely organized. But see, for examples, http://www.transitionnetwork.org/ (U.K. based) and http://transitionus.org/ (U.S. based). In much the same spirit, but with a broader and more political focus, see Holtzman et al., "Do It Yourself and the Movement beyond Capitalism."

58. Hopkins and Lipman, "Who We Are and What We Do," http://www.transitionnetwork.org/sites/default/files/WhoWeAreAndWhatWeDo-lowres.pdf; quotation is from 8.

59. The Invisible Committee, *Coming Insurrection*, 124.

60. Ibid.

61. Ibid., 117; but see also 102, 105, and 125.

62. Ibid., 105.

63. Ibid., 131.

64. Deleuze and Guattari, *A Thousand Plateaus*, 472.

65. Ibid., 417.

Appendix

1. Deleuze and Guattari, *What Is Philosophy?*, 100. See also the commentary on utopia and geophilosophy in Flaxman, "Politics of Non-Being," 27–39.

2. Jameson, *Archaeologies of the Future*.

3. Ibid., 72. For a similar (but less text-centric) distinction between what he calls the "utopianism of social process" and "utopias as spatial form," see Harvey, *Spaces of Hope*, esp. 164–81. Deleuze and Guattari, in a somewhat different vein, insist on the "need to distinguish between authoritarian utopias, or utopias of transcendence, and immanent, revolutionary . . . utopias" in *What Is Philosophy?*, 100.

4. Jameson, *Archaeologies of the Future*, 54–56; see also 212–14.

5. Ibid., 178.

6. Ibid., xiii.

7. Ibid., 180. Marin, *Utopics*.

8. Jameson, *Archaeologies of the Future*, 179.

9. Ibid., 180.

10. Ibid., 85.

11. Ibid., 178.

12. Ibid.

13. Elliott, *Shape of Utopia.*

14. Jameson, *Archaeologies of the Future,* 211. Jameson's commitment to negativity is clear from the start: "it is a mistake to approach Utopias with positive expectations, as though they offered visions of happy worlds, spaces of fulfillment and cooperation. . . . The confusion arises from the formal properties of these texts, which . . . seem to offer blueprints: these are however maps and plans to be read negatively" (12).

15. In *Utopics,* Marin defines the utopian genre in terms of a process he calls *neutralization* (from the Latin *ne uter,* "neither one nor the other"), whereby (to cite Jameson's account) "the Utopian text is not a synthesis of opposites . . . [but] rather . . . a synthesis of their negations or in other words a neutral term" (29). Jameson uses the Greimasian semiotic rectangle to plot the semantics of utopia throughout *Archaeologies of the Future* (see esp. chapters 3 and 11); see also his original review essay on Marin's genre study, "Of Islands and Trenches."

16. See esp. Gibson-Graham, *End of Capitalism.*

17. Jameson, *Archaeologies of the Future,* xiii.

18. On this distinction, see Williams, "Base and Superstructure in Marxist Critical Theory."

19. Jameson, *Archaeologies of the Future,* 11.

20. Friedman, *Utopies réalisables.* From the perspective of affirmative nomadology, Nozick's approach (also mentioned by Jameson) is fatally compromised from the start by his atomistic individualism.

21. Robinson, *Mars Trilogy.*

22. For a similar approach, see Carlsson, *Nowtopia.*

23. Jameson cites Braudel, *Mediterranean and the Mediterranean World in the Age of Philip II*; but see also Glissant, *Traité du tout-monde,* esp. the chapter on Martinique, 226–33, and Deleuze and Guattari's own extended treatment of (classical) Greek philosophy (which draws on the work of Jean-Pierre Vernant as well as Braudel) in the context of the Mediterranean in *What Is Philosophy?,* 86–113.

24. Jameson, *Archaeologies of the Future,* 225. Boxed into his alternatives of federalism and anarchism, Jameson's commitment to totality forces him to hitch his methodological wagon to the forces of nationalism, of all things, citing Žižek's psychological explanation (in *Tarrying with the Negative*) for its appeal: "Federalism would seem to lack that passionate investment which nationalism preeminently possesses. . . . Nationalism is at the very least the most dramatic and successful operative paradigm of a great collective project and of collective movements and politics: this is by no means to endorse it as a political idea, but rather a reason to utilize it as an instrument for measuring other collective possibilities" (226).

25. In addition to Deleuze and Guattari's *Anti-Oedipus,* see my *Deleuze and Guattari's Anti-Oedipus*; *Baudelaire and Schizoanalysis,* where such indexical reference is called *metonymic*; and "Representation and Misrepresentation in Postcolonial Literature and Theory."

26. The problem of renewing belief in this world echoes as a kind of refrain in Deleuze's later works. "It may be that believing in this world, in this life," write Deleuze and Guattari, *What Is Philosophy?*, 75, 74, "becomes our most difficult task. . . . It is possible that the problem [for philosophy] now concerns the one who believes in the world . . . [and] in its possibilities of movements and intensities, so as once again to give birth to new modes of existence." In *Cinema 2: The Time-Image*, Deleuze addresses the problem of "restoring our belief in the world" by saying, "It is doubtful if cinema is sufficient for this; but, if the world has become a bad cinema, in which we no longer believe, surely a true cinema can contribute to giving us back reasons to believe in the world and in vanished bodies? . . . The problem is not that of a presence of bodies, but that of a belief which is capable of restoring the world and the body to us" (220–21).

27. Jameson, *Archaeologies of the Future*, 278–79.

28. Ibid., 278.

29. See Hardt and Negri, *Empire*.

30. See Bloch, *Principle of Hope*, 1:199. Further on, Bloch stresses that "the subjective factor is the unenclosed potency to turn things here, the objective factor is the unenclosed potentiality of turnability. . . . Both factors are always interwoven with one another in dialectical interaction. . . . Subjective potency coincides not only with what is turning, but also with what is realizing in history, and it coincides with it all the more, the more men become conscious producers of their history. Objective potentiality coincides not only with what is changeable, but with what is realizable in history, and it coincides with this all the more, the more the external world independent of man is also one which is increasingly mediated with him" (1:247–48).

31. Hardt and Negri, *Empire*, 64.

32. Ibid., 321.

33. Ibid., 210; emphasis original.

34. Ibid., 395; emphasis added.

35. See Piercy, *Woman on the Edge of Time*, 197–98; quoted in Jameson, *Archaeologies of the Future*, 233.

36. Jameson, *Archaeologies of the Future*, 30–31, considers revolutionary or utopian enthusiasm to be "highly suspicious."

Adams, Frank T. *Putting Democracy to Work: A Practical Guide for Starting and Managing Worker-Owned Businesses.* San Francisco: Eugene Berrett-Koehler, 1992.

Agamben, Giorgio. *The Coming Community.* Minneapolis: University of Minnesota Press, 1993.

Allen, Amy. "Rethinking Power." *Hypatia* 13 (Winter 1998): 21–40.

Altemeyer, Bob. *The Authoritarian Specter.* Cambridge, Mass.: Harvard University Press, 1996.

———. *Enemies of Freedom: Understanding Right-Wing Authoritarianism.* San Francisco: Jossey-Bass, 1988.

Althusser, Louis. *For Marx.* London: Verso, 1977.

———. *Philosophy of the Encounter: Later Writings, 1978–1987.* Edited by François Matheron and Oliver Corpet. London: Verso, 2006.

Althusser, Louis, and Étienne Balibar. *Reading Capital.* London: New Left Books, 1970.

Anderson, Benedict. *Imagined Communities: Reflections on the Origin and Spread of Nationalism.* London: Verso, 1991.

Ansell-Pearson, Keith, ed. *Deleuze and Philosophy: The Difference Engineer.* London: Routledge, 1977.

Appadurai, Arjun. "Full Attachment." *Public Culture* 10 (1998): 443–49.

———. "Patriotism and Its Futures." *Public Culture* 5 (1993): 411–29.

Archer, Robin. *Economic Democracy: The Politics of Feasible Socialism.* Oxford: Clarendon Press, 1995.

Archibugi, Daniele, David Held, and Martin Köhler, eds. *Re-imagining Political Community: Studies in Cosmopolitan Democracy.* Palo Alto, Calif.: Stanford University Press, 1998.

Arendt, Hannah. *On Revolution.* New York: Viking, 1965.

———. *On Violence.* New York: Harcourt, Brace, Jovanovich, 1970.

Bacon, Sir Francis. *The Advancement of Learning.* 1605. Reprint, Oxford: Clarendon, 2000.

Bailey, Derek. *Musical Improvisation: Its Nature and Practice in Music*. Englewood Cliffs, N.J.: Prentice Hall, 1982.

Balibar, Etienne. "The Infinite Contradiction." *Yale French Studies* 88 (1995): 142–64.

Balibar, Etienne, and Immanuel Wallerstein. *Race, Nation, Class: Ambiguous Identities*. London: Verso, 1991.

Baran, Paul, and Paul Sweezy. *Monopoly Capital; an Essay on the American Economic and Social Order*. New York: Monthly Review Press, 1966.

Barry, Norman. "The Tradition of Spontaneous Order." *Literature of Liberty* 5, no. 2 (1982): 7–58.

Bataille, Georges. *The Accursed Share: An Essay on General Economy*. New York: Zone Books, 1988.

Baudrillard, Jean. *The Mirror of Production*. St. Louis, Mo.: Telos Press, 1975.

Beiner, Ronald, ed. *Theorizing Citizenship*. Albany: State University of New York Press, 1995.

Bell, Jeffrey A. *Deleuze's Hume: Philosophy, Culture, and the Scottish Enlightenment*. Edinburgh: Edinburgh University Press, 2009.

———. "Of the Rise and Progress of Historical Concepts: Deleuze's Humean Historiography." In *Deleuze and History*, edited by Jeffrey Bell and Claire Colebrook, 54–71. Edinburgh: Edinburgh University Press, 2009.

———. *Philosophy at the Edge of Chaos: Gilles Deleuze and the Philosophy of Difference*. Toronto, Ont., Canada: University of Toronto Press, 2006.

Bell, Jeffrey, and Claire Colebrook, eds. *Deleuze and History*. Edinburgh: Edinburgh University Press, 2009.

Benjamin, Andrew, and Peter Osborne, eds. *Walter Benjamin's Philosophy: Destruction and Experience*. Manchester, U.K.: Clinamen Press, 2000.

Benjamin, Walter. "Critique of Violence." In *Reflections: Essays, Aphorisms, Autobiographical Writings*, edited by Peter Demetz, 277–300. New York: Harcourt Brace Jovanovich, 1978.

Benkler, Yochai. "Coase's Penguin, or, Linux and 'The Nature of the Firm.'" *Yale Law Journal* 112, no. 3 (2002): 369–446.

———. "From Consumers to Users: Shifting the Deeper Structures of Regulation toward Sustainable Commons and User Access." *Federal Communications Law Journal* 52, no. 3 (2000): 561–79.

———. "Sharing Nicely: On Shareable Goods and the Emergence of Sharing as a Modality of Economic Production." *Yale Law Journal* 114, no. 2 (2004): 273–358.

———. *The Wealth of Networks: How Social Production Transforms Markets and Freedom*. New Haven, Conn.: Yale University Press, 2006.

Berlant, Lauren. *The Anatomy of National Fantasy: Hawthorne, Utopia, and Everyday Life*. Chicago: University of Chicago Press, 1991.

———. *The Queen of America Goes to Washington City: Essays on Sex and*

Citizenship. Durham, N.C.: Duke University Press, 1997.

Berman, Marshall. *All That Is Solid Melts into Air: The Experience of Modernity.* New York: Simon and Schuster, 1982.

Bey, Hakim. *T.A.Z.: The Temporary Autonomous Zone, Ontological Anarchy, Poetic Terrorism.* New York: Autonomedia, 2003.

———. "The Temporary Autonomous Zone." In *Crypto-Anarchy, Cyberstates, and Pirate Utopias,* edited by Peter Ludlow, 401–34. Cambridge, Mass.: MIT Press, 2001.

Bloch, Ernst. *The Principle of Hope.* 3 vols. Cambridge, Mass.: MIT Press, 1995.

Boltanski, Luc, and Eve Chapello. *The New Spirit of Capitalism.* London: Verso, 2005.

Boundas, Constantin, ed. *Gilles Deleuze: The Intensive Reduction.* London: Continuum, 2009.

Boundas, Constantin, and Dorothea Olkowski, eds. *Gilles Deleuze and the Theater of Philosophy.* New York: Routledge, 1994.

Bourne, Randolph. *War and the Intellectuals.* New York: Harper and Row, 1964.

Boyle, James. "The Second Enclosure Movement and the Construction of the Public Domain." *Law and Contemporary Problems* 66, nos. 1–2 (2003): 33–74.

Bradley, Keith, and Alan H. Gelb. *Cooperation at Work: The Mondragón Experience.* London: Heinemann Educational, 1983.

Braidotti, Rosi. "Biomacht und nekro-Politik: Uberlegungen zu einer Ethik der Nachhaltigkeit." *Springerin, Hefte fur Gegenwartskunst* 13, no. 2 (2007): 18–23.

———. "Becoming-Woman: Rethinking the Positivity of Difference." In *Feminist Consequences: Theory for the New Century,* edited by Elisabeth Bronfen and Misha Kavka, 381–413. New York: Columbia University Press, 2001.

———. *Metamorphoses: Towards a Materialist Theory of Becoming.* Cambridge: Polity, 2002.

———. *Nomadic Subjects: Embodiment and Sexual Difference in Contemporary Feminist Theory.* New York: Columbia University Press, 1994.

———. "Toward a New Nomadism: Feminist Deleuzian Tracks; or, Metaphysics and Metabolism." In *Gilles Deleuze and the Theater of Philosophy,* edited by Constantin Boundas and Dorothea Olkowski, 157–86. New York: Routledge, 1994.

Braudel, Fernand. *Capitalism and Material Life: 1400–1800.* New York: Harper and Row, 1973.

———. *The Mediterranean and the Mediterranean World in the Age of Philip II.* Berkeley: University of California Press, 1995.

————. *On History.* Chicago: University of Chicago Press, 1982.

Bronfen, Elisabeth, and Misha Kavka, eds. *Feminist Consequences: Theory for the New Century.* New York: Columbia University Press, 2001.

Brown, Norman O. *Life against Death: The Psychoanalytic Meaning of History.* Middletown, Conn.: Wesleyan University Press, 1959.

Brown, Wendy. *States of Injury: Power and Freedom in Late Modernity.* Princeton, N.J.: Princeton University Press, 1995.

Brown, William. *The Rochdale Pioneers: A Century of Co-operation.* Manchester, U.K.: Co-operative Wholesale Society, 1944.

Buber, Martin. "Society and the State." In *Pointing the Way,* 161–76. New York: Harper, 1957.

Buchanan, Ian. "Becoming-Woman and the World-Historical." In *Deleuzism: A Metacommentary,* 93–116. Durham, N.C.: Duke University Press, 2000.

————. "Treatise on Militarism." In *Deleuze and the Contemporary World,* edited by Ian Buchanan and Adrian Parr, 21–41. Edinburgh: University of Edinburgh Press, 2006.

Buchanan, Ian, and Adrian Parr, eds. *Deleuze and the Contemporary World.* Edinburgh: University of Edinburgh Press, 2006.

Buchanan, Ian, and Marcel Swiboda, eds. *Deleuze and Music.* Edinburgh: Edinburgh University Press, 2004.

Buchanan, Ian, and Nicholas Thoburn, eds. *Deleuze and Politics.* Edinburgh: Edinburgh University Press, 2008.

Bullock, Alan. *Hitler: A Study in Tyranny.* New York: Harper, 1952.

Canneti, Elias. *Crowds and Power.* New York: Viking, 1962.

Carlsson, Chris. *Nowtopia: How Pirate Programmers, Outlaw Bicyclists, and Vacant-Lot Gardeners Are Inventing the Future.* Oakland, Calif.: AK Press, 2008.

Carroll, Berenice. "Peace Research: The Cult of Power." *Journal of Conflict Resolution* 4 (1972): 585–616.

Cassirer, Ernst. *The Myth of the State.* Garden City, N.Y.: Doubleday, 1955.

Cheney, George. *Values at Work: Employee Participation Meets Market Pressure at Mondragón.* Ithaca, N.Y.: ILR Press, 1999.

Clastres, Pierre. *Archaeology of Violence.* New York: Semiotext(e), 1994.

————. *Society against the State: The Leader as Servant and the Humane Uses of Power among the Indians of the Americas.* New York: Urizen Books, 1987.

Coase, Ronald. *The Firm, the Market, and the Law.* Chicago: University of Chicago Press, 1988.

Colebrook, Claire, and Ian Buchanan, eds. *Deleuze and Feminist Theory.* Edinburgh: Edinburgh University Press, 2000.

Connolly, William. *Identity/Difference.* Ithaca, N.Y.: Cornell University Press, 1993.

———. *The Terms of Political Discourse.* 3rd ed. Princeton, N.J.: Princeton University Press, 1993.

Cooper, Terry. *An Ethic of Citizenship for Public Administration.* Englewood Cliffs, N.J.: Prentice Hall, 1991.

Cornell, Drucilla, Michel Rosenfeld, and David Gray Carlson, eds. *Deconstruction and the Possibility of Justice.* New York: Routledge, 1992.

Crozier, Michel, Samuel P. Huntington, and Joji Watanuki. *The Crisis of Democracy: Report on the Governability of Democracies to the Trilateral Commission.* New York: New York University Press, 1975.

Davis, Mike. *City of Quartz: Excavating the Future in Los Angeles.* London: Verso, 1990.

Davis, Walter A. *Death's Dream Kingdom.* London: Pluto Press, 2006.

———. *Deracination: Historicity, Hiroshima, and the Tragic Imperative.* Albany: State University of New York Press, 2001.

Day, Richard. *Gramsci Is Dead: Anarchist Currents in the Newest Social Movements.* London: Pluto Press, 2005.

Dean, John. *Conservatives without Conscience.* New York: Viking, 2006.

de Certeau, Michel. *The Practice of Everyday Life.* Berkeley: University of California Press, 1984.

DeLanda, Manuel. *Intensive Science and Virtual Philosophy.* London: Continuum, 2002.

———. "Markets and Antimarkets in the World Economy." In *Technoscience and Cyberculture,* edited by Stanley Aronowitz, 181–94. New York: Routledge, 1996.

———. "Meshworks, Hierarchies, and Interfaces." In *The Virtual Dimension: Architecture, Representation, and Crash Culture,* 274–85. New York: Princeton Architectural Press, 1998.

———. *A Thousand Years of Nonlinear History.* New York: Zone Books, 1997.

Deleuze, Gilles. *Cinema 2: The Time-Image.* Minneapolis: University of Minnesota Press, 1989.

———. *Desert Islands and Other Texts, 1953–1974.* Los Angeles: Semiotext(e), 2004.

———. *Difference and Repetition.* New York: Columbia University Press, 1994.

———. *Foucault.* London: Athlone, 1988.

———. *The Logic of Sense.* New York: Columbia University Press, 1990.

———. *Negotiations.* New York: Columbia University Press, 1995.

———. *Nietzsche and Philosophy.* New York: Columbia University Press, 1983.

Deleuze, Gilles, and Michel Foucault. "Intellectuals and Power." In *Desert*

Islands, edited by Gilles Deleuze, 206–13. Los Angeles: Semiotext(e), 2004.

Deleuze, Gilles, and Félix Guattari. *Anti-Oedipus.* Minneapolis: University of Minnesota Press, 1983.

———. *Mille Plateaux.* Paris: Minuit, 1980.

———. *A Thousand Plateaus.* Minneapolis: University of Minnesota Press, 1987.

———. *What Is Philosophy?* New York: Columbia University Press, 1994.

Derrida, Jacques. "Force of Law: The 'Mystical Foundation of Authority.'" In *Deconstruction and the Possibility of Justice,* edited by Drucilla Cornell, Michel Rosenfeld, and David Gray Carlson, 3–67. New York: Routledge, 1992.

———. *Politics of Friendship.* London: Verso, 1997.

D'Orfeuil, Henri Rouille. *Économie, le réveil des citoyens: Les alternatives à la mondialisation libérale.* Paris: Découverte, 2002.

Dow, Gregory. *Governing the Firm: Workers' Control in Theory and Practice.* Cambridge: Cambridge University Press, 2003.

Drucker, Peter F. *Landmarks of Tomorrow: A Report on the New "Post-modern" World.* London: Transaction, 1996.

Eagleton, Terry. *The Meaning of Life.* Oxford: Oxford University Press, 2007.

Ellerman, David. *The Democratic Worker-Owned Firm: A New Model for the East and West.* Boston: Unwin Hyman, 1990.

Elliott, Robert. *The Shape of Utopia: Studies in a Literary Genre.* Chicago: University of Chicago Press, 1970.

Federici, Sylvia. *Caliban and the Witch: Women, the Body, and Primitive Accumulation.* New York: Autonomedia, 2004.

———. "Wages against Housework." In *The Politics of Housework,* edited by Ellen Malos, 187–94. Cheltenham, U.K.: New Clarion Press, 1995.

Fichte, Johann. *Addresses to the German Nation.* 1808. Reprint, Chicago: Open Court, 1922.

Flaxman, Gregory. "The Politics of Non-being." In *Deleuzian Encounters: Studies in Contemporary Social Issues,* edited by Anna Hickey-Moody and Peta Malins, 27–39. New York: Palgrave Macmillan, 2007.

Follett, Mary Parker. *Dynamic Administration: The Collected Papers of Mary Parker Follett.* Edited by Elliot M. Fox and L. Urwick. London: Pitman, 1973.

———. *Freedom and Coordination: Lectures in Business Organisation.* London: Management Publications Trust, 1949.

———. *Mary Parker Follett—Prophet of Management: A Celebration of Writings from the 1920s.* Edited by Pauline Graham. Boston: Harvard Business School Press, 1995.

———. *The New State: Group Organization the Solution of Popular*

Government. University Park: Pennsylvania State University Press, 1998.

Foucault, Michel. *The Birth of Biopolitics: Lectures at the Collège de France, 1978–79.* New York: Palgrave Macmillan, 2008.

————. *History of Sexuality.* Volume 1. New York: Pantheon, 1978.

————. "Intellectuals and Power: A Conversation between Michel Foucault and Gilles Deleuze." In *Language, Counter-memory, Practice: Selected Essays and Interviews,* 205–17. Ithaca, N.Y.: Cornell University Press, 1977.

————. *Language, Counter-memory, Practice: Selected Essays and Interviews.* Ithaca, N.Y.: Cornell University Press, 1977.

————. *Society Must Be Defended.* New York: Picador, 2003.

Freeman, Caroline. "When Is a Wage Not a Wage?" In *The Politics of Housework,* edited by Ellen Malos, 142–48. Cheltenham, U.K.: New Clarion Press, 1995.

Friedman, Yona. *Utopies réalisables.* Paris: Union générale d'éditions, 1975.

Furubotn, Eirik G., and Rudolf Richter, eds. *Institutions and Economic Theory: The Contribution of the New Institutional Economics.* Ann Arbor: University of Michigan Press, 2005.

Fuss, Diana. *Essentially Speaking: Feminism, Nature, and Difference.* New York: Routledge, 1989.

Galloway, Alexander. *Protocol: How Control Exists after Decentralization.* Cambridge, Mass.: MIT Press, 2004.

Gibson-Graham, J. K. *The End of Capitalism (as We Knew It).* Oxford: Blackwell, 1996.

————. *A Postcapitalist Politics.* Minneapolis: University of Minnesota Press, 2006.

Giles, Jim. "Internet Encyclopaedias Go Head to Head." *Nature* 438, no. 7070 (2005): 900–901.

Glissant, Edouard. *Traité du tout-monde.* Paris: Gallimard, 1997.

Gorz, André. *The Division of Labor: The Labor Process and Class-Struggle in Modern Capitalism.* Atlantic Highlands, N.J.: Humanities Press, 1976.

Gould, Stephen Jay. *The Structure of Evolutionary Theory.* Cambridge, Mass.: Harvard University Press, 2002.

————. *Wonderful Life: The Burgess Shale and the Nature of History.* New York: W. W. Norton, 1990.

Goux, Jean-Joseph. *Symbolic Economies: After Marx and Freud.* Ithaca, N.Y.: Cornell University Press, 1990.

Grosz, Elizabeth. "A Thousand Tiny Sexes: Feminism and Rhizomatics." In *Gilles Deleuze and the Theater of Philosophy,* edited by Constantin Boundas and Dorothea Olkowski, 187–212. New York: Routledge, 1994.

————. *Time Travels: Feminism, Nature, Power.* Durham, N.C.: Duke University Press, 2005.

———. *Volatile Bodies: Toward a Corporeal Feminism*. Bloomington: Indiana University Press, 1994.

Hage, Ghassan. *Against Paranoid Nationalism: Searching for Hope in a Shrinking Society*. Annandale, N.S.W., Australia: Merlin Press, 2003.

Hamacher, Wener. "Afformative, Strike: Benjamin's 'Critique of Violence.'" In *Walter Benjamin's Philosophy: Destruction and Experience*, edited by Andrew Benjamin and Peter Osborne, 110–38. Manchester, U.K.: Clinamen Press, 2000.

Hanagan, Michael, and Charles Tilly. *Extending Citizenship, Reconfiguring States*. Lanham, Md.: Rowman and Littlefield, 1999.

Haraway, Donna. *Simians, Cyborgs, and Women: The Reinvention of Nature*. New York: Routledge, 1991.

Hardt, Michael, and Antonio Negri. *Empire*. Cambridge, Mass.: Harvard University Press, 2000.

———. *Labor of Dionysus: A Critique of the State-Form*. Minneapolis: University of Minnesota Press, 1994.

———. *Multitude: War and Democracy in the Age of Empire*. New York: Penguin Press, 2004.

Hartsock, Nancy. "Political Change: Two Perspectives on Power." *Quest* 1 (1974): 10–25.

Harvey, David. *A Brief History of Neoliberalism*. Oxford: Oxford University Press, 2005.

———. *The Limits to Capital*. London: Verso, 2006.

———. *Spaces of Hope*. Berkeley: University of California Press, 2000.

Harvie, David. "Commons and Communities in the University." *The Commoner* 9 (2004): 1–10.

Healy, Kevin. *Llamas, Weaving, and Organic Chocolate: Multicultural Grassroots Development in the Andes and Amazon of Bolivia*. Notre Dame, Ind.: University of Notre Dame Press, 2001.

Hedges, Chris. *American Fascists: The Christian Right and the War on America*. New York: Free Press, 2007.

Hegel, Georg. *Philosophy of Right*. 1831. Reprint, Amherst, Mass.: Prometheus Books, 1996.

Herzogenrath, Bernd. "The 'Weather of Music': Sounding Nature in the Twentieth and Twenty-first Centuries." In *Deleuze/Guattari and Ecology*, edited by Bernd Herzogenrath, 216–32. Basingstoke, U.K.: Palgrave Macmillan, 2009.

Hickey-Moody, Anna, and Peta Malins, eds. *Deleuzian Encounters: Studies in Contemporary Social Issues*. New York: Palgrave Macmillan, 2007.

Hjelmslev, Louis. *Prolegomena to a Theory of Language*. Madison: University of Wisconsin Press, 1961.

Hjelmslev, Louis, and Hans Jørgen Uldall. *Outline of Glossematics: A Study in the Methodology of the Humanities with Special Reference to Linguistics.* Copenhagen: Nordisk Sprog-og Kulturforlag, 1957.

Hobbes, Thomas. *De Cive.* 1642. Reprint, Oxford: Oxford University Press, 1983.

Holland, Eugene W. "Affective Citizenship and the Death-State." In *Deleuze and the Contemporary World,* edited by Adrian Parr and Ian Buchanan, 161–74. Edinburgh: Edinburgh University Press, 2006.

———. "Affirmative Nomadology and the War Machine." In *Gilles Deleuze: The Intensive Reduction,* edited by Constantin Boundas, 218–25. London: Continuum, 2009.

———. *Baudelaire and Schizoanalysis: The Sociopoetics of Modernism.* Cambridge: Cambridge University Press, 1993.

———. *Deleuze and Guattari's Anti-Oedipus: Introduction to Schizoanalysis.* New York: Routledge, 1999.

———. "Infinite Subjective Representation and the Perversion of Death." *Angelaki: Journal of the Theoretical Humanities* 5, no. 2 (2000): 85–91.

———. "'Introduction to the Non-Fascist Life': Deleuze and Guattari's 'Revolutionary' Semiotics." *L'Esprit Créateur* 27, no. 2 (1987): 19–29.

———. "Jazz Improvisation: Music of the People-to-Come." In *Deleuze, Guattari, and the Production of the New,* edited by Simon O'Sullivan and Stephen Zepke, 196–205. London: Continuum, 2008.

———. "Karl Marx." In *Deleuze's Philosophical Lineage,* edited by Graham Jones and Jon Roffe, 147–66. Edinburgh: Edinburgh University Press, 2009.

———. "Narcissism from Baudelaire to Sartre: Ego-Psychology and Literary History." In *Narcissism and the Text: Studies in Literature and the Psychology of the Self,* edited by Lynne Layton and Barbara Ann Shapiro, 149–69. New York: New York University Press, 1986.

———. "Nonlinear Historical Materialism and Postmodern Marxism." *Culture, Theory, Critique* 47, no. 2 (2006): 181–96.

———. "Representation and Misrepresentation in Postcolonial Literature and Theory." *Research in African Literatures* 34, no. 1 (2003): 159–73.

———. "Schizoanalysis, Nomadology, Fascism." In *Deleuze and Politics,* edited by Ian Buchanan and Nicholas Thoburn, 74–97. Edinburgh: Edinburgh University Press, 2008.

———. "Studies in Applied Nomadology: Jazz Improvisation and Postcapitalist Markets." In *Deleuze and Music,* edited by Ian Buchanan and Marcel Swiboda, 20–35. Edinburgh: Edinburgh University Press, 2004.

———. "The Utopian Dimension of Thought in Deleuze and Guattari." In *Imagining the Future: Utopia and Dystopia,* edited by Andrew Milner, Matthew Ryan, and Robert Savage, 217–42. North Carlton, Vic., Australia: Arena, 2006.

Holloway, John. *Change the World without Taking Power.* London: Pluto Press, 2005.

Holloway, John, and Sol Picciotto, eds. *State and Capital: A Marxist Debate* Austin: University of Texas Press, 1978.

Holtzman, Ben, Craig Hughes, and Kevin van Meter. "Do It Yourself and the Movement beyond Capitalism." In *Constituent Imagination: Militant Investigations, Collective Theorizations*, edited by Stephen Shukaitis and David Graeber, with Erika Biddle, 44–61. Oakland, Calif.: AK Press, 2007.

Holyoake, George Jacob. *The History of the Rochdale Pioneers, 1844–1892.* London: G. Allen and Unwin, 1907.

Hopkins, Rob, and Peter Lipman. "Who We Are and What We Do." http://www.transitionnetwork.org/sites/default/files/WhoWeAreAndWhatWeDo-lowres.pdf.

Horwitz, Morton J. *The Transformation of American Law, 1780–1860.* Cambridge, Mass.: Harvard University Press, 1977.

Howard, Philip H. "Central Coast Consumers Want More Food-Related Information, from Safety to Ethics." *California Agriculture* 60, no. 1 (2006): 14–19.

Howard, Philip H., and Patricia Allen. "Beyond Organic and Fair Trade? An Analysis of Ecolabel Preferences in the United States." *Rural Sociology* 75, no. 2 (2010): 244–69.

———. "Consumer Willingness to Pay for Domestic 'Fair Trade': Evidence from the United States." *Renewable Agriculture and Food Systems* 23, no. 3 (2008): 235–42.

Invisible Committee, The. *The Coming Insurrection.* Los Angeles, Calif.: Semiotext(e), 2009.

Jacobs, Jane. *The Death and Life of Great American Cities.* New York: Random House, 1961.

———. "The Use of Sidewalks." In *Metropolis: Center and Symbol of our Time,* edited by Philip Kasinitz, 111–25. New York: New York University Press, 1995.

Jameson, Fredric. *Archaeologies of the Future: The Desire Called Utopia and Other Science Fictions.* London: Verso, 2005.

———. "Of Islands and Trenches." In *The Ideologies of Theory,* 2:75–101. Minneapolis: University of Minnesota Press, 1988.

Johnson, Steven. *Emergence: The Connected Lives of Ants, Brains, Cities, and Software.* New York: Scribner, 2001.

Jones, Graham, and Jon Roffe, eds. *Deleuze's Philosophical Lineage.* Edinburgh: Edinburgh University Press, 2009.

Jost, John T., Jack Glaser, Arie W. Kruglanski, and Frank J. Sulloway. "Political Conservatism as Motivated Social Cognition." *Psychological Bulletin* 129, no. 3 (2003): 339–75.

Kasinitz, Philip, ed. *Metropolis: Center and Symbol of Our Time.* New York: New York University Press, 1995.

Kasmir, Sharryn. *The Myth of Mondragón: Cooperatives, Politics, and Working-Class Life in a Basque Town.* Albany: State University of New York Press, 1996.

Kauffman, Stuart. *At Home in the Universe: The Search for Laws of Self-Organization and Complexity.* New York: Oxford University Press, 1995.

———. *The Origins of Order: Self-Organization and Selection in Evolution.* New York: Oxford University Press, 1993.

Keller, Evelyn Fox. *Making Sense of Life: Explaining Biological Development with Models, Metaphors, and Machines.* Cambridge, Mass.: Harvard University Press, 2002.

Kennedy, James F., Russell C. Eberhart, and Yuhui Shi. *Swarm Intelligence.* San Francisco: Morgan Kaufmann, 2001.

Klein, Naomi. *The Shock Doctrine: The Rise of Disaster Capitalism.* New York: Henry Holt, 2007.

Knowles, Rob. *Political Economy from Below: Economic Thought in Communitarian Anarchism, 1840–1914.* New York: Routledge, 2004.

Koch, Andrew. "Poststructuralism and the Epistemological Basis of Anarchism." *Philosophy of the Social Sciences* 23, no. 3 (1993): 327–51.

Kozinn, Allan. "Orpheus Group to Do without Director, Too." *New York Times,* May 4, 2002.

Lacan, Jacques. "The Function and Field of Speech and Language in Psychoanalysis." In *Écrits: A Selection,* 31–106. New York: W. W. Norton, 2002.

Lakoff, George. *Moral Politics: How Liberals and Conservatives Think.* Chicago: University of Chicago Press, 2002.

Landes, Joan. "Wages for Housework: Political and Theoretical Considerations." In *The Politics of Housework,* edited by Ellen Malos, 195–205. Cheltenham, U.K.: New Clarion Press, 1995.

Laplanche, Jean-Bertrand, and Jean Pontalis. "Fantasy and the Origins of Sexuality." *International Journal of Psychoanalysis* 49 (1968): 1–18.

———. *The Language of Psycho-analysis.* New York: W. W. Norton, 1973.

Layton, Lynne, and Barbara Ann Shapiro, eds. *Narcissism and the Text: Studies in Literature and the Psychology of the Self.* New York: New York University Press, 1986.

Le Corbusier. *The City of To-morrow and Its Planning.* Cambridge, Mass.: MIT Press, 1986.

Lefebvre, Henri. *The Urban Revolution.* Minneapolis: University of Minnesota Press, 2003.

Ludlow, Peter, ed. *Crypto-Anarchy, Cyberstates, and Pirate Utopias.* Cambridge, Mass.: MIT Press, 2001.

Luxemburg, Rosa. *The Accumulation of Capital.* 1913. Reprint, London: Routledge and Kegan Paul, 1951.

Mainzer, Klaus. *Thinking in Complexity: The Computational Dynamics of Matter, Mind, and Mankind.* Berlin: Springer, 2004.

Malos, Ellen, ed. *The Politics of Housework.* Cheltenham, U.K.: New Clarion Press, 1995.

Marcuse, Herbert. *Eros and Civilization: A Philosophical Inquiry into Freud.* Boston: Beacon Press, 1974.

Marin, Louis. *Utopics: Spatial Play.* Atlantic Highlands, N.J.: Humanities Press, 1984.

Marshall, T. H. "Citizenship and Social Class." In *Class, Citizenship, and Social Development: Essays by T. H. Marshall,* 65–122. Garden City, N.Y.: Doubleday, 1964.

Marvin, Carolyn, and David Ingle. *Blood Sacrifice and the Nation: Totem Rituals and the American Flag.* Cambridge: Cambridge University Press, 1999.

Marx, Karl, and Frederick Engels. *Collected Works.* 50 vols. New York: International, 1975.

Massumi, Brian. *Parables for the Virtual.* Durham, N.C.: Duke University Press, 2002.

———. *User's Guide to Capitalism and Schizophrenia: Deviations from Deleuze and Guattari.* Cambridge, Mass.: MIT Press, 1992.

May, Todd. "Is Post-structuralist Political Theory Anarchist?" *Philosophy and Social Criticism* 15, no. 3 (1989): 167–81.

———. *The Political Philosophy of Poststructuralist Anarchism.* University Park: Pennsylvania State University Press, 1994.

Mbembe, Achille. "Necropolitics." *Public Culture* 15, no. 1 (2003): 11–40.

McIntyre, Robert S., and T. D. Coo Nguyen. "Corporate Income Taxes in the Bush Years." Citizens for Tax Justice and the Institute on Taxation and Economic Policy. http://www.ctj.org/corpfed04an.pdf.

Meltzer, Albert. *Anarchism: Arguments For and Against.* Edinburgh: AK Press, 2000.

Ménard, Claude, ed. *Institutions, Contracts, and Organizations: Perspectives from New Institutional Economics.* Cheltenham, U.K.: Edward Elgar, 2000.

Miami Theory Collective, The. *Community at Loose Ends.* Minneapolis: University of Minnesota Press, 1991.

Mies, Maria. *Patriarchy and Accumulation on a World Scale.* London: Zed Books, 1998.

Miller, Daniel, ed. *Acknowledging Consumption; a Review of New Studies.* London: Routledge, 1994.

Milner, Andrew, Matthew Ryan, and Robert Savage, eds. *Imagining the Future: Utopia and Dystopia.* North Carlton, Vic., Australia: Arena, 2006.

Moglen, Eben. "Anarchism Triumphant: Free Software and the Death of Copyright." *First Monday: Peer-Reviewed Journal on the Internet* 4,

no. 8 (1999). http://firstmonday.org/htbin/cgiwrap/bin/ojs/index.php/
fm/article/view/684/594.

―――. "The dotCommunist Manifesto." http://emoglen.law.columbia.edu/
publications/dcm.html.

―――. "Free Software Matters: Free Software or Open Source." http://emo-
glen.law.columbia.edu/publications/lu-07.pdf.

―――. "Freeing the Mind: Free Software and the Death of Proprietary Culture." http://emoglen.law.columbia.edu/publications/maine-speech.html.

Nancy, Jean-Luc. *The Experience of Freedom.* Palo Alto, Calif.: Stanford University Press, 1993.

―――. *The Inoperative Community.* Minneapolis: University of Minnesota
Press, 1991.

―――. *Multiple Arts: The Muses II.* Palo Alto, Calif.: Stanford University
Press, 2006.

Negri, Antonio. *Marx beyond Marx: Lessons on the Grundrisse.* South Had-
ley, Mass.: Bergin and Garvey, 1984.

―――. *The Savage Anomaly: The Power of Spinoza's Metaphysics and Politics.* Minneapolis: University of Minnesota Press, 1991.

O'Sullivan, Simon, and Stephen Zepke, eds. *Deleuze, Guattari, and the Production of the New.* London: Continuum, 2008.

Parr, Adrian, and Ian Buchanan, eds. *Deleuze and the Contemporary World.*
Edinburgh: Edinburgh University Press, 2006.

Patton, Paul. *Deleuze and the Political.* London: Routledge, 2000.

Pease, Donald. *The New American Exceptionalism.* Minneapolis: University
of Minnesota Press, 2009.

Perelman, Michael. *The Invention of Capitalism: Classical Political Economy
and the Secret History of Primitive Accumulation.* Durham, N.C.: Duke
University Press, 2000.

Peters, Tom. *Liberation Management: Necessary Disorganization for the
Nanosecond Nineties.* New York: Knopf, 1992.

Piercy, Marge. *Woman on the Edge of Time.* New York: Knopf, 1976.

Poster, Mark. *Critical Theory of the Family.* New York: Seabury Press, 1978.

Postone, Moishe. *Time, Labor, and Social Domination: A Reinterpretation of
Marx's Critical Theory.* Cambridge: Cambridge University Press, 1993.

Protevi, John. *Political Affect: Connecting the Social and the Somatic.* Minneapolis: University of Minnesota Press, 2009.

―――. *Political Physics: Deleuze, Derrida, and the Body Politic.* London:
Athlone Press, 2001.

Protevi, John, and Mark Bonta. *Deleuze and Geophilosophy: A Guide and
Glossary.* Edinburgh: Edinburgh University Press, 2004.

Purkis, Jonathan, and James Bowen, eds. *Changing Anarchism: Anarchist
Theory and Practice in a Global Age.* Manchester, U.K.: Manchester
University Press, 2004.

Read, Jason. "Primitive Accumulation: The Aleatory Foundation of Capitalism." *Rethinking Marxism* 14, no. 2 (2002): 24–49.

Reddy, William. *Money and Liberty in Modern Europe.* Cambridge: Cambridge University Press, 1987.

Rheingold, Howard. *Smart Mobs.* Cambridge: Basic Books, 2002.

Robinson, Kim Stanley. *Mars Trilogy.* New York: Bantam Books, 1996.

Roozen, Nico, and Frans van der Hoff. *L'Aventure du Commerce Equitable.* Paris: J.-C. Lattès, 2002.

Rosanvallon, Pierre. *Democracy Past and Future.* New York: Columbia University Press, 2006.

———. *L'âge de l'autogestion: Ou, La politique au poste de commandement.* Paris: Seuil, 1976.

Rose, Jacqueline. *States of Fantasy.* Oxford: Clarendon Press, 1996.

Sandel, Michael. *Democracy's Discontent: America in Search of a Public Philosophy.* Cambridge, Mass.: Harvard University Press, 1996.

Schivelbusch, Wolfgang. *Three New Deals: Reflections on Roosevelt's American, Mussolini's Italy, and Hitler's Germany, 1933–1939.* New York: Henry Holt, 2006.

Schmitt, Carl. *The Concept of the Political.* Chicago: University of Chicago Press, 2007.

———. "Theory of the Partisan." *CR: The New Centennial Review* 4, no. 3 (1963): 1–78.

Seifter, Harvey, and Peter Economy. *Leadership Ensemble: Lessons in Collaborative Management from the World's Only Conductorless Orchestra.* New York: Henry Holt, 2001.

Sennett, Richard. *The Fall of Public Man.* New York: Random House, 1974.

Shotter, John. "Psychology and Citizenship: Identity and Belonging." In *Citizenship and Social Theory,* edited by Bryan Turner, 115–38. London: Sage, 1993.

Simondon, Gilbert. *Du mode d'existence des objets techniques.* Paris: Aubier, 1958.

Sohn-Rethel, Alfred. *Intellectual and Manual Labor: A Critique of Epistemology.* Atlantic Highlands, N.J.: Humanities Press, 1978.

Starhawk. *Truth or Dare.* New York: HarperCollins, 1990.

Stolle, Dietlind, Marc Hooghe, and Michele Micheletti. "Politics in the Supermarket: Political Consumerism as a Form of Political Participation." *International Political Science Review / Revue internationale de science politique* 26, no. 3 (2005): 245–69.

Strozier, Charles. *Apocalypse: On the Psychology of Fundamentalism in America.* Boston: Beacon Press, 1994.

Surowiecki, James. "The Science of Success." *New Yorker,* July 9, 2007.

———. *The Wisdom of Crowds.* New York: Doubleday, 2004.

Taylor, Charles. *Hegel and Modern Society.* Cambridge: Cambridge University Press, 1979.

Taylor, Frederick. *The Principles of Scientific Management.* 1911. Reprint, New York: W. W. Norton, 1967.

Taylor, Mark. *The Moment of Complexity.* Chicago: University of Chicago Press, 2001.

Taylor, Michael. *The Possibility of Cooperation.* Cambridge: Cambridge University Press, 1987.

Theweleit, Klaus. *Male Fantasies.* 2 vols. Minneapolis: University of Minnesota Press, 1987–89.

Thoburn, Nicholas. *Deleuze, Marx, and Politics.* London: Routledge, 2003.

Tilly, Charles. *Coercion, Capital, and European States, A.D. 990–1992.* London: Blackwell, 1992.

Trott, Ben. "Walking in the Right Direction?" http://turbulence.org.uk/turbulence-1/walking-in-the-right-direction/.

van Gunsteren, Herman. *A Theory of Citizenship: Organizing Plurality in Contemporary Democracies.* Boulder, Colo.: Westview Press, 1998.

Virno, Paolo. "Virtuosity and Revolution: The Political Theory of Exodus." In *Radical Thought in Italy: A Potential Politics,* edited by Paolo Virno and Michael Hardt, 189–212. Minneapolis: University of Minnesota Press, 1996.

von Hayek, Friedrich. *Law, Legislation, and Liberty.* Vol. 2, *The Mirage of Social Justice.* Chicago: University of Chicago Press, 1976.

———. "The Use of Knowledge in Society." *American Economic Review* 35, no. 4 (1945): 519–30.

———. "Why I Am Not a Conservative." In *The Constitution of Liberty,* 397–414. Chicago: University of Chicago Press, 1978.

Wallerstein, Immanuel. "Bourgeois(ie) as Concept and Reality." In *Race, Nation, Class: Ambiguous Identities,* 135–52. London: Verso, 1991.

———. "The Global Possibilities: 1945–2025." In *The Age of Transition: Trajectory of the World-System, 1945–2025,* edited by Terence K. Hopkins and Immanuel Wallerstein, with John Casparis, 226–43. London: Zed Books, 1996.

———. *The Politics of the World-Economy: The States, the Movements, and the Civilizations.* Cambridge: Cambridge University Press, 1984.

Ward, Colin. *Anarchism: A Very Short Introduction.* Oxford: Oxford University Press, 2004.

Watson, Janell. "Oil Wars, or Extrastate Conflict 'beyond the Line': Schmitt's Nomos, Deleuze's War Machine, and the New Order of the Earth." *South Atlantic Quarterly* 104, no. 2 (2005): 349–57.

Weber, Max. *Politics as a Vocation.* Philadelphia: Fortress Press, 1965.

———. *The Theory of Social and Economic Organization*. New York: Free Press, 1964.

Whyte, William Foote, and Kathleen King Whyte. *Making Mondragon: The Growth and Dynamics of the Worker Cooperative Complex*. Ithaca, N.Y.: ILR Press, 1991.

Williams, Michael. *Neighborhood Organization: Seeds of a New Urban Life*. Westport, Conn.: Greenwood Press, 1985.

Williams, Raymond. "Base and Superstructure in Marxist Critical Theory." In *Problems in Materialism and Culture*, 31–49. London: Verso, 1980.

Williamson, Oliver. *Markets and Hierarchies: Analysis and Antitrust Implications*. New York: Free Press, 1975.

Williamson, Oliver E., and Sidney G. Winter, eds. *The Nature of the Firm: Origins, Evolution, and Development*. New York: Oxford University Press, 1991.

Wittgenstein, Ludwig. *Philosophical Investigations*. New York: Macmillan, 1953.

Young, Iris Marion. "City Life and Difference." In *Metropolis: Center and Symbol of Our Time*, edited by Philip Kasinitz, 250–79. New York: New York University Press, 1995.

———. *Inclusion and Democracy*. Oxford: Oxford University Press, 2000.

———. *Justice and the Politics of Difference*. Princeton, N.J.: Princeton University Press, 1990.

———. "Responsibility and Global Justice: A Social Connection Model." *Social Philosophy and Policy* 23, no. 1 (2006): 102–30.

Žižek, Slavoj. *Violence: Six Sideways Reflections*. New York: Picador, 2008.

Eugene W. Holland is professor and chair of comparative studies at The Ohio State University. He is the author of *Baudelaire and Schizoanalysis: The Sociopoetics of Modernism* and *Deleuze and Guattari's Anti-Oedipus: Introduction to Schizoanalysis* and coeditor (with Dan Smith and Charles Stivale) of *Gilles Deleuze: Image and Text*.